READING BETWEEN THE LINES

TURNING POINT Christian Worldview Series
Marvin Olasky, General Editor

Turning Point: A Christian Worldview Declaration
by Herbert Schlossberg and Marvin Olasky

Prodigal Press: The Anti-Christian Bias of the American News Media
by Marvin Olasky

Freedom, Justice, and Hope:
Toward a Strategy for the Poor and the Oppressed
by Marvin Olasky, Herbert Schlossberg,
Pierre Berthoud, and Clark H. Pinnock

Beyond Good Intentions: A Biblical View of Politics
by Doug Bandow

Prosperity and Poverty: The Compassionate Use
of Resources in a World of Scarcity
by E. Calvin Beisner

The Seductive Image: A Christian Critique
of the World of Film
by K. L. Billingsley

All God's Children and Blue Suede Shoes:
Christians and Popular Culture
by Kenneth A. Myers

A World Without Tyranny:
Christian Faith and International Politics
by Dean C. Curry

Prospects for Growth:
A Biblical View of Population,
Resources and the Future
by E. Calvin Beisner

More Than Kindness:
A Compassionate Approach to Crisis Childbearing
by Susan Olasky and Marvin Olasky

Reading Between the Lines:
A Christian Guide to Literature
by Gene Edward Veith, Jr.

READING BETWEEN THE LINES

*A Christian Guide
to Literature*

Gene Edward Veith, Jr.

CROSSWAY BOOKS • WHEATON, ILLINOIS
A DIVISION OF GOOD NEWS PUBLISHERS

Reading Between the Lines: A Christian Guide to Literature.

Copyright © 1990 by Gene Edward Veith, Jr.

Published by Crossway Books, a division of
Good News Publishers, Wheaton, Illinois 60187.

 Published in association with the
Fieldstead Institute
P.O. Box 19061,
Irvine, California 92713

Cover illustration: Guy Wolek

Printed in the United States of America

Unless otherwise noted, Bible quotations are taken from *Holy Bible: New
International Version,* copyright © 1978 by the New York International Bible
Society. Used by permission of Zondervan Bible Publishers.

Scripture quotations taken from the *Revised Standard Version* are identified RSV.
Copyright 1946, 1953 © 1971, 1973 by the Division of Christian Education of
the National Council of Churches in the USA.

Library of Congress Cataloging-in-Publication Data

Veith, Gene Edward, 1951-
    Reading between the lines : a Christian guide to literature
by Gene Edward Veith, Jr.
        p. cm.
        "Published in association with the Fieldstead Institute . . . Irvine, California"—T.p. verso
    Includes bibliographical references (.).
    Includes indexes.
    ISBN 0-89107-582-8
    1. Christianity and literature. 2. Literature and morals.
3. Literature, Immoral. I. Title.   809'.93382--DC20
PN49.V45 1990   90-80623

11	10	09	08	07	06	05	04	03	02	01	00	99	98
20	19	18	17	16	15	14	13	12	11	10	9	8	7	6	5	4	3

The author and the publisher gratefully acknowledge permission to reprint material from the following:

Matthew Arnold, "Dover Beach" from *Matthew Arnold,* ed. Miriam Allott and
    Robert H. Super (New York: Oxford University Press, 1976) by permission.
Bruno Bettelheim, *The Uses of Enchantment: The Meaning and Importance of
    Fairy Tales* © 1975, 1976 by Bruno Bettelheim. Reprinted by permission
    of Alfred A. Knopf, Inc.
E. K. Chambers, *The Medieval Stage* (London: Oxford University Press, 1903)
    by permission.

For my students,
who have heard much of this before

T A B L E O F

CONTENTS

ACKNOWLEDGMENTS	xi
PREFACE	xiii
1 The Word and the Image: The Importance of Reading	17
2 Vicarious Experience and Vicarious Sin: The Importance of Criticism	27

THE FORMS OF LITERATURE

3 Nonfiction: The Art of Truth-Telling	49
4 Fiction: The Art of Story-Telling	59
5 Poetry: The Art of Singing	79

THE MODES OF LITERATURE

6 Tragedy and Comedy: The Literature of Damnation and Salvation	101
7 Realism: Literature as a Mirror	117
8 Fantasy: Literature as a Lamp	129

THE TRADITIONS OF LITERATURE

9 The Middle Ages and the Reformation: The Literature of Belief	151
10 The Enlightenment and Romanticism: The Literature of Nature and the Self	169
11 Modernism and Postmodernism: The Literature of Consciousness and Self-Consciousness	191
12 The Makers of Literature: Writers, Publishers, and Readers	213
APPENDIX: A Reading List	225
NOTES	231
SCRIPTURE INDEX	247
GENERAL INDEX	249

ACKNOWLEDGMENTS

Most books have their origin when the author has an idea and convinces an editor to publish the results. This book came into being the opposite way. Marvin Olasky, editor of the Turning Point Christian Worldview Series, had an idea of what he wanted and convinced me to write the book. He is therefore partially responsible for what you will be reading. I thank him for asking me, for his ideas, and for his timely help and attention throughout the writing process.

I should also acknowledge two Christian thinkers who showed me the relationships between Christianity and literature. I stumbled upon Leland Ryken's books at a critical time when I was studying literature at graduate school and first discovering the possibilities of Biblical thought. His writings helped direct me on the course I have taken, and I appreciate his example and his influence. James Sire showed me how to read slowly (to allude to one of his books) and introduced me to the possibilities of worldview criticism. As an editor, he also encouraged me to write about these things and was responsible for publishing my first book. Breaking into print for the first time is the greatest obstacle for a writer; after the first time, it gets easier. I will always be grateful to him for getting me started, both as a critic and as an author. The influence of Leland Ryken and James Sire will be evident on every page of this book.

I am also grateful to Dr. R. John Buuck, president of Concordia University-Wisconsin, and to the Board of Regents for granting me a sabbatical to work on this project. Thanks too, as always, to my wife Jackquelyn and to Paul, Joanna, and Mary.

P R E F A C E

This book is written to help people be better readers. The title, *Reading Between the Lines,* perhaps suggests a note of suspicion, that we need to scrutinize everything we read for sinister hidden meanings. My purpose *is* to promote critical reading, the habit of reading with discernment and an awareness of larger contexts and deeper implications. I will be attacking books that I consider morally, theologically, or aesthetically bad. I come, though, to praise books, not to bury them. The capacity to read is a precious gift of God, and this book is designed to encourage people to use this gift to its fullest.

Nor does reading between the lines imply an over-emphasis upon mere interpretation of literature. Although I hope to show readers how to read closely and understand what they read, I resist treating a poem or a novel like a puzzle that has to be figured out. Once the meaning is deciphered, under this view, we can put aside the book, perhaps wondering why its author did not just come out and tell us the idea in the first place. I contend that the imaginative activity that takes place as the eyes scan the page provides both the pleasure and the intellectual value of reading. Interpretation is important, but appreciation and enjoyment must come first.

Reading between the lines is a figure of speech. Attending to the empty spaces between the lines of print refers to what is left unsaid, to the values and assumptions that are an important dimension of what we read. We might also think of lines of demarcation, or even of battle lines. This book takes the reader between the lines of Christian and non-Christian literature, fantasy and realism, comedy and tragedy. Its method is to draw lines—distinguishing between words and images, the Greek and the Hebraic, the Modern and the Postmodern—and to show how Christianity intersects with them all.

The habit of reading is absolutely critical today, particularly for Christians. As television turns our society into an increasingly image-dominated culture, Christians must continue to be people of the Word. When we read, we cultivate a sustained attention span, an active imagination, a capacity for logical analysis and critical thinking, and a rich inner life. Each of these qualities, which have proven themselves essential to a free people, is under assault in our TV-dominated culture. Christians, to maintain their Word-centered perspective in an image-driven world, must become readers.

This is often difficult. We live in a society which sponsors both a mass culture that minimizes reading and an elite intellectual culture which is highly literate but hostile to Christianity. This book is designed to help Christians recover the art of reading and to help them navigate their way through both the classics and the bestseller lists.

Some Christians do not realize that they are heirs to a great literary tradition. From the beginnings of the church to the present day, Christian writers have explored their faith in books, and in doing so have nourished their fellow believers. Some of the best writers who have ever lived have been Christians, working explicitly out of the Christian worldview. To their loss, many contemporary Christians are unaware of Christian writers—both those from past generations and those writing today. This book will introduce readers to these authors who can offer hours and years of pleasure and enrichment.

Although the subject of the book is literature, a host of other subjects will also be addressed. This is because literature, by its very nature, involves its readers in a wide range of issues, provoking thought in many directions. Our discussions of style and literary history will lead to the abortion controversy. Our discussions of comedy and tragedy will lead into the theology of Heaven and Hell. Our discussions of fairy tales will lead to child psychology. Reading can break us out of the tunnel vision of a narrow specialty and lead us into many intriguing and important avenues of thought, a process this book will try to model as well as to explain.

As a "guide to literature," this book may be read in different ways. I hope that it can bear a sustained reading from beginning to end. It can also be read in parts. Each section and each chapter is somewhat self-contained. Someone curious about how comedy works or what post-modernism involves can turn to those chapters. With its index to authors, movements, and issues, the book can function as a reference work.

Several kinds of readers should find something of value in this book. Those with little background in literature, including students of various levels, will learn about the techniques of literature and how to read with greater understanding and appreciation. Those with more experience in reading already know such things, but they may find other topics of interest: the contrast between the classical and the Hebraic traditions; the tragic sense of life as opposed to the comic sense of life; my analysis of the role of existentialism and fascism in Modernist and Postmodernist culture. I also address those who wish to take their place in the Christian literary tradition as poets or novelists. I try to show them how Christian authors in every age have used the writing styles common in their day to express the Christian faith.

This book does not deal with all of the theoretical issues involved in the relationship between Christianity and literature. Other books do that well, and I highly recommend them.[1] I hope readers will consult the footnotes as well as the text and that some will go on to read the works of scholarship I cite. I have been free with my quotations in order to give readers a taste of what there is to read. My own approach is that of a literary historian, eclectic critic, and voracious reader for whom Christianity and literature have proven mutually illuminating.[2]

The first chapter explores why reading has always been so important to Christianity. Words and images promote two totally different mind-sets. Christians must be people of the Word, although the old temptation to succumb to "graven images" is present in a new form in the television age. The second chapter describes the good and the bad pleasures that reading can promote. It discusses such topics as the different kinds of "bad language" and the need to cultivate the art of criticism and to acquire a taste for excellence.

The next section contains chapters on each of the major genres of literature: nonfiction, fiction, and poetry. Each chapter explains the inner workings of the form and focuses on Christian writers who excel in each genre.

The next section examines the diverse modes of literary expression: tragedy, comedy, realism, and fantasy. Whether a work of literature makes the reader cry or laugh, whether it imitates the world or creates a new one—each mode of literature can open the mind and the imagination in significant ways.

The next section surveys literary history. Chapters on Medieval and Reformation literature, Enlightenment and Romantic literature, and Modern and Postmodern literature show how and why literature has changed, and how Christian writers have managed to be relevant in every age.

The last chapter explores the relationship between authors, publishers, and readers. It examines the workings of the literary establishment and the Christian alternatives. It shows how Christian readers, by patronizing worthy writers, can have a major impact on the literary marketplace and thus on the culture as a whole.

The Ethiopian eunuch was reading a good book, but that was

not enough. Philip asked him, "Do you understand what you are reading?"

He replied, "How can I . . . unless someone explains it to me?" (Acts 8:30, 31).

Philip should perhaps be the patron saint of literary critics. The critic simply hopes to do the work of Philip, offering explanations and interpretations as he and the reader bounce along in the chariot. The center of attention should be the book—ultimately, the Book—through which the Living Word, "the author and finisher of our faith," reveals Himself (Hebrews 12:2 KJV).

This particular book, by the same token, is meant to call attention to other books, and ultimately to the depths of truth and meaning expressed in the written words of Scripture. My central purpose will be served if through this book a reader discovers the poetry of George Herbert or the children's stories of Walter Wangerin, gains insight into Scripture by noticing its parallelism or nonvisual imagery, or turns off the TV one night to settle down with a good book.

THE WORD
AND THE IMAGE:
The Importance of Reading

Will reading become obsolete? Some people think that with the explosion of video technology, the age of the book is almost over. Television monitors, fed by cable networks and video recorders, dominate our culture today. Our fads and fashions, politics and morals, entertainment and leisure time are all shaped and controlled by whatever is transmitted on the diode screen. As electronic communication develops at an astonishing rate, who is to say that such arcane skills as reading and writing can or even need to survive?

One thing, however, is certain: Reading can never die out among Christians. This is because the whole Christian revelation centers around a Book. God chose to reveal Himself to us in the most personal way through His Word—the Bible. The word *Bible* is simply the Greek word for "the Book." Indeed the Bible is the primal Book, the most ancient of all literary texts and the source of all literacy. Reading the Bible tends to lead to reading other books, and thus to some important habits of mind.

PEOPLE OF THE BOOK

The centrality of the Bible means that the very act of reading can have spiritual significance. Whereas other religions may stress visions, experiences, or even the silence of meditation as the way to achieve contact with the divine, Christianity insists on the role of language.[1]

Language is the basis for all communication and so lies at the

heart of any personal relationship.[2] We can never know anyone intimately by simply being in that person's presence. We need to have a
conversation in order to share our thoughts and our personalities. By
the same token, we need a conversation with God—two-way communication through language—in order to know Him on a personal basis.
Just as human beings address God by means of language through
prayer, God addresses human beings by means of language in the pages
of Scripture. Prayer and Bible reading are central to a personal relationship with God. Christians have to be, in some sense, readers.

Creation itself was accomplished by God's Word (Hebrews 11:3),
and Jesus Christ Himself is none other than the living Word of God
(John 1:1). The Word of the gospel, the good news that Jesus died for
sinners and offers them eternal life, is a message in human language
which calls people to salvation. "Faith comes from hearing the message, and the message is heard through the word of Christ" (Romans
10:17).[3] God's Word is written down in the pages of the Bible. Human
beings, inspired by the Holy Spirit, have recorded what God has
revealed about Himself and His acts in history. In the Bible, God reveals
His relationship to us, setting forth the law by which we should live
and the gospel of forgiveness through Christ. As we read the Bible, God
addresses us in the most intimate way, as one Person speaking to
another.

When we read the Bible, we are not simply learning doctrines or
studying history—although we *are* doing those things. "The word of
God is living and active. Sharper than any double-edged sword, it pen-
etrates even to dividing soul and spirit, joints and marrow; it judges
the thoughts and attitudes of the heart" (Hebrews 4:12). As we read
the Bible, all of the senses of "The Word of God" come
together—God's creative power, His judgment, Jesus Christ, and
proclamation of the gospel—and are imprinted in our minds and souls.
In the Word, the Holy Spirit is at work.

Certainly the Word of the gospel can be proclaimed orally and
not in writing alone. In church we hear the Word of God preached,
and even in casual witnessing, the Word of God is being shared. In cultures that lack Bibles or people who know how to read them, the
church has managed to survive through the oral proclamation of the
Word, although often with many errors and difficulties. Still, the priority that God places on language and the idea that God's Word is personally accessible to us in a book has meant that Christians have
always valued reading and writing.

Even when books were rare and expensive, having to be copied
out by hand, so that common people remained uneducated, at least
the priests had to know how to read. The Reformation was providen-
tially accompanied by the invention of the printing press, enabling

books to be cheaply mass-produced. This meant that the Bible could be put into the hands of every Christian. Every Christian, therefore, needed to learn how to read. Universal literacy, taken for granted today, was a direct result of the Reformation's reemphasis upon the centrality of Bible reading, not only for theologians but for the spiritual life of every Christian.

Missionaries to nonliterate cultures often begin by mastering the people's language and giving them a system of writing. They then translate the Bible and teach the people how to read it in their own language. The Word of God begins to transform its readers. Once people know how to read the Bible, of course, they can read anything. Tribes go on to discover modern health care and the need for social change, just as the Reformation Christians, empowered by Bible reading, went on to develop scientific technology, economic growth, and democratic institutions.

When ideas and experiences can be written down, they are, in effect, stored permanently. People are no longer bound by their own limited insights and experiences, but they can draw on those of other people as well. Instead of continually starting over again, people can build upon what others have discovered and have written down. Technological, economic, and social progress become possible. The impact of writing can be seen plainly by comparing nonliterate cultures, many of which still exist on the Stone Age level, with those that have had the gift of writing. Nonliterate peoples tend to exist in static, unchanging societies, whereas literate societies tend toward rapid change and technological growth.

Christians, along with Jews and Moslems, are considered "people of the Book." Such reverence for reading and writing has profoundly shaped even our secular society. Certainly, non-Biblical cultures have made great use of writing, but this was almost always reserved for the elite. The religious idea that everyone should learn how to read in order to study the Bible (a view implicit in the Hebrew *bar mitzvah* and carried out in the Reformation school systems) would have radical consequences in the West. Universal education has led to the breaking of class systems, the ability of individual citizens to exercise political power, and a great pooling of minds that would result in the technological achievements of the last four hundred years. It is no exaggeration to say that reading has shaped our civilization more than almost any other factor and that a major impetus to reading has been the Bible.

ELECTRONICALLY GRAVEN IMAGES

Reading has been essential to our civilization, yet today its centrality is under attack by the new electronic media. If reading has had vast social and intellectual repercussions, we should wonder about the repercussions of the new media. Can democratic institutions survive without a literate—that is, a reading—populace, or will the new modes of thinking lend themselves to new forms of totalitarianism? Can educational and intellectual progress continue if visual imagery supplants reading, or will the new information technologies, ironically, subvert the scientific thinking that created them, resulting in anti-intellectualism and mass ignorance?

Such issues are critical for the culture as a whole, but they are especially urgent for the church. Is it possible for Biblical faith to flourish in a society that no longer values reading, or will the newly dominant images lead to new manifestations of the most primitive paganism? Ever since the Old Testament, graven images have tempted God's people to abandon the true God and His Word. Today the images are graven by electrons on cathode ray tubes.

Neil Postman is a media scholar and one of the most astute social critics of our time. His writings focus, with great sophistication, on how different forms of communication shape people's thinking and culture. Postman says that he first discovered the connection between media and culture in the Bible: "In studying the Bible as a young man, I found intimations of the idea that forms of media favor particular kinds of content and therefore are capable of taking command of a culture." He found this concept in the Ten Commandments: "You shall not make for yourself a graven image, or any likeness of anything that is in heaven above, or that is in the earth beneath, or that is in the water under the earth" (Exodus 20:4 RSV).

I wondered then, as so many others have, as to why the God of these people would have included instructions on how they were to symbolize, or not symbolize, their experience. It is a strange injunction to include as part of an ethical system *unless its author assumed a connection between forms of human communication and the quality of a culture.* We may hazard a guess that a people who are being asked to embrace an abstract, universal deity would be rendered unfit to do so by the habit of drawing pictures or making statues or depicting their ideas in any concrete, iconographic forms. The God of the Jews was to exist in the Word and through the Word, an unprecedented conception requiring the highest order of abstract thinking. Iconography thus became blasphemy so that a new kind of God could enter a culture. People like ourselves who are in the process of converting their culture from word-centered to image-centered might profit by reflecting on this Mosaic injunction.[4]

According to Postman, "word-centered" people think in a completely different mode from "image-centered" people. His distinction is especially important for Christians, for whom the "Mosaic injunction" is eternally valid.

In an important book on education, Postman explores the differences between the mental processes involved in reading and those involved in television watching. Reading demands sustained concentration, whereas television promotes a very short attention span. Reading involves (and teaches) logical reasoning, whereas television involves (and teaches) purely emotional responses. Reading promotes continuity, the gradual accumulation of knowledge, and sustained exploration of ideas. Television, on the other hand, fosters fragmentation, anti-intellectualism, and immediate gratification.[5]

Postman does not criticize the content of television—the typical worries about "sex and violence" or the need for quality programming. Rather, the problem is in the properties of the form itself. Language is cognitive, appealing to the mind; images are affective, appealing to the emotions.

> This difference between symbols that demand conceptualization and reflection and symbols that evoke feeling has many implications, one of the most important being that the content of the TV curriculum is irrefutable. You can dislike it, but you cannot disagree with it. . . . There is no way to show that the feelings evoked by the imagery of a McDonald's commercial are false, or indeed, true. Such words as *true* and *false* come out of a different universe of symbolism altogether. Propositions are true or false. Pictures are not.[6]

Postman goes on to connect the newly emerging dominance of electronic images over words to habits of mind that are having monumental social consequences: to the undermining of authority, the loss of a sense of history, hostility to science, pleasure-centeredness, and the emergence of new values based on instant gratification and the need to be continually entertained. The new media direct us "to search for time-compressed experience, short-term relationships, present-oriented accomplishment, simple and immediate solutions. Thus, the teaching of the media curriculum must lead inevitably to a disbelief in long-term planning, in deferred gratification, in the relevance of tradition, and in the need for confronting complexity."[7] The social acceptance of sexual immorality, the soaring divorce rates, and the pathology of drug abuse may well be related to this pursuit of instant pleasure at all costs.

And yet, human beings—made as we are for higher purposes—can scarcely live this way. The untrammeled emotionalism, the isolation, and the fragmentation of mind encouraged by the new information environment lead to mental illness, suicide, and emotional collapse. "Articulate language," on the other hand, according to Postman, "is our chief weapon against mental disturbance."[8] If the trends he sees continue to develop, Postman foresees a future in which we have "people who are 'in touch with their feelings,' who are spontaneous and musical, and who live in an existential world of immediate experience but who, at the same time, cannot 'think' in the way we customarily use that word. In other words, people whose state of mind is somewhat analogous to that of a modern-day baboon."[9]

The impact of the TV mentality on politics is already clearly evident. Rational, sustained debate of issues has been replaced by "soundbites"—brief "media events" that can play on the evening news. Political campaigns are managed by "image consultants," and candidates are chosen for their charisma and the way they appear on TV rather than for their ideas and policies.[10] American democracy was the creation of a word-centered culture and a literate populace.[11] Whether the traditions of freedom and democracy can be sustained without that basis is questionable. An easily manipulated population that cares mostly for its own amusement may be more ready for tyranny (which can keep the masses happy with "bread and circuses") than for the arduous responsibilities of self-government.

The impact of the new mentality upon religion is even more significant. The appeal of the New Age movement with its almost comical irrationalism is evidence that categories such as true or false, revelation or superstition, have become irrelevant for many people.[12] The sophisticated and affluent pay large sums of money to hear the wisdom of ancient Egyptian warriors or extra-terrestrial aliens purportedly taking over the bodies of the "channelers." Well-educated socialites plan their lives by horoscopes. Trendy movie stars solve their problems by means of magical crystals. How can anyone believe such things? If people stop thinking about religion in propositional terms (part of the heritage of "the Word"), abandoning truth or falsehood as religious categories, then belief hardly enters into it. Even among Christians today, religious discussions often focus upon "what I like" rather than "what is true." Those whose main concern is self-gratification search in exactly the same way for religious gratification.

Of course, Christians know that there is nothing "new" in the New Age movement, which the Bible terms demon possession, divination, and idolatry. The New Age movement is simply the paganism of the Old Age. Such primitive and oppressive superstitions squelched human progress for millennia. Ironically, our advanced technology is resulting in a new primitivism, in which the gains of thousands of years of civilization are glibly rejected by a post-literate culture that closely resembles pre-literate ones. Even infanticide, a commonplace practice of pagan societies, has become socially acceptable in the form of abortion on demand. As Scripture warns, graven images can lead to paganism of the most horrific kind.

And yet, evangelicals too have been seduced by the electrical graven images of television and the kind of spirituality that it encourages. In his study of contemporary "TV ministries," Postman is remarkably charitable towards television evangelists, but he shows how the medium itself inevitably distorts the Christian message:

> On television, religion, like everything else, is presented, quite simply and without apology, as an entertainment. Everything that makes religion an historic, profound, and sacred human activity is stripped away; there is no ritual, no dogma, no tradition, no theology, and above all, no sense of spiritual transcendence. On these shows, the preacher is tops. God comes out as second banana.[13]

Postman quotes a religious broadcaster who admits that in order to attract an audience, TV ministries must offer people something they want.

> You will note, I am sure, that this is an unusual religious credo. There is no great religious leader—from the Buddha to Moses to Jesus to Mohammed to Luther—who offered people what they want. Only what they need. But television is not well suited to offering people what they need. It is "user friendly." It is too easy to turn off. It is at its most alluring when it speaks the language of dynamic visual imagery. It does not accommodate complex language or stringent demands. As a consequence, what is preached on television is not anything like the Sermon on the Mount. Religious programs are filled with good cheer. They celebrate affluence. Their featured players become celebrities. . . . I believe I am not mistaken in saying that Christianity is a demanding and serious religion. When it is delivered as easy and amusing, it is another kind of religion altogether.[14]

Since Postman wrote these words, we have seen the collapse of various television ministries. The moral and spiritual failures of the TV preachers may well be a symptom of the shallowness of the TV theology, which lured them away from the spirituality of the Word.

The problem, however, is not only for TV ministries. As evangelicals, we too are tempted to conform to the world rather than to the Word, just as the children of Israel were tempted by their neighbors' graven images and the thought-forms these embodied. We too often stress feeling rather than truth. We tend to seek emotional religious experiences rather than the cross of Jesus Christ. Because we expect worldly "blessings," we do not know how to endure suffering. We want to "name it and claim it"—instantly—rather than submit ourselves without reservation to the will of God. We are impatient with theology, and we dismiss history, thus disdaining the faith of our brothers and sisters who have gone before us and neglecting what they could teach us. We want entertaining worship services—on the order of a good TV show—rather than worship that focuses on the holiness of God and His Word. We want God to speak to us in visions and inner voices rather than in the pages of His Word. We believe in the Bible, but we do not read it very much.

Like the ancient Israelites, we live in "the land of graven images," amidst people who are "mad upon their idols" (Jeremiah 50:38).[15] Also like them, we subtly drift into the ways of "the people of the land" unless we are rescued by the Word of God.

THE IMPORTANCE OF READING

Postman may well be exaggerating the dangers of television and its impact on our lives. He himself does not advocate the elimination of television, as if that were possible or desirable. Instead, he argues that its worst effects can be countered by a reemphasis upon language in our schools and culture, providing a stabilizing balance to the role of the media.[16]

The electronic media still employ language. The gospel can be effectually proclaimed in a television or radio broadcast. For that reason, Christians can and should become involved with the new electronic media. The radio is intrinsically an oral medium, and so is quite appropriate for the oral proclamation of the Word. Straightforward Biblical exposition and preaching can be effectually broadcast on television, although presentations that feature people speaking instead of images are often derided as "talking heads" by media experts. Billy Graham does not stage "media-events"; rather, he broadcasts actual revival services in front of real people in real cities. Christian journalists should by all means produce Christian news and documentary programs. Religious drama, a time-honored contribution of Christian literature, especially deserves expression on television and film.

The Word of God proclaimed orally has always been central in evangelism and in the life of the church, and the electronic media can transmit that Word to the ears of millions of listeners. Nor are all "images" necessarily in opposition to God's Word. I have elsewhere written about what the Bible says about the arts, and I have found that sheer iconoclasm—the rejection of all artistic images as idolatrous—is not Biblical.[17]

However, God's people have always had to be very cautious lest, without thinking, they slip into the ways of their pagan neighbors. The forms can distort the message—an evangelist broadcasting over the airwaves is not exactly the same as a pastor addressing his congregation or a Christian personally witnessing to a friend. The intimacy, the person-to-person presence is lost in an electronic broadcast, and the temptation may be to manipulate the unseen audience or to entertain them by sub-Biblical teachings. This need not happen, but religious broadcasters will have to struggle against the demands of the electronic media. Christians must become conscious of how the image-centered culture is pulling them in non-Christian directions. The priority of language for Christians must be absolute. As the rest of society abandons language-centeredness for image-centeredness, we can expect to feel the pressures and temptations to conform, but we must resist.

One way to do this is simply to read. A growing problem is illiteracy—many people do not know how to read. A more severe problem, though, is "aliteracy"—a vast number of people know how to read but never do it. If we cultivate reading—if we read habitually and for pleasure, reading the Bible, newspapers, the great works of the past and the present, the wide-ranging "promiscuous reading" advocated by the Christian poet Milton[18]—we will reinforce the patterns of the mind that support Christian faith and lead to a healthy and free society.

Even if the masses sink into illiteracy and drug themselves by "amusement," the influential and the powerful will still be readers, as they are today. In the ancient pagan world, reading was a zealously guarded secret for the priests and the ruling elite, who, because they had access to knowledge, had access to power. Postman explores the paradox of a society increasingly dependent upon its scientists but undermining the literate thought-forms science demands. "It is improbable that scientists will disappear," he concludes, "but we shall quite likely have fewer of them, and they are likely to form, even in the short run, an elite class who, like priests of the pictographic age, will be believed to possess mystical powers."[19]

Thinking, planning, imagining, creating—processes encouraged by reading—remain essential to society. Even television shows must have writers. Without people oriented toward language, very little would be accomplished. The point is, the wielders of influence will always be those who read and write, who still work within the framework of language. If Christians remain true to their heritage, if they train themselves to be people of the Word and pursue the disciplines of reading and writing, their influence will be felt once again as it was in the formative moments of our civilization.

VICARIOUS EXPERIENCE AND VICARIOUS SIN:
The Importance of Criticism

*T*urning off the television and picking up a book is a good beginning. And yet Christians who pick up a typical best-selling paperback and read a few chapters might think it better to turn the television set back on. The cover depicts a handsome gentleman in period costume ripping off the period costume worn by the young woman swooning in his arms (this genre of historical romance is often referred to in the business as a "bodice-ripper"). Inside we are treated to a play-by-play account of the characters' sexual activities rendered in breathless prose. Or other covers might invite us to try other successful formulas: the evil child (a cute little girl with malevolent eyes stares out from the cover, holding a doll in one hand and a bloody axe in the other); the "epic saga" of a rich and powerful family (five hundred pages of social climbing, back stabbing, and consumerism); the angst-ridden personal problem tract (about abandoning one's family in a depressing quest for personal fulfillment); the action-adventure techno-thriller (featuring spies, detectives, soldiers, or spacemen thwarting attempts to take over the world).

Some of the most popular books are starkly bad—bad in their content, bad in their effect, and, in a related way, bad aesthetically. Television has at least a few restraints—books seemingly have none. Wrapped in the mantle of the Freedom of the Press, books seem to have no qualms about obscene language, pornographic or sadomasochistic displays, and tasteless, mindless sensationalism. Books can engage the inner mind more deeply than the external images of television and film;

therefore, in some ways they might seem even more insidious, more corrupting.

But apart from their content, some of the most popular titles are badly written. The characters are predictable stereotypes; the plots are churned out according to a formula; the styles are ludicrous or inept. These books give their readers almost nothing of value for their investment of money and time. Such books cannot stand up to a second reading—once we know what happens, there is no point in reading it again. They do not provoke any thought either during or after they are read. The most that even their biggest fans can say for them is that they kill time. As with other products of a mass culture, such as fast food and disposable merchandise, they are aimed at "consumers" who do not so much read as "consume" new titles.[1]

Popular literature today has been profoundly shaped by the television mind-set and by the larger dynamics of our contemporary mass culture. Just as television is an "attention-centered medium," much writing today exists solely to win attention for itself. This is why so many books play with the obscene and the pornographic. Few of them are works of art, exploring the depths of human behavior. Most are simply trying to keep the readers' attention by titillating them with sexual fantasies, stirring scandals, and grotesque brutality. Such material is ridiculously easy to write—there is nothing to it. Original sin has great marketing potential.

The answer to bad books is good books. Readers need to be able to tell the difference. The problem is not "reading for pleasure" or "recreational reading." Pleasure and recreation are excellent reasons to read. Nor is the problem simply the content of certain books—sex, violence, or immoral subjects. Such topics may be explored with morality and taste. Nor is the problem with certain genres of books. First-rate authors old and new have written superb works of art in the various popular genres—romances (Emily and Charlotte Brontë), science fiction (C. S. Lewis and Ray Bradbury), thrillers (Edgar Allan Poe and Graham Greene), and mysteries (Dorothy Sayers and P. D. James).

The problem is the way bad books are written: badly. Good books—even those written by non-Christians or dealing only with secular themes—must be written according to the aesthetic laws that are part of the created order. As such, Christians can see them in the light of God, who is not only the source of all truth, but also the source of all beauty and all perfection (James 1:17). Conversely, books that are morally bad will tend to be aesthetically bad as well. Great works of literature may not always articulate an explicitly Christian worldview, but they will still usually be worth reading for their intrinsic merit and will often give unwitting testimony to God's sovereignty over all of life.

In emphasizing "good books" and the importance of aesthetic

quality, I am not being elitist nor do I intend to denigrate merely reading for pleasure. Literature is supposed to give pleasure. Curling up with a good book on a rainy afternoon, going to the theater, singing a song, staying up late reading a mystery thriller that is too exciting to put down—these are precious human experiences. That reading is also beneficial, that it can instruct us in various ways, is a pleasant side effect. Bad books can give us superficial gratification; good books can give us far deeper pleasure.

In fact, I am often suspicious of books that do not give me pleasure. The Victorian critic Matthew Arnold, convinced that modern people would no longer be able to believe in Christianity, thought that poetry would take the place of religion.[2] For many writers and readers in the "high culture" of the intellectual elite, this has happened. They turn to Art to give meaning and direction to life. Unfortunately, when literature and the arts substitute for religion, they become self-important, pontificating, and dismal. Novels become world-weary philosophical discourses on the meaninglessness of life; poetry becomes esoteric and pretentious; reading becomes an ascetic duty rather than an aesthetic pleasure.

Thus we have a curious dichotomy in the modern literary scene. Whereas the popular culture gives us books that offer entertainment but no ideas, the "high culture" gives us books that offer ideas but no entertainment. There are many books—in my opinion the best books—which manage to do both. Christian writers and readers may be in a position to help heal this literary schizophrenia. Those of us who know God are freed to enjoy literature on its own terms, without requiring it to be either overly "serious" or overly trivial.

The pleasures of reading are, for the most part, good for us. We might even say that the reason we enjoy a book is that it is doing something good for us. We can benefit not only from a book's themes and ideas; we can benefit from the very pleasures that impel us to keep turning the pages. Christians realize that although all pleasures are made possible by God and are thus good in themselves, human beings can turn every kind of pleasure into a sinful perversion. The quest for pleasure alone, outside of God's provision, can violate the love we owe to God, to our neighbor, and to ourselves. Literature likewise is often misused for erotic, hateful, or egotistic ends.

This chapter will discuss the pleasures of the imagination, both the life-affirming and God-affirming ones that make us more sensitive and aware, and those which can deaden our hearts. Our reading habits, as well as the other pleasures of our lives, need to be disciplined. That discipline must be based on knowledge, understanding, and a cultivated taste. Modern bookstores are filled with shallow, salacious, badly written books that are travesties of true literary art. Today more than ever, Christians need to learn how to discern the good and the bad in what they read, to recognize quality, and to train their sensibilities so that they enjoy what is excellent. In other words, they need to be critics and not simply consumers.

IMAGINATIVE EXPERIENCE

Reading—besides involving the mental disciplines of logic, critical thinking, and sustained thought—operates on our imaginations. As human beings, we have the capacity to picture things in our minds. We can conjure up memories from the past (a particular Christmas morning when we were very young) or plans for the future (what next summer's vacation will be like). We can picture things that are real (the maple tree with its fall colors in the backyard) or things that have no reality in themselves (a maple tree with purple bark and plaid leaves).

Today the term imagination has connotations of artistic creativity, so that some people lament that they have none. This is to misunderstand the term. Everyone can call forth complex mental images, rich textures of sights, sounds, smells, tastes, feelings, and ideas. Nearly every waking moment and at night when we dream, we are using our imaginations. A carpenter must imagine what he is going to build. A scientist must imagine a model that would account for the data. An engineer must imagine the solution of a problem or the possibilities of a new invention. What goes on in our minds when we are daydreaming, making plans, or "just thinking" is imagination—an extraordinary gift of God, which we usually take completely for granted.

When we read, the words on the page work upon our imaginations. Mental images are created in our minds. When we watch television, the images are presented to us ready-made; we simply take them in passively. Reading, however, merely offers us marks on paper; for them to mean anything, we must *actively* employ our personal imaginations. The result is that we construct and enter into a vast world of actions, feelings, and experiences taking place nowhere else but in our minds.

Reading *exercises* the imagination in a very literal way. Just as lifting weights builds up the body's physical strength, reading builds up the mind's imaginative strength. The energy expended in lifting weights could be used for more productive purposes on a loading dock, but exercise is beneficial to one's overall health and strength. In the same way, even reading inferior books is probably beneficial. When my children read Nancy Drew or Tarzan or young romance novels, I am so happy that they are not watching TV that I seldom complain that they are not reading more substantial fare. A more sophisticated taste can come from more experience in reading, but I am glad that their imaginations are getting a workout.

The imagination has a moral dimension as well. We are told to: "Rejoice with those who rejoice; mourn with those who mourn" (Romans 12:15). Such empathy, identifying with the joys and sorrows of others, is a special application of the imagination. The ability to imagine what it would be like to experience what someone else is experiencing, to project ourselves into someone else's point of view, can be crucial to moral sensitivity. When we read a novel, we are ushered into the point of view of various characters and are gladdened by their victories and saddened by their tragedies. Reading provides mental training for empathizing with real people.

Reading offers vicarious experience. We can have the sensation of experiencing something without actually having to experience it firsthand. We can read a historical narrative about the Civil War, a novel about life on a whaling ship, or a poem about courtly love in a medieval castle. While we read, we imaginatively experience the battles, the mysteries of the sea, the fervor of love. Such vicarious experiences are pleasurable because they allow us to extend ourselves into situations, times, and places that we could never enter apart from books. Reading satisfies our curiosity, our thirst for adventure, our delight in new phenomena, our need, in C. S. Lewis's words, "to enlarge our being."³

Vicarious experience can be more pleasurable than real experience. Reading about a Civil War battle may be exciting; actually being in a Civil War battle would be terrifying. Reading the novel *Moby Dick* may evoke the mystery of the sea, but actually living on a whaling boat might seem boring and brutal. Reading a medieval love poem may conjure up the beauty of hopeless love, although no one enjoys having a broken heart in real life. Extreme sensations or dangerous undertakings may be experimented with in safety. Our imaginations can launch off into hair-raising adventures or emotionally wrenching ordeals, while at the same time we enjoy the security of our own easy chairs.

Just as we can learn from real experiences, we can learn from secondhand ones. People who have risked their lives in combat usually learn from what they have gone through. Reading *The Red Badge of Courage, All Quiet on the Western Front,* or *The Iliad* is not the same as actually facing an enemy on the battlefield, but the reader of these books can still learn something of what the combat veteran knows. Having a wide range of experiences can enlarge and deepen our personalities, which is why reading can enrich our lives.

This is not to say that books are a substitute for real experiences. People rightly complain about those who know the world only through books. Books, though, can mediate real experiences that we may have later and can enable us to sample experiences that would be undesirable or even impossible to have in real life. Vicarious experience of the impossible—the alternate universes of fantasy and science fiction—stretches our imaginations and thus builds our minds.

Walter Wangerin has defined art as a "composed experience." As a writer, he selects details and expresses them in language in such a way that the reader experiences something significant.[4] Often we seek out "composed experiences" that are trivial—we are only interested in a momentary thrill, a literary roller coaster ride. Other times we can seek out more substantial literary experiences. What would it be like to live in ancient Greece? Histories, historical novels, and literary masterpieces of the past can place us, vicariously, into another place and time. What would it be like to struggle through poverty, hopelessness, persecution, or other obstacles? What might war or atheism or missionary work feel like, and how would my own faith respond to them? Books can provide access to all of these experiences.

VICARIOUS SIN

Some experiences, on the other hand, are forbidden. Too often readers turn to books so they can vicariously experience sin. They are interested in books that pander to their sexual fantasies, to their dreams of wealth and power, to their dark, secret obsessions with sadistic violence or occult nightmares. Many such readers would never actually carry out the sorts of depravity they love to read about (although some do). Reading the pornographic descriptions and the lovingly described acts of brutality gratifies their secret desires, giving them perverted pleasures in the privacy of their own imaginations.

What takes place in the imagination has moral and spiritual significance. Jesus Himself tells us so in the Sermon on the Mount: "You have heard that it was said, 'Do not commit adultery.' But I tell you that anyone who looks at a woman lustfully has already committed adultery with her in his heart" (Matthew 5:27, 28). Committing adultery is not a matter only of overt action. The inner passion of lust is what corrupts. The evil in the heart brings forth evil actions (Matthew 15:19, 20). If the action is hindered because of the constraints of law or opportunity, the inner sinfulness remains. Jesus makes the same point about violence: Being angry with your brother can make you guilty of murder, as far as God's judgment is concerned (Matthew 5: 21, 22).

The application is inescapable. Just as we must avoid sinful actions, we must avoid sinful imaginings. Jesus puts this in no uncertain terms: If our eyes lead us into sin, it is better to gouge them out than to allow them to lead us to Hell (Matthew 5:29, 30). We must not water down these solemn warnings from Jesus Christ Himself. The Sermon on the Mount proves that sin is a condition of our inmost being; although our sinful nature is atoned for in the cross and our failures freely forgiven, we must never willingly cultivate habits that Scripture condemns. Lustful and angry fantasies are clearly forbidden by Scripture. It would follow that the imagination can be a source of evil as well as good. Indeed, Scripture says as much, speaking of the time before the Flood: "The LORD saw that the wickedness of man was great in the earth, and that every imagination of the thoughts of his heart was only evil continually" (Genesis 6:5 RSV).

Many experts extol the powerful impact of good literature in forming moral values, strong minds, and healthy personalities. And yet when it comes to pornography, for example, they change their tune and deny that it has any impact. If good literature can have a positive effect on the individual and on society as a whole, surely bad literature can have a negative effect. The imagination is an integral facet of our inner lives; as such it can be used to degrade our minds as well as to build them up.

Does this mean Christians should not read literature that leads them into vicarious sin? I would say yes. If our Lord would have us go so far as to gouge out our eyes or cut off our hands to avoid sin, surely a limitation to our reading practices is not too severe. If His words are metaphorical, that does not diminish their force or their scope, but rather increases them.

And yet, some distinctions should be made. The Sermon on the Mount does not imply that the *subjects* of sexuality or violence are forbidden for Christians to contemplate. Notice that our Lord's own words—gouging out eyes and cutting off hands—are gruesomely violent in their imagery. And yet, these words, imagined in our minds, are not equivalent to actually mutilating someone. Christ's words certainly do not fill their readers with anger, hatred, or evil thoughts toward anyone else. The Bible is never delicate when it comes to specifying sexual sin or sanctioning marital love. The Bible's depictions of sexuality, however, are unlikely to induce immorality in their readers.

To apply the principle to literature, what might render a work harmful is how it affects a reader. One reader may experience lust when he reads a particular novel. Other novels might provoke in a reader hate-filled fantasies of revenge or sadistic domination. Another reader may find that a book dredges up dark occult yearnings. Another reader may be tempted into covetousness, worldliness, pride, or other sins. In each case, the reader should "pluck his eyes" out of that book.

And yet, another reader may be morally unaffected by a passage that is a serious moral stumbling block to someone else. As a trained and experienced reader with perhaps a jaded imagination, I find that I react to many of the "obligatory sex scenes" of contemporary fiction with boredom. My usual thought is, *Here we go again,* as the writing becomes more and more ludicrous and the author's sexual fantasies rage out of artistic control. I do not think I am being harmed simply by reading them.

Some readers are, though. Writers should be more careful, lest they incur the horrible judgment reserved for those who cause "a little one" to sin (Luke 17:1, 2). At the same time, some people are so tormented by lust that *any* mention of sex inflames them, even when the treatment of sexuality is morally and artistically legitimate (as in The Song of Solomon). This may not be the fault of the author or the book, but a problem in the reader. Those so affected should avoid the occasion for sin, but they should not necessarily try to suppress the work for everyone.

In evaluating the morality of a work of literature, we must realize that to depict sin is not necessarily to advocate sin. As Susan Gallagher and Roger Lundin point out, we must consider the work's purpose and its point of view. Does the work depict sin in order to show its evil (as the Bible does), or does it depict sin "in order to encourage its practice" (as pornography does)?

> A story that contains an act of adultery is not necessarily immoral or obscene. If the perspective of the story implies that adultery is an acceptable social practice that harms no one, the story advocates an immoral position with which we would disagree.[5]

The Bible's account of David and Bathsheba or the story of Lancelot and Guinevere depict adultery in such a way that the reader comes to understand why it is evil. Works that depict immorality in an honest way may help us to see through its superficial appeal and thereby arm us against it.

Gallagher and Lundin also remind us that sexual immorality or profane language is only a small part of the moral universe:

> Sometimes we get so concerned with offensive language or sex that we overlook many other kinds of depictions of sin that may prove far more tempting and harmful for us to read. If we think about the immoral acts depicted in literature that pose the most temptation to us, are profanity and sexual sin really the most dangerous? Aren't we far more likely to be influenced by our society's ideals of self-centeredness; the glorification of alcoholic or drug-induced irrationality; the importance of money, clothing, and physical possessions; the need to be beautiful and have a perfect body; or the assumption that cheating and manipulation are acceptable practices? . . . Some of the most dangerous immorality in texts today has nothing to do with sex or profanity. It lies instead in the accep-

tance of materialism, the encouragement of egotism, and the glorification of violence.[6]

Just as reading can exercise our moral faculties, it can also corrupt them. We must observe the effect that our reading is having on us.

Some literature is abhorrent in itself. A song popular recently is entitled "Treat Her Like a Prostitute." Its purpose and its point of view do nothing to redeem the message of its title. Slasher movies, pornography, and "Lifestyles of the Rich and Famous" also seem to me to be intrinsically evil. Christians are right to condemn worldliness, pornographic degradation of women, and violence that hardens our hearts to human suffering. Christians must scrutinize themselves in their reading as well as in every other area of their lives, learning how "to distinguish good from evil" (Hebrews 5:14).

BAD LANGUAGE

To that end, it might be helpful to define the terms often used to describe the evils in literature. Words such as *obscenity, pornography, vulgarity,* and *profanity* each mean something completely different and can help us understand the various issues that deserve our scrutiny.

The word *obscene* can be thought of as meaning "out of the scene" or "offstage."[7] In ancient Greek drama, certain actions could not be performed onstage for fear of violating the decorum, the appropriate aesthetic effect, of the play. Specifically, Greek drama forbade presenting violence onstage. When the plot of a tragedy demanded that a character commit suicide or murder, the violent action was never shown. Rather, the characters affected simply left the stage; later a messenger came to report the horrible news.

Why this reticence? The Greeks were hardly prudish or moralistic. The reason was a sound aesthetic one. When the audience is enthralled by a dramatic action, involved in the characters and their dilemmas, the spectacle of overt violence literally breaks the aesthetic mood. The audience may become totally involved with the suffering of Oedipus, but if it then must witness the actor poking out his eyes, the reaction shifts from tragic pathos to shock and revulsion. The delicate evocation of vicarious experience is disrupted by grisly special effects.

The same principle is evident in contemporary films. The audience is introduced to the characters and their situations; the story becomes more and more absorbing; the suspense builds—and then someone takes out a chain saw and splatters someone's guts all over the screen. How does the audience react? Some viewers say, "Ooooh, gross!"; some cover their eyes; some try to figure out the special effects;

some start to laugh. The aesthetic experience, at any rate, is finished. The violence could be considered "obscene"; that is, it should not have been shown on screen because it violates aesthetic decorum.

The same is true of graphic sexual depictions. When an actor and an actress take off their clothes in a movie, viewers begin reacting sexually instead of aesthetically. The dramatic effect is interrupted and displaced by the sexual effect. Stimulating an audience artistically takes skill and craft; stimulating them sexually is far easier.

The Greeks did not shy away from dealing with sexuality or violence. *Oedipus Rex* deals with incest, patricide, self-mutilation, and suicide. It somehow manages to deal with such scarifying topics while maintaining taste, dignity, and a serious moral tone. How? By maintaining decorum, by presenting the characters' actions and anguish in language of exalted poetry, but never explicitly presenting the horrors onstage. Obscenity is not only a moral fault; as the Greeks understood, it is also an artistic fault. Insensitivity to aesthetic decorum is perhaps one of the worst weaknesses of contemporary literature.[8]

The aesthetic problem of sexual obscenity can be seen in the history of the way sex has been depicted in literature. What was once merely alluded to—whether discreetly or bawdily—gradually became more and more graphic, escalating to the point that many writers today seem to be attempting to create sexual pleasure in their readers rather than aesthetic pleasure. The skilled writers of the "high culture" led the way for the lesser writers of the "mass culture." In the early part of the twentieth century, people were shocked at James Joyce's *Ulysses*, which by current standards is extremely mild, and by the frank eroticism of D. H. Lawrence's *Lady Chatterly's Lover*. These novels by admittedly great writers provoked court battles that cast down most legal restraints and made explicit sexual descriptions completely acceptable in literary circles. Pornography had existed for centuries, but now it was in the mainstream.

As writers began to appeal to readers' sexual pleasure instead of aesthetic pleasure, the intrinsic limitations of the pornographic imagination cheapened their work. Characters became coarsened and stereotyped. Pornography depends upon sexual fantasies—beautiful, pliant women who eagerly satisfy the insatiable desires of the macho heroes. The result will be superficial characterizations such as are found everywhere in today's literature—Mickey Spillane mysteries, "adult" Westerns, family-saga romances, and works by "serious" writers. Such one-dimensional and predictable characters inhibit realism, complexity, and sophisticated aesthetic effects.

As the readers' threshold of stimulation keeps getting higher, writers of the erotic must always be going beyond the earlier boundaries. If the desire is to titillate the increasingly jaded reader, normal sexuality begins to seem too tame, lacking the "tang" of the forbidden. The sex described must become wilder, more exotic, and more perverse. The sexual imagination begins to rule over the aesthetic imagination.

The moral problem with obscenity is even more significant than the aesthetic problem. We might think of the "obscene," in the Greek sense, as portrayals of what should be kept private. Sexuality is for the private intimacy of marriage, not for public eyes. Striptease shows are obscene, not because nudity is wrong but because nudity is private. To pay a woman to take her clothes off in front of crowds of ogling men is to violate her in a very brutal way. Public sex is obscene, not because sex is evil but because sex is sacred. As William Kirk Kilpatrick says, "Unless you understand that Christianity considers sexual love to be a sacred thing, you can never fully understand why it insists that sex be set about with exclusions and restrictions. All sacred things are. It is not that it thinks sex a bad thing but a high thing."9

Obscene violence is also a moral desecration. A popular video consists of actual footage of executions, automobile accidents, murder scenes, and autopsies. Renting this tape and sitting down with a bowl of popcorn for an evening's entertainment is obscene. Taking pleasure in death is monstrous. Trivializing and enjoying our neighbors' suffering violates the love we owe them (Matthew 22:39). Such obscenity desensitizes its viewers, making them immune to normal human impulses of compassion and love, turning their hearts to stone (see Zechariah 7:9-12).

The word *pornography*, by the way, is derived from two Greek words which together literally mean "prostitute-writing."10 Pornography is a type of obscenity consisting of graphic sexual descriptions designed to arouse the reader with vicarious sexual experiences. Satisfying one's sexual cravings by patronizing prostitutes is very similar to using books or movies for that purpose. Both involve the buying and selling of sex. Both dislocate sexuality away from the personal relationship of marriage. Pornography, like prostitution, abuses women, rendering them as nonhuman objects of lust and conditioning men to treat real women in this way. Pornographic films and magazines exploit sexually the real human beings who appear in them. Porn stars, enticed by their yearning for glamour and big money, are debauched, humiliated, and used. The writers of pornography are also prostituting themselves, selling their imaginations the way some women sell their bodies.

Again, in order to keep its readers stimulated, obscenity and pornography must become more and more extreme. Heroin addicts after awhile become less and less sensitive to the drug. They require ever larger doses to achieve their high—until finally an overdose kills them. The same holds true for those addicted to pornography and obscene violence. Since the "tang of evil" is part of the thrill, and since these addicts become desensitized to ordinary pleasure, they must continually push the boundary. Pictures of naked women after awhile are not enough; pictures of people having sex come next. Then perverted sex. Then sadism. Then—children being especially innocent and thus providing a greater "tang of evil"—child pornography. Then what? Snuff movies (pornographic films that conclude with an actual murder)? Carrying out these vicarious experiences in real life? Those who ruin their lives by fornication and perversion often speak of having started with pornography. Many rapists tell the same story. So do serial killers.[11]

Such obscenity and pornography is a social problem and not only an aesthetic issue. Human nature is filled with dark secrets and horrifically evil potential. Pornography and obscenity deaden the senses, the imagination, and the conscience. They tap into dangerous impulses. The issue is not simply the effect these have on children. I worry about the effect on adults.

The *vulgar* is a much milder form of offensive language than obscenity. The term literally means "the common people." Reflecting the ancient social hierarchies, the implication is that the lower classes exhibit behavior and conversation that cultivated people would avoid. Vulgar talk would include references that are embarrassing, rude, or inappropriate for the time, the place, and the company. Mild sexual innuendos, allusions to having to go to the bathroom, and other "naughty" language (the sort of thing that children giggle at) are not necessarily obscene, but they are usually vulgar.

Notice that in the original sense of the word, vulgarity is embarrassing not so much to the hearers but to the speaker. Someone who is vulgar reveals a poor education and subservient social position. Today, society has changed. Common people still tend to find certain words offensive; the upper classes are often the most foul-mouthed of them all. Thus the elite are now vulgar, revealing a "low" sensibility and an utter lack of taste.

Vulgarity is not necessarily sinful, however. The degree to which one may refer to "bodily functions," for example, varies historically. Chaucer's *Canterbury Tales* is not really obscene, but its medieval lack of prudery means that it is occasionally vulgar by our standards. Even Christian writers of the past often seem startlingly coarse in their language. Luther is enormously edifying to read, yet when he attacks abuses in the church or in society he pulls no punches. It has been said that some of Luther's writings could not today be published in Lutheran periodicals. Certain Victorians even considered the Bible to be too embarrassing. Modern Christians should not mistake their post-Victorian sense of propriety for moral purity. Vulgarity may exhibit poor taste and should be avoided by Christians on aesthetic grounds, but it is seldom sinful.

More problematic for Christians is *profanity*. This word comes from another Latin construction meaning "outside the temple."[12] If something were profane—that is, ceremonially unclean—it would not be allowed inside the Temple. *Profane* is the opposite of *sacred*. In the present context, profanity violates what is holy. Profanity uses religious language in a way that desecrates or trivializes its sacred meaning. The Bible says relatively little about obscenity, pornography, or vulgarity, but it condemns profanity in the strongest terms. "You shall not misuse the name of the LORD your God, for the LORD will not hold anyone guiltless who misuses his name" (Exodus 20:7). Nor are we to swear (Matthew 5:34; James 5:12). Nor are we to curse our fellow human beings (James 3:10).

To do so is a grave misuse of language. A Christian can never say, "those are just words," implying (with the modern view) that mere words have little importance. In the Christian consciousness, words are of staggering significance, underlying existence itself, defining personality and enabling relationships to occur. God created by His Word; His Word became flesh in Jesus Christ; He reveals Himself to us through the writing and the proclamation of His Word. Moreover, "it is with your mouth that you confess and are saved" (Romans 10:10). Our continuing relationship with God is centered in the language of prayer. No wonder James excoriates those who profanely misuse such a monumental gift as language: "With the tongue we praise our Lord and Father, and with it we curse men, who have been made in God's likeness. Out of the same mouth come praise and cursing. My brothers, this should not be" (James 3:9, 10).

Profane language would include irreverent invocations of the name of God ("Oh my God!"); insincere promises based on holy things ("I swear on a stack of Bibles!"); the calling down of God's wrath upon another human being ("God damn you!"). Apparently, God sees these expressions as prayers. He takes them seriously even if we do not. Ironically, such expressions seem mild and inoffensive today. We might be shocked at "bathroom language" or four-letter sexual obscenities, but not at an "oh God" when someone is surprised or a "go to Hell" when someone is angry. Here, as so often, our worldly standards and those of Scripture are turned upside down. What seems shocking to us may mean little to God, and what may seem minor to us may be a grave offense to God's holiness.

Profanity is not a matter of language alone. The violation of the holy occurs in other ways. The sex scene in the film *The Last Temptation of Christ* is profane. So is George Burns playing the role of God—rendering the Consuming Fire in terms of a domesticated nice guy spouting pop psychology and comic shtick. A corrupt evangelist using God's name to swindle people out of their money is profane in a deeper sense. I wonder whether some of the products sold in Christian bookstores might verge on profanity. Only what is religious risks being profane.

Blasphemy—overt denigration of God—is an extreme case of profanity, and it is not uncommon in contemporary literature. Andres Serrano's photograph of a crucifix immersed in urine was described by one critic as "a fairly conventional piece of post-surrealist blasphemy,"[13] and there are many literary equivalents. Moslems consider Salman Rushdie's *Satanic Verses* blasphemous, and they are surely right, in that it ridicules Mohammed and their sacred Koran. Their response—to try to kill the author—is not an option for Christians affronted by blasphemy, who must bless and pray for their enemies and persecutors, overcoming evil with good (Romans 12:14-21). And yet this sin is especially horrible. Dante placed blasphemers in that section of Hell that also punishes violence against nature and art.[14] According to Dante, blasphemy is violence against God, although such violence is pathetically futile. It is profoundly unnatural to malign the source of our very existence. To lash out in hatred at the Person who created us, makes possible all of our joys, and sustains our very existence is vicious and perverse.

If profanity is so evil, what does this mean for literature? In Shakespeare's time, officials felt that the mere mentioning of God in a dramatic production was a violation of the commandment against taking the Lord's name in vain. The characters in a play were not real, they reasoned. Therefore, for them to invoke God in a fictional context was insincere, false, and "in vain." As a result, any explicit references to God were routinely censored.[15] The playwrights would get around the injunction (enforced more for stage versions than for written texts) in several ways. They would allude to pagan deities which were made to symbolize the true God (Jove could not be profaned). They replaced the word *God* with an associated word such as *Heaven* (as in "Heaven forgive thee," rather than "God forgive thee").[16] And they used elegant language that tiptoes around the sacred name, as in these lines from Shakespeare:

> Why all the souls that were, were forfeit once;
> And He that might the vantage best have took
> Found out the remedy. How would you be,
> If He, which is the top of judgment, should
> But judge you as you are? O, think on that;
> And mercy then will breathe within your lips,
> Like man new made.
>
> (*Measure for Measure*, 2.2.73-79)[17]

Such an extreme fear of profanity is surely going too far (although we might hesitate to question an age that was both more religious and more artistic than our own). It might remind us that purely "secular" writing may be more harmless than ostensibly "religious" writing, just as the Reformation was more suspicious of religious art than of purely secular art such as portraits and landscapes.

In a society that has lost all sense of the sacred, we should not be too surprised to hear sacred language treated profanely. We who find this language meaningful should be offended at its misuse. The sin inheres in the speaking (or writing) of profanity, not in its hearing (or reading). A Christian should never use profanity, but I do not think hearing or reading profane language is necessarily sinful, just as witnessing a sin is not necessarily condoning it. Encountering profanity in a book is unlikely to provoke vicarious sin in a Christian, except when its repetition starts to deaden our own reverence at hearing the sacred name of our Lord. As long as we wince at the profanity, it is probably not hurting us. The irritation we feel "when we hear one rack the name of God"[18] is evidence that those words are not profane to us. Christians should excoriate profanity whenever they encounter it, but they need not be afraid of language which properly belongs to them. Nor should they miss the irony of godless people incessantly calling upon God.

The Christian novelist Flannery O'Connor has a character in *Wise Blood,* Hazel Motes, who is trying to run away from God. He seeks out the company of the most depraved people he can find. Every profanity they utter, though, is a pointed reminder of the Person he is trying desperately to avoid. He goes to a used car lot. The operator's boy is always cursing: "'Jesus on the cross,' the boy said. 'Christ nailed.'" Such words make Hazel grow pale. As Hazel and the used car dealer bargain for a car, in the background the boy keeps muttering, "'Sweet Jesus, sweet Jesus, sweet Jesus.'" Finally, Hazel cannot take it anymore: "'Why don't he shut up?' Haze said suddenly. 'What's he keep talking like that for?'"[19]

In the fictional world of the novel, the boy is being profane. And yet, O'Connor's novel is not being profane. She means the terms literally and in their most sacred sense. The boy's profanity ironically reminds Hazel of the reality of Jesus Christ. Haze is wondering with the psalmist, "Where can I flee from Your presence?" and he is discovering that even in the depths of human sinfulness he cannot escape from his God (Psalm 139:7). Where Hazel least expects to hear them, the sacred words find him out.

The apparent profanity in O'Connor's novel is a brilliant and profound example of irony—the literary technique in which the surface meaning is contradicted by the actual meaning. (As when the messenger in *Oedipus* announces "Good News!" as he delivers the information that is going to ruin everyone's lives. Sarcasm is another form of irony, as in, "That's just great—I love to get stuck in traffic.") Irony can exist on several levels, even when it is not intended. A carpenter who hammers his finger and blurts out the name of Jesus Christ, a teenager who continually invokes the Deity in a conversation about a shopping mall, a man who prays that his lawn mower be eternally condemned to Hell because it won't start—all of them display serious spiritual confusion, but they bear evidence that human nature at a very deep, instinctual level, recognizes God's sovereignty and His connection to pain, pleasure, and judgment.

The Scriptures clearly warn against "bad language" in all of its manifestations:

> But fornication and all impurity or covetousness must not even be named among you, as is fitting among saints. Let there be no filthiness, nor silly talk, nor levity, which are not fitting, but instead let there be thanksgiving. Be sure of this, that no fornicator or impure man, or one who is covetous (that is, an idolater), has any inheritance in the kingdom of Christ and of God. Let no one deceive you with empty words, for it is because of these things that the wrath of God comes upon the sons of disobedience. . . . Take no part in the unfruitful works of darkness, but instead expose them. For it is a shame even to speak of the things that they do in secret (Ephesians 5:3-6, 11, 12 RSV).

This passage condemns not only sinful action but sinful language: speaking and deceiving through empty words.

CENSORSHIP AND SELECTIVITY

Should a book be suppressed for its sinfulness? Should Christians work to outlaw offensive writing? Christians must be very cautious here. Freedom of the press and freedom of speech are precious rights and must be affirmed, if for no other reason than that the most censored book is the Bible and the most persecuted speech is proclamation of the gospel. The legal niceties restricting censorship must be respected as part of the God-ordained secular authority designed for our good (Romans 13:1-7).

And yet, if certain books are truly evil in themselves and in their effect on others, condoning them would be an abdication of our responsibility to love our neighbors and to work for a healthy society. The legal remedies available against obscenity should be pursued. Child pornography, at least, is against the law, as is obscenity. "Adult bookstores" (a ludicrous name) should be harassed by zoning ordinances and other legal means. Prosecuting illegal actions involved in producing pornography—for example, charging child pornographers with child abuse and charging the makers of pornographic films with prostitution—is another fruitful legal avenue that leaves First Amendment rights intact.

Except in certain extreme cases, the state may not outlaw the publications of a free press. The selection of those publications, especially in schools and libraries, can be controversial. No one can buy every book, and it is not legally censoring a publication to refuse to buy it. A librarian, a teacher, a school board, or a parent chooses books for someone else to read. Is it censorship to refuse to select certain books because of their moral effect?

Unfortunately, when Christians have tried to ban books from libraries and classrooms, they have often engaged in the wrong battles and fought them in self-defeating ways. Efforts have been made to ban *The Lion, the Witch, and the Wardrobe* by C. S. Lewis, a Christian allegory that clearly presents the gospel and through which hundreds of children and adults have been brought to Christ. Why would Christians object to such a book? Because the title has a witch in it and thus might be an entry point for occult powers. Obviously the protestors were simply skimming titles and had never read or understood Lewis's novel.

Other times would-be censors focus on relatively trivial issues. Should *The Wizard of Oz* be banned because it speaks of a "good witch"? Certainly the term is a contradiction (I have this conversation with my children every year), but the error in terminology should not be exaggerated and turned into an excuse for banning a wholesome book. Nor should Christians waste their energies fighting books such as *Tom Sawyer* (because it shows disrespect for authority) or John Steinbeck's *Of Mice and Men* (because of occasional vulgar language). To do so shows a lack of perspective, a straining at a gnat (Matthew 23:24). Such efforts are never successful and only invite contempt for Christianity.

Conservative Christians are not the only ones who try to engage in censorship. Liberal factions are probably the most successful censors, and their agenda seldom attracts the indignation of the American Civil Liberties Union. Whereas conservatives tend to focus on questions of personal morality, liberals tend to focus on questions of social morality. *Huckleberry Finn* is attacked not by conservatives (as the media often implies), but by liberals who believe it promotes racial stereotyping. Conservatives are offended by obscene language (which never fails to invite ridicule from the press). Liberals, by the same token, are offended by Mark Twain's use of *nigger*. The word is indeed offensive, just as obscenities are offensive and for the same reason. To take the word out of its nineteenth-century context, when it was not as pejorative as it is today, is unfair to the author's original meaning. Moreover, the theme that permeates every page of *Huckleberry Finn* is that racism is evil. Those who would ban one of the greatest American novels on the basis of these misinterpreted details betray the same type of closed-minded failure to read with understanding as the Christians who would ban *The Lion, the Witch, and the Wardrobe.*

In the same way, fairy tales are suppressed because they portray "sexual stereotypes." "Cinderella" is censored because it "unfairly depicts nontraditional families"; in other words, it includes a wicked stepmother. Any sympathetic treatment of religion, of course, is purged out of textbooks and curricula with the thoroughness of the Inquisition. As Milton said, "if it come to prohibiting, there is not aught more likely to be prohibited than truth itself."[20] Milton—a Puritan, by the way—makes that point in his great Christian defense of freedom of the press, entitled "Areopagitica" (which deserves close reading by contemporary Christians concerned with this issue).

And yet both sides have legitimate concerns. The question in selecting schoolbooks is not necessarily one of censorship, but one of appropriateness. I would never censor or ban *Huckleberry Finn,* but if I were teaching junior high students, I would question whether they were sophisticated enough to fully understand it. If there were racial conflicts in the class already, I might avoid the occasion for hurt feelings and derision that could arise from Mark Twain's nineteenth-century racial epithets. I would pick something else. I do teach *Huckleberry Finn* in college and encourage younger readers who understand good liter-ature to read it. Nor would I teach *The Canterbury Tales,* one of my favorite books, to people who would only giggle at its "naughty" lan-guage. I do not believe in throwing pearls to swine—that is, in present-ing something of value to those unable to appreciate it (Matthew 7:6).

Christians should present their concerns in a temperate and knowledgeable way, addressing issues of appropriateness and educa-tional levels rather than strident scatter-shot denunciation. They should also clearly affirm their commitment to freedom of the press and free-dom of speech. To be successful, they will have to express their com-plaints in other than theological terms. For example, when complaining about a book that contains pornographic scenes, they might demon-strate how the offending passages demean women. When complaining about the anti-Christian bias of a book, they might point out how it perpetuates offensive stereotypes of religious minorities. (I agree that theological language is far better than such social-science jargon, but the authorities must be addressed in a language they will understand.)

Selectivity should not be confused with censorship. Parents and educators are right to use judgment in choosing literature for children, and they should consider moral implications no less than educational and psychological ones. They should also consider aesthetic implications. Poorly written textbooks—earnestly realistic and didactic primers that offer nothing more inspiring than the importance of brushing one's teeth—can make a child hate to read. There are many reasons not to buy a bad book.

Nor should criticism be confused with censorship. Christians affronted by a work of literature need not try to censor it. Outlawing the book, calling for its suppression, or attempting reprisals on its author are usually futile and illegal gestures. Christians can, however, bring to bear their powers of criticism, complaint, and derision. Professional critics are always excoriating worthless writing, while never denying its legal right to exist. Christians can do the same, counterattacking the assaults on their values and their aesthetic sensibilities. They can loudly take offense without calling for censorship. The moral outrage spurred by the civil rights movement and its offspring have meant that publishers now are very careful about the way they portray blacks, Jews, women, the handicapped, and other minority groups. Perhaps the media moguls can develop the same sensitivity in regard to Christians and their beliefs.

The power of the marketplace is also formidable in influencing culture, especially for popular works (such as film and television) whose only reason for being made is to attract large audiences. Refusing to patronize scurrilous material (and its sponsors) is a way of voting with one's wallet and confronting the mass culture in a way it understands.

This does not mean that Christians should be overscrupulous. It does mean they should save their money for works of excellence. A well-written book or a well-made film may deal with sex or violence, but almost never in a prurient way. Serious literary art tends to be honest; as such, it often confronts realities—the search for love, the ugliness of evil, the futility of life without God, the mysterious splendors of ordinary life—that Christians can recognize as part of the human condition and what God has ordained in the created order.

Christians should make their presence known in the marketplace. This means refusing to waste money on worthless entertainment and actively supporting quality work. Perhaps we could start by renting classic videos instead of the latest slasher movie. We could also turn off the TV more often and read more good books.

GOOD BOOKS

What is a good book? Are not "matters of taste" purely subjective? Not completely. Our tastes, like other facets of our lives, must be trained. We must learn how to delight in what is good. Just as morally bad books are usually aesthetically bad as well, good books—even those by non-Christians—are usually in accord with God's created order both morally and aesthetically.

To fully recognize both excellence and mediocrity requires experience and knowledge. Mortimer Adler, writing about beauty, distinguishes between "the enjoyable" and the "admirable." The enjoyable is subjective—what one person enjoys another might not, and there are many reasons why someone may find pleasure in a given experience. The admirable, on the other hand, refers to objective qualities, to what Adler describes as "an intrinsic excellence or perfection appropriate to that kind of thing."[21]

Many people find slasher movies "enjoyable," but even their fans would probably not consider them "admirable," either morally or aesthetically. A movie, to be objectively "admirable," would feature among other "perfections" skillful acting, effective editing and cinematography, a well-written script, a thought-provoking theme. To recognize these "perfections" requires knowledge of the techniques and aesthetics of film-making. Once viewers attain that knowledge, they find themselves enjoying movies even more, although they are no longer satisfied by third-rate products. Similarly, people who do not enjoy classical music usually do not understand it. Once they are taught how to listen to classical music—understanding its techniques, its forms, its history, and its meaning—the enjoyment comes.

This process of learning how to enjoy (subjectively) what is admirable (objectively) is known as the cultivation of taste. The rest of this book will explore the different forms and styles of literature with a view toward cultivating taste. Obscenity is "tasteless." Preferring ugliness to beauty is "bad taste." Solomon observes that "a fool finds pleasure in evil conduct," whereas "a man of understanding delights in wisdom" (Proverbs 10:23). What we delight in has a spiritual dimension. For contemporary Christians, at sea in a mass culture, taking pleasure in excellence may be an important survival skill.

THE FORMS OF LITERATURE

The Bible contains nearly every type of writing and every literary form. From the statistical record keeping of the book of Numbers to the complex theological discussions of Paul's epistles, God employs writing in nearly all of its forms to reveal Himself. The Bible is a library of sixty-six separate books—history, law, theology, social criticism, and personal reflection. They make use of nearly every literary type: historical nonfiction (the depiction of actual concrete events), philosophical nonfiction (the explanation and analysis of abstract ideas), fiction (the method of the parables), and poetry (the method of the psalms).

There is no need for Christians to defend any of these forms or to worry about whether poetry or fiction are legitimate for Christians to read or to write. If God thought it proper to use them in Scripture, they have to be legitimate. Worldly rationalism might attack the practicality of fiction or the propriety of poetry, but Christians, insofar as they place themselves under God's Word, cannot.

And yet, these different types of writing are often misunderstood. For example, it is widely assumed that if a text is poetry, then it must not be true. Bible scholars who make such assumptions are also quick to label passages "mythological," or even "fictional," without a clear understanding of what myth and fiction actually involve. Misunderstanding literary form can result in misunderstanding Scripture.

In reading outside of the Bible, a knowledge of the dynamics of literary forms such as fiction and poetry can also be helpful. Knowing the artistry involved in nonfiction, in supposedly "factual" writing, can help us to understand the hidden biases and worldviews implicit in any piece of writing. Such understanding can help us to appreciate excellent writing and to become better communicators ourselves. Knowing something about the technique of fiction-writing can increase our pleasure and understanding when we read a novel or short story. Knowing how to read poetry—almost a forgotten art for contemporary readers—can open up whole realms of pleasure and insight.

Understanding how literature works can help us to be more discerning—to sort out quality writing from the trash that fills the bookstores and to cultivate a taste for what is "excellent," as Philippians 4:8 recommends. Awareness of literary technique is also essential for Christian writers who wish to leave their own mark on the reading public.

The following three chapters will explore the nature of the three main categories of literature—nonfiction, fiction, and poetry. Just as physical laws apply to Christians and non-Christians alike (Matthew 5:45), the laws of art apply universally. Aesthetic principles, no less than scientific principles, are grounded in the created order and are a manifestation of God's design. Thus, whether the author is a Christian or a non-Christian, the elements of skillful writing will remain the same. Each chapter, however, will give examples of Christian authors who have mastered their craft and who merit further reading.

NONFICTION:
The Art of Truth-Telling

M any people would probably not, at first glance, consider
nonfiction to be an art form. Historians, philosophers, essayists,
or journalists simply need to write down the truth as they see it. They
are not supposed to make things up with their imaginations or to orna-
ment their facts with elaborate word-play. And yet, writing down the
truth involves selection of detail and selection of words. These words
must be arranged into a meaningful pattern, and they must communicate effectively with their readers. Nonfiction must be persuasive,
whether in trying to convince its readers of the validity of its claims
or in the more aggressive goal of trying to change the readers' beliefs
and actions. Such selection, patterning, and calculation of effect are
at the essence of art.

RHETORIC AND SEMANTICS

The ancient Greeks and Romans knew this well. Their explorations
of "rhetoric," the art of persuasion, remain unsurpassed.[1] They knew
that the ability to persuade people can lead to enormous power, for
good or evil. Today, the term "rhetoric" is often used in a derogatory
sense to mean words that are empty and deceiving ("that speech is just
a lot of rhetoric"). That is probably a testimony to the poor quality
of modern discourse, but, properly speaking, rhetoric simply refers to
the art of speaking or writing effectively. That rhetoric may be used
for evil purposes (as in much political propaganda) or for good purposes (as in many sermons) only heightens its importance.

Whether nonfiction involves facts or ideas, the author must

choose which facts to include and which words to use to describe them. Marvin Olasky has shown how even supposedly objective journalists, in their selection of details to report and in the language that they use, often convey an anti-Christian bias.[2] Whenever there is selection, there must be some criteria for choosing what is important and what is not. Usually, those criteria arise from the author's worldview.

Words convey meaning in a complicated way. Nonfiction can shape (or manipulate) the way people think by adept (or unscrupulous) use of words. The study of how words carry meaning is called "semantics." Familiarity with basic principles of semantics can help beleaguered Christians cut through the sophistry and language games practiced by the secular culture.

Semanticists speak of two types of meanings that exist in words. The "denotation" of a word is its literal definition. Words also tend to acquire some "connotations," a set of associations that accompany the word. Thus *house* and *home* have similar denotations—the place where one lives—but *home* carries with it connotations of family, security, and a wealth of personal feelings, memories, and associations. *Politician* and *statesman* have similar denotations—both words mean people involved in the government. There is a genuine difference, though, in the way these words are taken. *Politician* tends to carry associations of corruption, self-interest, and sleaziness. *Statesman,* on the other hand, has connotations of honesty, patriotism, and accomplishment.

Such connotations change over time (*politician* used to be a respectable word) and sometimes vary from person to person. (Terms such as *conservative* or *liberal* are negative for some people and positive for others.) These associations are subtle, nonreflective, and emotion-based. As such, they are very powerful, so that use of "loaded language" can often short-circuit any rational debate.

Words with a bad connotation may be replaced by words with a good connotation. This is called "euphemism." When a child's pet is euthanized, the parents do not say, "The doctor killed Fluffy." Rather, they say, "The doctor put Fluffy to sleep." *Kill* has a negative connotation; *sleep* has a positive connotation. The parents want to "soften the blow," and they do so by language. At its best, euphemism can be a way to be tasteful ("going to the restroom" instead of more vulgar versions) or tactful (describing a child as "husky" or "big-boned" rather than "fat"). At its worst, euphemism can be manipulative and deceiving, a way to hide the truth behind a pleasant mask. Politicians (or statesmen) speak of "revenue enhancements" rather than tax increases. Terrorists see themselves as members of a People's Liberation Army; when they murder civilians, they think of it as "taking action against imperialism."

Some words are so powerful, conveying such overwhelmingly positive connotations, that they are called "god-terms." For Americans, words that conjure up patriotic ideals such as *freedom, democracy,* and *rights* are very commanding, summarizing as they do the essence of American ideology. And yet "god-terms" can be artificially attached to more problematic issues so that the powerful connotations of the language actually shape the way people think.

An American could hardly be opposed to "voting rights," or "equal rights," or "human rights." When considering an issue such as abortion, the question of whether the fetus is a human being or not may be completely ignored if the question is phrased in terms of "abortion *rights.*" People may say that they are personally opposed to abortion, but then they go on to support "the woman's right to choose." When such language defines the terms of the debate, those opposed to abortion are cast as opponents of human "rights," thereby caricatured as totalitarian and anti-American. The language used determines the result of the argument. When the sacred language of the civil religion is invoked, rational analysis and moral debate become impossible. The very terms of the debate are shifted away from the concrete issues—is a fetus a human life and should it be protected?—into the realm of sacred and therefore unquestionable absolutes.

Such rhetoric, although it purports to be secular, is nonetheless religious. It makes use, not of Christian categories, but of the civil religion that tends to develop within a society. It short-circuits thought in a way that can enable almost any idea to attract defenders. If there is such a thing as "human rights," why not "animal rights"? Today, child molesters can sway some people by speaking of "the sexual rights of children."

The major social and moral debates are often simply battles over language.[3] Indeed, whichever side succeeds in choosing the words our culture uses to discuss these issues will control the way people think about them. Abortionists speak of "terminating a pregnancy" instead of killing a baby (or is it "a fetus" or even simply "fetal tissue"?). "Having an affair," with its connotations of glamour and lack of consequences, is a euphemism for adultery. The semantic shift away from "sodomy" (with its Biblical allusion to sin and judgment) to "homosexual" (a medical-sounding, pathological term) to "gay" (denoting happiness, joy, and celebration) has made this "sexual orientation" seem perfectly acceptable and moral.

A person who thinks in terms of the Biblical language may be less likely to commit the sin than the person who thinks in terms of soap opera language. We think with words. Our attitudes and our behavior are shaped by the language that we choose, or that we pick up unconsciously from the world around us. For this reason, Christians need to cultivate a sensitivity to language. Reading and reflecting upon literature is perhaps the best means to that end.

GOOD AND BAD NONFICTION

When we read nonfiction—journalism, scholarship, essays, and argumentation—we need to pay attention not only to the subject matter of the piece and to its internal argumentation, but also to its language. The writing style may well be the key, not only for our aesthetic enjoyment, but also for our full understanding of the work. What are the characteristics of well-written nonfiction?

Whether the writing expresses a view that I agree with or that I find abhorrent, I want the writing to be clear, honest, and piercing. Good nonfiction reveals, rather than hides, its meaning. Bad writing equivocates, hiding its implications behind a facade of authoritative-sounding abstractions.

This is not to say that good writing is always easy to read. Sometimes complex ideas require complex explanations. But when a writer is describing a difficult subject—nuclear physics, for example—it is even more important that the language itself not get in the way. Every field has its technical language, but such terminology can be deciphered. As Jacques Barzun has observed, "The failure of all 'difficult' writing without exception lies elsewhere than in the technicalities. In such writing it is the common words that are misused, the sentence structure that is ramshackle, and the organization that is wild or nonexistent."[4] Language should always help communication, not impede it. Difficult concepts demand clear explanations, so that the difficulty inheres in the subject and not the words.

What often happens is the reverse: simple ideas are expressed in difficult language. Instead of "Keep off the ice," we have, "All persons must terminate using any body of water for any ice-related recreation."[5] Instead of "Call an ambulance," we have, "Activate the EMS system."

Bad nonfiction garbs simple ideas in overly complex language or scientific-sounding jargon. It is wordy. It sounds ugly. One has to read it over and over again to decipher it. Such writing is arrogant in its pseudo-learning and in the way it neglects its readers' needs. Bad writing is usually impersonal; that is, it lacks a human voice and speaks of human beings as if they were only numbers or machines. The droning, lifeless jargon of much modern writing—like a computer idiotically spitting out data—is a product of the mechanistic worldview that dominates our time. Christians, bound by their faith to affirm life and the Personality who underlies all of reality, should never imitate that sort of prose.

Good nonfiction can be transparent, achieving such clarity that we become caught up in what is being said and fail to notice the skillful style that creates this effect. Or good writing can be expressive, using words that do call attention to themselves because they so aptly and so piercingly impart the author's mind.

Good nonfiction will be interesting. It has been said that any subject can be made interesting by a good writer. I have found myself enthralled by articles discussing things that I never had an interest in—bureaucracies, office politics, clothing, germs, dirt. Conversely, I suppose, any subject can be made dull by an inept writer, including that most endlessly fascinating and most inexhaustible of all topics: Christianity.

Part of the secret of effective nonfiction is avoiding clichés. A good writer will avoid the stultifying language that readers have heard over and over so often that the words mean nothing anymore. Rather, the writer will try to express the subject in a fresh way, so that readers confront it again as if for the first time.

A CHRISTIAN NONFICTION WRITER

A good model for contemporary Christian writers is C. S. Lewis. He is such an effective apologist for the Christian faith precisely because he is such a good writer. Consider how he writes about Jesus Christ:

> The things He says are very different from what any other teacher has said. Others say, "This is the truth about the Universe. This is the way you ought to go," but He says, "*I* am the Truth, and the Way, and the Life." He says, "No man can reach absolute reality, except through Me. Try to retain your own life and you will be inevitably ruined. Give yourself away and you will be saved." He says, "If you are ashamed of Me, if, when you hear this call, you turn the other way, I also will look the other way when I come again as God without disguise. If anything whatever is keeping you from God and from Me, whatever it is, throw it away. If it is your eye, pull it out. If it is your hand, cut it off. If you put yourself first, you will be last. Come to Me everyone who is carrying a heavy load, I will set that right. Your sins, all of them, are wiped out, I can do that. I am Re-birth, I am Life. Eat Me, drink Me, I am your Food. And finally, do not be afraid, I have overcome the whole Universe."[6]

Here is no Sunday school language (with all due respect to Sunday schools). We have heard so much about Jesus that we sometimes forget the magnitude of His claims. Lewis uses modern categories ("absolute reality" and "Universe"), but he waters down nothing. In fact, his purpose is to restore the astonishing, radical statements of Christ, to undomesticate them, so that we experience them as both startling and compelling, as His first listeners did. The rhythm of the passage builds and quickens, culminating in a sentence that interrupts itself twice to convey the personal urgency in Christ's voice: "Your sins, all of them, are wiped out, I can do that."

Lewis's style is always lucid, engaging, and even entertaining. His logic is masterful (especially striking in an age that generally minimizes logic). At the same time, he can call forth powerful emotions. He always grounds his ideas in vivid examples, and even in the depths of a serious issue, he is not afraid to be funny. Consider, for example, the logic, the passion, and the wit of these lines about the claims of Christ, which have helped so many people to become Christians:

> A man who was merely a man and said the sort of things Jesus said would not be a great moral teacher. He would either be a lunatic—on a level with the man who says he is a poached egg—or else he would be the Devil of Hell. You must make your choice. Either this man was, and is, the Son of God: or else a madman or something worse. You can shut Him up for a fool, you can spit at Him and kill Him as a demon; or you can fall at His feet and call Him Lord and God.[7]

Lewis balances the three possibilities about the identity of Christ with three possible responses on the part of human beings, impelling the reader to a commitment: "You must make your choice." The carefully constructed logic is not allowed to be abstract; rather, the passage is grounded in vivid details: if He is a demon, spit at Him; if He is God, fall at His feet. The whole discussion, for all of its fervor and urgency, is leavened with humor. In describing lunacy, he could have used obvious illustrations, but instead posits a man who thinks he is a poached egg. The passage, for all of its truth, is consummately artistic.

Lewis does not, in my opinion, argue people into the faith, as if that were possible. What he does so well is simply to explain what Christianity is. The Bible indicates that whenever the gospel of Christ is proclaimed by human beings, the Word of God itself is at work, and the Holy Spirit is active in the hearts of its hearers to bring them to faith (Hebrews 4:12; Romans 10:17).

What Lewis does is to present that Word in a way that is dazzlingly clear. His style cuts through his readers' confusions, preconceptions, and biases about Christianity. Moreover, Lewis's writing tears down the obstacles to faith. As Paul says, "We demolish arguments and every pretension that sets itself up against the knowledge of God"

(2 Corinthians 10:5). The false assumptions of human philosophy and pride must be cast down to prepare the way for Christ. Human words can be a vehicle for the Word of God.

NONFICTION TODAY

William Zinsser, the noted author and editor, argues that nonfiction is the dominant literary form of the late twentieth century.[8] Nevertheless, many people still do not think of nonfiction as "literature":

> Those of us who are trying to write well about the world we live in, or to teach students to write well about the world *they* live in, are caught in a time warp, where literature by definition consists of forms that were certified as "literary" in the nineteenth century: novels and short stories and poems. But in fact these have become quite rarefied forms in American life. The great preponderance of what writers now write and sell, what book and magazine publishers publish, and what readers demand is nonfiction.[9]

Some think that the late twentieth-century novel has become stale and repetitive; poetry has become too esoteric. Works of nonfiction, though—treatments of politics, history, science, and popular culture; investigative journalism and current events; scholarly enterprises such as biographies and social analysis written to engage the ordinary reader—are now blossoming.

For example, the "new journalists" are experimenting with "nonfiction novels," works about real people and real events using techniques borrowed from fiction. The new journalists, such as Tom Wolfe, do not just write about objective facts; rather, they attempt to recreate the point of view of the people involved and speculate about the meaning of the external events. The best of the new journalists combine meticulous research, narrative techniques borrowed from fiction, and a freewheeling style that results in extremely vivid descriptions, sharply expressed personal commentary, and, at least in Tom Wolfe's case, satirical humor. (See Tom Wolfe's *The Right Stuff* on America's first astronauts, *The Painted Word* on the art world, and his essay "Radical Chic" on the leftist pretensions of the very rich.)

The new journalism never claims to be unbiased, so readers must be cautious about accepting this sort of reporting uncritically. Misrepresenting real people (how can a writer know what someone was thinking at the time?) can lead to sensationalism and slander (as in the scurrilous biographies popular today). Facts can easily be distorted in the telling, and complicated people can be reduced to caricatures. At least the biases of the new journalists are on the surface where they are frankly admitted and easily detected, as opposed to journalists who hide their biases under the guise of "objective" reporting. New journalists may be suspect as objective journalists, but their "nonfiction novels"—long narratives using fictional techniques to explore actual events—are an intriguing literary concept, suggesting ways of integrating artistry and truth.

ANNIE DILLARD AND WALTER WANGERIN

Not only is nonfiction trespassing on the grounds once reserved for fiction, it is also in many ways usurping the domain of poetry. Many nonfiction writers are pushing language to its limits to capture experiences and to meditate on what they mean. Annie Dillard and Walter Wangerin, Jr., are two Christian writers making their mark on contemporary literature in this way.

Annie Dillard writes about the physical world and its spiritual significance. Her work is informed by scientific knowledge, careful observation, and deep personal reflection. She shrinks back from nothing—neither the appalling appetite of praying mantises nor the facts of human suffering—but she also affirms the reality, the mystery, and the utter majesty of God. Consider her version of a typical church service:

> The churchwomen all bring flowers for the altar; they haul in arrangements as big as hedges, of wayside herbs in season, and flowers from their gardens, huge bunches of foliage and blossoms as tall as I am, in vases the size of tubs, and the altar still looks empty, irredeemably linoleum, and beige. We had a wretched singer once, a guest from a Canadian congregation, a hulking blond girl with chopped hair and big shoulders, who wore tinted spectacles and a long lacy dress, and sang, grinning, to faltering accompaniment, an entirely secular song about mountains. Nothing could have been more apparent than that God loved this girl; nothing could more surely convince me of God's unending mercy than the continued existence on earth of the church.
>
> The higher Christian churches—where, if anywhere, I belong—come at God with an unwarranted air of professionalism, with authority and pomp, as though they knew what they were doing, as though people in themselves were an appropriate set of creatures to have dealings with God. I often think of the set pieces of liturgy as certain words which people have successfully addressed to God without their getting killed. In the high churches they saunter through the liturgy like Mohawks along a strand of scaffolding who have long since forgotten their danger. If God were to blast such a service to bits, the congregation would be, I believe,

genuinely shocked. But in the low churches you expect it any
minute. This is the beginning of wisdom.[10]

Dillard turns even the tackiness of the linoleum altar and the painful-
ness of the special music into a tribute to the love of God. She describes
worshipers with an unlikely and comic metaphor—Mohawks scram-
bling over scaffolding—and in doing so makes us reconsider a familiar
experience, helping us to understand what it means to come into the
presence of a holy God. In her word choice and in the way she orches-
trates her images throughout her books, her writing offers the vivid
imagery and the searching insights of the best poetry.

    Walter Wangerin, Jr., is also a poet in nonfiction. His accounts
of his experiences as a pastor in an inner-city parish are achingly moving.[11] He too plays with language for its sound, for its effect, and for
its power. In one short essay, he begins with what seems to be a biology
lesson. Spiders, he tells us, have no stomachs. They inject their digestive
juices into their prey.

> Through tiny punctures she injects into a bounded fly digestive
> juices; inside *his* body his organs and nerves and tissues are bro-
> ken down, dissolved, and turned to warm soup. This soup she
> swills—
>   —even as the most of us swill souls of one another after having
> cooked them in various enzymes: guilt, humiliations, subjectivities,
> cruel love—there are a number of fine, acidic mixes. And some
> among us are so skilled with the hypodermic word that our dear
> ones continue to sit up and to smile, quite as though they were still
> alive. But the evidence of eating is in our own fatness.[12]

Most spiders lay their eggs and leave, but there is another species of
spider. This one stays with her eggs:

> By the hundreds she gathers her brood upon her back so that she
> seems a grotesque sort of lump, rumpled and swollen. But such is
> love: it makes the lover ugly.
>   And when the children emerge, she feeds them; Her juices
> soften the meat to their diminutive snorkels. Yet even this care,
> peculiar among the spinsters, does not give her a name above all
> other names. Many mothers mother their children; that is not
> uncommon. Rather, it is the last supper which she reserves against
> necessity that astonishes the watcher and makes him wonder to see
> heaven in a tiny thing. . . .
>   Sometimes food grows scarce, and no amount of netting can
> snare the fly that isn't there. Sometimes tiny famine descends upon

the mother and her spiderlings, and then they starve, and then they may die, if they do not eat.

But then, privately, she performs the deed unique among the living.

Into her own body this spinster releases the juices that digest. Freely they run through her abdomen while she holds so still, digesting not some other meat, but her own, breaking down the parts of her that kept her once alive, until her eyes are flat.

She dies.

She becomes the stomach for her children, and she herself the food.

And Jesus said to those who stood around him, "I am the bread of life. I am the living bread which came down from heaven; if any one eats of this bread, he will live forever; and the bread which I will give for the life of the world is my flesh."

Take—and eat.

This one was different from all the rest of us: cooked on a cross.[13]

Wangerin meditates on something that we usually find repulsive. He finds in it an emblem of both human sinfulness and the glorious self-sacrifice of Jesus Christ. He translates this theological language into terms that are concrete, unflinching, and undeniably real.

Wangerin brings home the magnitude of Christ's sacrifice by employing figures of speech drawn from science (the symbol of the spider from entomology and words such as *enzymes* and *hypodermic* to describe human viciousness) and from ordinary life ("cooked on a cross"). In addition, like any other poet, he is luxuriating in the music of the language (the alliteration of "this soup she swills . . . as the most of us swill souls").

Dillard and Wangerin demonstrate a freshness of language—you will never find in them an unexamined cliché—and a toughness of mind that demand a hearing. Annie Dillard won the Pulitzer Prize. Walter Wangerin won the American Book Award. Both are read and respected by Christian and non-Christian alike. Both use the art of language to tell the truth.

FICTION:
The Art of Story-Telling

A lthough any piece of writing can be, in an important sense, literature, when we use the term, we usually think of fiction and poetry. (Drama too is a form of literature. When it is performed instead of read, it is unique, but insofar as it is "written," the structuring of its stories will be like other forms of fiction.) Fiction of one kind or another—including movies and television programs—comprises much of our entertainment and takes up much of our leisure time. We seem to have a need for stories.

DEFENDING FICTION

The capacity to invent stories is a function of the creative imagination. This power of the human mind is doubtless a remnant of the divine image given us by the Creator. That Jesus Christ was a storyteller, explaining the Kingdom of God by means of parables, is authority enough for Christians who might wonder whether stories are legitimate. (The word *parable* in Greek refers to a figurative or even symbolic comparison, requiring interpretation,[1] a use of language that is thus analogous to poetry as well.)

Some Christians simply do not understand how to read fiction. I have heard C. S. Lewis, an impeccably orthodox Christian, criticized for believing that people in Hell can take bus trips to Heaven where they might get a second chance (a failure to interpret the allegory and the symbolism of *The Great Divorce*). Those who seek to ban *The Lion, the Witch, and the Wardrobe* because of the witch in the title exhibit a similar problem. Such Christians may know how to read words, but they do not know how to read fiction, how to interpret its figurative and parable-like way of exploring reality.

Some Christians oppose fiction on principle.[2] Some are concerned about wasting time on trivialities or mere pleasure when there is important work to be done. Certainly, we can spend too much time doing just about anything. This is a matter of setting priorities. Some of us even spend too much time making a living. Working too much, as well as reading too much or gardening too much, can cause us to neglect our more important duties to our families, to our personal spiritual life, and to the Kingdom of God. The Scriptural principle of the Sabbath, however, should remind us that God requires us to rest as well as to work. Literature can help us to rest our minds, and it can even help us to nourish our spiritual lives.

Some Christians worry about whether fiction is a form of lying since fiction, by definition, is a story that is not true. Sir Philip Sidney in his *Apology for Poetry* answers this charge, giving perhaps the first Christian defense of literature. "To lie," he observes, "is to affirm that to be true which is false." The imaginative writer, though, never pretends that the stories are true. "He nothing affirms, and therefore never lieth."[3]

Historians, philosophers, and scientists, Sidney argues, can hardly avoid an occasional inadvertent lie—presenting as true something which in actuality turns out to be false. Poets or fiction writers, on the other hand, can almost never lie, because they present their work as imaginary. The poet is not

> laboring to tell you what is, or is not, but what should or should not be. And therefore, though he recount things not true, yet because he telleth them not for true, he lieth not. . . . What child is there that, coming to a play, and seeing *Thebes* written in great letters on an old door, doth believe that it is Thebes? If then a man can arrive, at that child's age, to know that the poets' persons and doings are but pictures of what should be, and not stories of what have been, they will never give the lie to things not affirmatively but allegorically and figuratively written. And therefore, as in history, looking for truth, they go away full fraught with falsehood, so in poesy, looking for fiction, they shall use the narration but as an imaginative ground-plot of a profitable invention.[4]

While affirming that literary art is essentially creative and not bound to external reality, Sidney suggests that there *is* a connection between artistic creation and truth. Fiction is related to truth, as in the manner of the parables, "allegorically and figuratively." The truth of a novel is in its meaning, not its facts.

Sidney makes another important point about literature: Its function is to teach and to delight.[5] Although it communicates figuratively, fiction does teach. More than simply informing us about good and evil—which most of us already know—literature can motivate us to pursue the good and to reject the evil. Part of the reason stories are such effective teachers, according to Sidney, is that they give pleasure.

> For he doth not only show the way, but giveth so sweet a prospect into the way, as will entice any man to enter into it. . . . He beginneth not with obscure definitions, which must blur the margent with interpretations and load the memory with doubtfulness; but he cometh to you with words set in delightful proportion . . . and with a tale forsooth he cometh unto you, with a tale which holdeth children from play, and old men from the chimney corner. And, pretending no more, doth intend the winning of the mind from wickedness to virtue: even as the child is often brought to take most wholesome things by hiding them in such other as have a pleasant taste.[6]

This is why stories are often better teachers than abstract discourses or straightforward exhortations (as preachers know, who usually fill their sermons with anecdotes and examples to illustrate their points and to move their congregations).

William Kirk Kilpatrick, the contemporary Christian psychologist and social critic, has shown how stories instill moral values by giving models for concrete ethical behavior. Stories motivate their readers to act morally by inspiring them to emulate the models.[7] Stories teach, not by being preachy or by tacking on a moral at the end, but by being good, gripping stories.

Kilpatrick shows how stories have always been the most important method of moral education. The Greeks, young and old, pored over Homer's *Iliad* and *Odyssey* and shaped their ideals and their behavior according to the nobility of their heroes. The Angles and Saxons of ancient England passed down their moral heritage in epic poems such as *Beowulf*, the story of a fearless warrior who became a self-sacrificing king, and in celebrations of history such as *The Battle of Maldon,* in which the warriors' courage grows as their strength lessens. The Bible, above all, offers not only abstract doctrines but stories. When we hear or read a story that stirs us, we want to play a part in that story.[8]

Today, our society, having drifted away from words, has abandoned the use of stories in moral education in favor of "values clarification" sessions. School children gather around and discuss how they would handle impossible moral dilemmas (whom they would exclude from a fall-out shelter, for example). What values clarification actually teaches is that morality is inherently problematic and only a matter of personal preference. Traditional stories (such as fairy tales, national legends, and most classic novels) present evil as repulsive, and goodness as alluring, a matter of objective law and heroic struggle. The values clarification view of morality is both a symptom and a cause of the moral chaos wrecking our culture. We need, says Kilpatrick, "stories to live by."

> Life is full and rich and complex like a story, not abstract and neat like a theory. The things that happen to us—the great joys, the intense sorrows, the surging passions—are too much like drama to be accounted for by anything less than drama. . . . What needs to be seen is that virtue in large part is also in the realm of imagination. Unless the moral imagination is hooked, the other moral faculties—will, emotion, and reason—are too often over-matched by fear, laziness, and self-interest. The great mistake of modern psychology lies in ignoring this obvious fact while it toys with values clarification and decision-making exercises. That is why I believe that our ancestors, both Christian and non-Christian, were the better psychologists. They knew that you must grasp the imagination, and they knew how to do it.[9]

"How to do it"—how the writers of stories "grasp the imagination" will be the subject of the rest of this chapter.

NARRATIVE

Fiction employs "narrative" writing. Whereas "expository" writing seeks to explain a fact or an idea, narrative seeks to recreate a sequence of events. Narrative presents an experience in chronological order from the point of view of someone involved in the action. As a result, the reader participates imaginatively in the unfolding action.

For example, a newspaper article is usually expository. You might read about a traffic accident: "Two people were injured Monday night when a car collided with a semi near the Silver Springs exit on I-43. Police report that the car was headed north in the southbound lane. Charges of driving while intoxicated have been filed against the driver, Jack Deer of 117 Maple Manor, who is in stable condition in the county hospital." The article will continue in this vein, including all of the facts, which are arranged not in chronological order but in their order of importance (so that the reader can quit reading at any time and so that the editor can cut the story at any point to fit the space allotted to it).

To present the same incident as a narrative, an author would describe the event as a sequence of details in chronological order from the point of view of someone in the car:

> Jack fumbled for his keys and tried to clear his head. He was always in a good mood after a few drinks, but now he was anxious to get home. He was thinking about how well his Bob Uecker imitation went over at the tavern when he saw the freeway ramp to his left. He thought the entry was up ahead past the traffic light, but his mind was a little blurry. He could see the interstate sign, although he could not quite make out the red sign. He made a very sharp turn.
>
> He drove slowly—he was always careful when he had been drinking—and kept to the right lane. Two headlights glared into his windshield. "Dim your lights!" he yelled out loud. The lights grew bigger and bigger, and he heard the blast of an air-horn and felt a sting of panic, but he could not remember what to do. As in slow motion, he could just make out the International Harvester emblem on the radiator of the semi as he felt himself jerked out of his seat into the windshield.

Notice how this account is working. It does not simply tell the reader about the action; rather, the reader enters the action. By describing the accident as it unfolds from the point of view of Jack Deer, the narrative causes the reader to *imagine* what happened from the inside and in living detail. Imagining an event is more than intellectually comprehending a set of objective facts. Imagination allows us to enter into the life of an event—its details, feelings, and meaning.

Notice too that Jack Deer's accident did not really happen. The account is completely fictional, but that does not detract from the truth of its meaning. I imagined and described a "typical" drunk driver, which makes the narrative applicable to many real drunk drivers. The narrative illustrates the general truth that drunk driving is very foolish. In the same way, a good writer of fiction can make up totally imaginary tales that illuminate the real world.

The techniques of writing narrative, the methods by which an author creates the illusion of an unfolding action, are really fairly simple. The writer employs dialogue, description, action, thoughts, and exposition. Dialogue creates the illusion that the reader is overhearing conversations and is thus in the presence of actual people. Description, depicting what the characters are seeing, enables the reader to "picture" what is happening. Continually depicting action—not just the action of the plot, but the casual gestures and movements of the characters—gives the reader the sensation of witnessing an actual event.

By depicting thoughts, writers bring the reader into the very minds of the characters and thus into the center of the story. Writers of narrative need not always be plunging readers into the maelstrom of the senses. They can also employ exposition—straight explanations at crucial points in the narrative to link scenes, to supply background information, or to comment upon the action. To organize their work, writers typically plan a series of scenes, recreated moments, which are linked by exposition and sequenced according to the demands of the plot.

Nonfiction can employ narrative—personal experiences or reconstructions of historical or current events. The experiments of the new journalists demonstrate the potential of narrative to help readers imagine truth directly. Narrative is, however, the essence of fiction, which also requires plot, character, setting, and theme.

PLOT

A story, of course, needs a plot; something has to happen. A plot is not just random action. First of all, a plot will almost always involve some sort of conflict. Every story will hinge upon a struggle, a problem, or a battle of contending forces or ideas. I used to put off my children's requests for a bedtime story by saying, "Once upon a time, there was a little boy and a little girl who lived in a castle in the deep woods. And they lived happily ever after." My children, astute literary critics at an early age, rightly complained, "That's not a *story*! Tell us a story." When I would bring a monster into the castle, or a wicked stepmother, or sibling rivalry, or some sort of difficulty that the characters would have to overcome, then we would have a story.

That there can be no meaningful story without a conflict of some kind is worth contemplating. If, as Kilpatrick suggests, our lives are actually a story (whose author and finisher is Christ), then our own conflicts may well be necessary for our lives to be meaningful. At any rate, discerning the conflict of a story is the key to understanding its significance.

There are many types of conflict. Many stories depend upon a straightforward, external conflict—a hero and a villain literally slugging it out. Much second-rate fiction—Saturday morning cartoons, car-chase movies, adventure tales, and drugstore paperbacks—often have little more to them than a simple, external conflict between "good guys" and "bad guys," with a few complications and the good guys winning at the end. Indeed, that is enough to make an involving and exciting plot, although such stories are generally so undemanding that the reader gains no more than a few moments of entertainment. Much first-rate fiction also employs external conflict—Homer's *Iliad, Beowulf, Pilgrim's Progress, The Red Badge of Courage, The Lord of the Rings*—although they also have conflicts of a more complicated kind.

Internal conflicts are often more riveting in the long run than mere physical fighting. Internal conflict takes place within the mind of a character. Often a character is torn between two different options. A classic example, occurring over and over again in literature, is the "lovers' triangle" plot. Here a person is in love with two different people and must choose between them.

In the King Arthur saga, Queen Guinevere is happily married to the king. She then falls in love with his greatest knight, Lancelot. Her conflict is between her moral obligation to be faithful to her husband and her passionate desire for Lancelot. Lancelot too is torn between his loyalty to his king (who is also his friend) and his overpowering obsession for the queen. The king too, when he discovers the ensuing affair, is torn apart by his hurt at their betrayal and his continuing love for both of them, and by his desire to be merciful and his sworn duty to uphold the law by punishing adulterous traitors.[10] Notice how the thread of one internal conflict, one agony of decision, becomes part of a whole tapestry of the human condition.

A plot can also be animated by a thematic conflict. The King Arthur story shows a clash between married love and illicit love, loyalty and selfishness, virtue and passion. A story can explore in concrete terms the battle between ideas and values. In *Pilgrim's Progress,* Christian must combat a host of monsters, giants, and deceivers, representing in precise psychological and theological terms the temptations all Christians must face in their journeys through life.

To take a more modern and more subtle example, Flannery O'Connor in *The Violent Bear It Away* sets up two characters with utterly contrary worldviews—a wild-eyed Christian prophet and a secular humanist psychologist—and requires a young man to choose between them. She puts the two worldviews together in a dramatic context and the result, like placing a positive charge next to a negative charge, is electricity.

Whether an author depicts an individual struggling against social pressures, fighting against nature for survival, or contending against the evil impulses within the human heart, conflict animates and propels the story. A television network executive once tried to answer critics of TV violence by saying that programs *have* to show people's lives in danger; otherwise, the plots would never be entertaining. What he was fumbling for, I think, is that plots do have to have conflict—a purely peaceful and happy story in which the characters have no problems and everyone is kind to each other is, in a very literal way, impossible. Crude violence, though, provides conflict of the most simple-minded kind. The best stories usually present many levels of conflicts orchestrated together in a thoughtful and thought-provoking way. Homer's *Iliad* has some great fight scenes, but its real subject is "the wrath of Achilles," the personality conflicts and the inner character of the heroes battling on the plains of Troy. Often an external conflict (Captain Ahab versus Moby Dick) becomes an occasion to explore far-reaching psychological and thematic issues.

Certainly some melodramas will have a "good guy" competing against a "bad guy," making at least some pretension of portraying a thematic conflict between good and evil, but often the good people seem no different from the bad. We can tell them apart only because one is ugly and wears black, and the other is handsome and wears white. The hero never shows any particular goodness—he is not particularly kind, sensitive, or compassionate. The villain, usually the most interesting character, at least has the motivation of wanting to take over the world. Both hero and villain are mainly concerned with bashing each other.

A true grappling of good and evil, though, would embody that conflict in characters facing specific moral issues: saving life versus destroying life, generosity versus selfishness, humility versus pride, forgiveness versus revenge. Today's habit of depicting good and evil only in abstract symbols is symptomatic of a culture that manages somehow to be both amoral and self-righteous.

In addition to conflict, a plot must have structure. That is, the action needs to lead somewhere. Simply recording the day-to-day activities of our hero with an occasional fight or inward struggle is not really a plot. Such narratives are termed "episodic," consisting merely of a sequence of unrelated episodes rather than a sustained plot. The structure of the plot can be simple or complex, but usually it will have a definite beginning, middle, and end.

The beginning of a story must introduce the reader to the characters and to the conflict. This is called the "exposition." As readers, we get to know the people in the story by watching them do things. (We meet King Arthur and his ideals for a new civilization; we witness his charming arranged marriage with Guinevere; we are introduced to Lancelot, with his noble deeds and chivalrous character.) When the conflict is introduced, we need to care about the characters enough so that we want to see what they will do. (Oh no—Lancelot and Guinevere fall in love!) The conflict then builds and develops in various ways as obstacles and complications are introduced into the story. (We see Guinevere fighting her feelings by scorning Lancelot, whose friendship with the king deepens; we see another woman, Elaine, falling hopelessly in love with Lancelot; we see the king innocently asking Lancelot to serve as the queen's personal guard.) The plot, as we say, thickens.

The conflict builds until, usually at the middle of the story, it reaches a turning point: the decision is made; the battle is won by one side or another; one of the contending forces seems to win. (Lancelot and the queen throw aside moral constraints and begin their adulterous affair.)

The story is not over yet. The movement from the exposition to the turning point, or climax, is only the "rising action." Now we see what happens when the conflict is supposedly resolved. The next phase of the plot, the "falling action," shows the consequences. (The lovers become torn by guilt and assailed by rumors that ruin the harmony of the Round Table.) Often, there will be a "reversal." (The king is forced to recognize the adultery and follow his own law by condemning the queen to be burned; Lancelot rescues her in the nick of time, but in doing so kills some of our favorite knights, plunging the whole realm into civil war.)

The story ends with a "denouement," the final unraveling of the action. Often a story ends with an "epiphany," a moment of revelation for both the characters and the readers. In a mystery story, we discover who really committed the murder, thus making sense of the whole complicated action that has gone before. Or the character undergoes a change or achieves, with the reader, an insight into truth. (Arthur dies and the ideals of Camelot are ended; Lancelot and Guinevere survey the ruin of a whole civilization caused by their adultery; repentant, Guinevere enters a convent and Lancelot becomes a monk.)

CHARACTER

A second element of fiction is character. The events of the story must happen to individuals with whom the reader can become involved.

Most people think of the plot as the most important facet of a story. In my opinion, character is usually the key to its success or failure. This holds true even for popular commercial writing, or even for a TV show. I have found that I can predict the commercial failure or success of a new TV series simply by evaluating the effectiveness of the characters. People become involved in soap operas not because of their plots, which are usually so convoluted as to be almost impossible to unravel, but because they become intrigued with the characters. The successful TV shows—think of "I Love Lucy," "M.A.S.H.," "Star Trek," "The Cosby Show"—manage to portray characters who seem unique, likeable, and engaging. We want to see what they will do and what will happen to them. The success of these programs is not because of their plots, which are often minimal or predictable (Lucy buys something which she does not want Ricky to find out about; Captain Kirk beams down to a planet, is imprisoned, and changes their civilization for the better). Rather, we find ourselves involved with the characters—Lucy, Ricky, Ethel and Fred; Kirk, McCoy, and Mr. Spock—all of whom we come to know and to care about, such is the illusion of fiction, as if they were our friends.

The networks often miss this point. After they canceled "Star Trek," they decided to do an even bigger science fiction series. They gave the new show a much bigger budget and the latest technology in special effects. The result? "Battlestar Galactica." The special effects were much better than "Star Trek's," the conception much more grandiose—and yet the characters simply did not work. The captain of the battlestar was played by Lorne Greene, whose success at playing the rancher in "Bonanza" belied his image as a space man, and the supporting cast was uniformly attractive and thus impossible to distinguish from each other. The result was a monumental failure. The secret of "Star Trek" was not its special effects nor its science-fiction premise but the chemistry between the characters (the ultra-rational Spock, the folksy Dr. McCoy, and the shrewd pragmatist Captain Kirk), aided by some imaginatively written scripts.

Special effects, car chases, explosions, murders, and suspense can never salvage a story when nobody cares about the characters. Aristotle, far before the special effects technology of Industrial Light and Magic, made exactly the same point. He criticized plays for relying too much on what he termed "spectacle":

> The Spectacle has, indeed, an emotional attraction of its own, but, of all the parts, it is the least artistic, and connected least with the art of poetry. For the power of Tragedy, we may be sure, is felt even apart from representation and actors. Besides, the production of spectacular effects depends more on the art of the stage machinist than on that of the poet.[11]

Aristotle also squelches dramas which confuse shocking their audiences with moving them by true "tragic wonder." His words apply strikingly well to contemporary horror movies which rely exclusively on gruesome special effects rather than story and atmosphere: "Those who employ spectacular means to create a sense, not of the terrible but only of the monstrous, are strangers to the purpose of Tragedy."[12]

Characters may be "flat" or "rounded." Flat characters exist only on the surface. Their appearance is generally the clue to how we are to interpret them (again, "good guys" are handsome; "bad guys" are ugly). Often these characters, although they too need to be vital and engaging, are simply stereotypes: the dumb blonde, the obsequious butler, the hard-boiled detective, the mad scientist. Such characters are often useful in supporting roles—because they are generic characters, they can be sketched very quickly and easily. Sometimes all the characters are one-dimensional, usually a mark of inept writing.

Rounded characters, on the other hand, are complex. They have more than one trait; they seem to have an inner life and, like an iceberg, there is more to them than is evident on the surface. The hero has good qualities, but he may also have some bad qualities which he is struggling against. The villain may be a good family man, an animal lover, a sensitive friend—whose line of work just happens to be that of a hired killer. In other words, rounded characters are often a mixture of good traits and bad traits, of normal feelings and odd idiosyncracies—just like real people.

Even the most successful popular fiction usually has characters of some complexity. Tarzan is both an Ape Man and an English aristocrat; Sherlock Holmes is a rational genius who is plagued by melancholy and an addiction to cocaine; John LeCarré's spies are typically overweight, rumpled bureaucrats who end up saving the free world from their shadowy counterparts. The characters in classic literary masterpieces—King Lear, Hamlet, Captain Ahab, Gatsby—manage to somehow be both unique and universal, unforgettably one-of-a-kind, yet also as familiar as ourselves.

SETTING

A third element of fiction, after plot and character, is setting. A story must take place somewhere, at a particular location in a particular moment. Setting is often thought of as part of the background—the stage upon which the characters perform. Actually, setting can provide one of the great delights of fiction, enabling the reader to imaginatively enter into another place and time.

The age of chivalry, the wild West, a World War II fighter squadron, the African rain forest, the lifestyles of the rich and famous, the struggles of the hopelessly poor all become accessible to us when we read. A skillful writer can recreate (with varying degrees of historical accuracy) what it might feel like to be in another time, another civilization. Or the writer could set the story in the present but in a world largely inaccessible except through the imagination: the worlds of crime, of power, of espionage, or of some subculture. City dwellers and small-town dwellers, northerners and southerners, business executives and farmers, the very rich and the very poor, ethnic Europeans and black people—all of these groups tend to be alien to each other, but literature is a way to enter someone else's world. Fiction writers can even create settings that do not exist. Science fiction writers can help us imagine new planets and alternate futures. Writers of fantasy can cause us to imagine worlds more beautiful and more terrible than our own.

Setting is partly a matter of description and partly point of view, but a vivid setting also has to do with atmosphere. That is, a good setting should convey the "feel" of a place. A typical novel set in the American West might describe the people and the landscape, but a better novel might also convey the taste of the dust on the trails, the sense of a people both at home in nature and struggling against it, the combination of toughness and idealism necessary in those so bold as to settle in the western wilderness. A good setting, even when completely imaginary or impossible, will seem real. Although we can recognize and relate to the place, it will also communicate a sense of "otherness." Conversely, a realistic setting—one which seems ordinary to us—will be not only recognizable, but also somewhat strange, enabling us to see our own surroundings in a fresh light.

Literature is often condemned for being "escapist." People who read a lot are charged with trying to escape from their real lives, retreating into a never-never land of fantasies and daydreams. The escape offered by fiction, usually a function of setting, can, like most human capacities, be used for either evil or good.

To be sure, some readers are tempted to ignore the challenges of their own lives and to live completely in the alternative reality of books. This can be dangerous and sinful, a rejection of the real world in which God has placed us. On the other hand, no one disputes the value of taking time off from work occasionally for a vacation. Travel "broadens the mind," and taking a break from one's routine is healthy, stimulating, and refreshing, enabling us to come back into our work with renewed energy. A book can provide a mental vacation (at a great savings of time and money).

The best writing—whether "realistic" or "fantasy"—tends to involve us in life more deeply. This may be another mark of excellence in writing as opposed to the racks and racks of lurid romances, formula science fiction, predictable thrillers, and breathless fantasies of wealth, sex, and power that clutter up the drugstores and bestseller lists. Good literature may give us escape, but it also brings us back, rearmed with insight for our everyday experiences and with a new appreciation for the texture of actual life. Bad literature makes us despise our lives, wishing we could be like the fictional people we read about and causing us to regard ordinary living as boring. Good literature makes us understand and appreciate our lives, opening our eyes to the drama and significance of the story we are living.

The metaphor involved in the charge of escapism has another dimension as well. According to J. R. R. Tolkien, a Christian author who is the master of fantasy, escape is not necessarily an irresponsible running away from reality. Escape can be eminently practical and sensible—if you are in a prison. There is a difference, Tolkien writes, between "the flight of a deserter" and "the escape of a prisoner." "Why should a man be scorned if, finding himself in prison, he tries to get out and go home? Or if, when he cannot do so, he thinks and talks about other topics than jailers and prison-walls?"[13]

Literature enables people to escape from the prison of the here-and-now, the day-to-day drudgery that can become so stifling and ener-vating. Christians, in particular, know that we are in fact imprisoned—by the flesh and by the world. Our sinful condition and environment hinder our awareness of the larger spiritual realm which comprises true reality. The worldviews that dominate our culture today exclude the mysteries and complexities affirmed by Scripture. According to messages that assail us, only the material truly exists. Nothing lies beyond the limits of our senses. Only the physical is real. The result is a claustrophobic universe, a narrow, limiting vision that minimizes nearly everything human beings have always considered most important. Love, goodness, and beauty are reduced to banalities of biological forces and social conventions. Mystery, purpose, and ide-als are all eliminated, leaving only bare matter in all of its dullness.

Literature can be a means of escape from this materialistic prison. Christians can escape the straitjackets of modern thought by reading books from other times, which provide a context for a more compre-hensive and Biblically informed way of thinking. Even modern books have a way of working against the worldviews that try to squelch the human spirit, of questioning the modern assumptions and pointing to something more. Perhaps language itself works against materialism—one can hardly read any work of fiction without sensing that the tex-ture of life is rich and somehow purposeful, that good and evil are more than names, and that the universe is wider and more wondrous than we could ever expect. Reading some fantasy can send us soaring through the prison bars. Reading a realistic novel can force us to rec-ognize the prison for what it is, enabling us to dig deeper and deeper until we have tunneled our way out.

THEME

A fourth element of fiction (after plot, character, and setting) is theme. A story will generally have some sort of point; that is, it will be written for some purpose, to convey certain ideas and provoke in the reader certain thoughts.

Sometimes a writer will start with an overt theme—a plan to write a story denouncing war, promoting love, or exposing some social evil. Most themes, though, cannot be reduced to a truism or to a simple "lesson in life" (with the notable exception of *Aesop's Fables*). Most writers find themselves exploring ideas, not simply stating them. A writer might want to explore a conflict between love and friendship, or how war might affect a young man's life, or the downfall that can come from pride. Characters are then placed into situations, and the writer imagines how they might act and where their actions might lead them. Along the way, both the author and the reader make discoveries.

As we have seen, the lovers' triangle in the King Arthur story raises hosts of issues—conflicts between friendship and love, love and honor, reason and passion, sin and virtue. When the story ends, the reader is left pondering the awful consequences of Lancelot and Guinevere's adultery, how a single sin—at first so understandable, so seemingly excusable—leads to the annihilation of a noble civilization. This is one theme of the King Arthur story, and the reader can then abstract its principles and apply them on many levels: how sexual immorality can destroy not only Camelot but TV ministries; how any personal sin, unrepented, can grow in magnitude and in destructive power. The story, though, does not really preach; rather, it simply depicts human beings and what happened to them. Throughout, the characters and the consequences of their actions are consistent with human nature so that they are believable. The reader then thinks about the story, interprets its significance, and draws conclusions.

Sidney said that the function of literature is to teach and to delight; if he is right, a work of literature cannot help but teach, despite itself. Often authors intend certain themes to emerge from their works. Sometimes, however, a reader can notice unintended themes implicit in the work. For example, slasher movies have a theme. They explore what it might be like to butcher other human beings. Whereas the King Arthur story deals with the evil of adultery, other stories present adultery as something liberating and glamorous. The authors' overt purpose may be simply to make lots of money. Yet, intentional or not, their writings do teach, although the theme may be abhorrent.

Interpreting the theme of a story is thus of great importance for Christians. Some cautions, though, are in order. Often Christians become involved in outcries against literary works before they fully understand them. Again, simply presenting a moral evil is not the same as condoning or teaching it. The King Arthur legend deals with adultery, but certainly does not advocate it—quite the contrary. There is a witch in Lewis's *The Lion, the Witch, and the Wardrobe,* but the work does not advocate witchcraft. *Huckleberry Finn* is about a boy who plays hookey from school and who lives in a society that keeps slaves. Mark Twain, however, is not advocating illiteracy and, far from promoting racism, he is attacking it with a vengeance. Many Christians seize upon a detail or a subject dealt with by a book, take it completely out of context, and fail to do the necessary labor of thinking about the work and interpreting it thematically.

Christians should also remember that they are not necessarily contaminated by being exposed to a viewpoint they disagree with. I can listen to my agnostic friends explaining the way they look at the world without succumbing to their unbelief. In fact, these conversations help me understand them and give me an occasion to answer and to witness to them. By the same token, I should be able to read a book by a non-Christian without danger to my faith. I should be able to understand what it is saying and then disagree with it, in whole or in part, just as I can with any other statement.

One of the great benefits of literature, as C. S. Lewis points out, is that it provides a way for us to enter into other people's minds for a while, to allow us to understand what it feels like to live in a certain time or to hold to a certain worldview.[14] Reading works by rationalists or naturalists or Marxists or existentialists can help us to understand these perspectives better from the inside and to identify the human needs they address (and fail to address). Such understanding is necessary whether we are attempting to refute these limiting worldviews or simply to communicate more effectively to the modern mind. Reading works by non-Christians can thus can be healthy for Christians, if—and only if—they have a firm grasp of Biblical truth and a well-sharpened critical sensibility, which comes from studying literature.

On the other hand, fiction can be more powerful than nonfiction (and potentially more subversive to Christianity) precisely because, as Sidney says, it "moves" us by our delight into accepting what it teaches. Unsophisticated readers—children, for example, and those weak in their faith—may well be misled by non-Christian writings. Christians need to learn how to be sophisticated readers. If we become aware of how literary techniques work upon our imaginations and if we become practiced interpreters of literary themes, we can sort out the good from the bad and view whatever we read from a Christian perspective.

Most of the spiritually bad literature is also aesthetically bad. Writers are often tempted to sell out their art in a bid for commercial success. As a result, they try to appeal to the lowest pleasures of a mass market, offering nothing more than time-killing titillation. Pornography, psychotic violence, neurotic cynicism, and hedonistic fantasies are easy to write, once you have the knack. They demand nothing from their readers and give nothing of value in return. Editors may demand "obligatory sex scenes" in an effort to sell more books, and talented authors despise themselves for giving in. The corruption in these books manifests itself in hackneyed plots, one-dimensional characters, ludicrous settings, and decadent themes.

Serious writers, on the other hand, even when they themselves are lost in their sins or hopelessly searching for some meaning in life, tend to portray a complexity of experience and theme that Christians can recognize. Whereas the glitzy and shallow writers pretend that life without God is great fun, real artists know otherwise. Jean Paul Sartre was no Christian when he wrote *Nausea* or *No Exit* (although he supposedly experienced a deathbed conversion), but these works show unforgettably the emptiness and the "nausea" of life without God. Melville was probably as spiritually confused as his main characters, but his portrait of Ahab in *Moby Dick* shows a human being rebelling against existence itself. The futility, madness, and tragedy of this rebellion have a special resonance for Christians, whose perspective is also presented in the novel. Christians can be confident that because God is the author of all truth, any flash of insight into that truth, no matter what its source, will be in full harmony with the revelation of Scripture.

The truth of the Christian faith is so profound that often non-Christians, if they are honest, must acknowledge what Scripture reveals. God's moral law is universal, written on the heart even of unbelievers (Romans 2:14-15). This means that whenever the human heart is honestly explored, one will run right into the bedrock of God's law.[15] Thus, even works by pre-Christian writers, such as Sophocles and Virgil, were hailed by the early church as containing sound moral teaching. Similarly, works by the best writers—those with integrity, honesty, and imaginative insight (not simply those acclaimed by the world)—will tend to accord startlingly well with parts of Scriptural revelation, even though their authors tragically do not know Christ. Moreover, as Augustine suggests, the aesthetic laws—the standards of beauty, the psychology of literary form, and the requirements of language itself—will tend to draw authors even against their natural inclinations into creating structures in harmony with the *logos* of God which underlies everything that is real.[16]

CHRISTIAN FICTION WRITERS

Writing good fiction is a craft. A Christian automobile mechanic may or may not be more skilled in fixing an automobile than a non-Christian mechanic; in the same way, a writer's personal faith may or may not result in superior writing. Still, Christian authors can offer readers a range of insight that escapes even the best of secular writers. If God's law is universal and is evident even to Gentiles, the gospel of Christ is particular, distinctive, and scandalous. Non-Christians can speak eloquently about ethics and can even alert us to our lost condition, but the staggering message of Jesus Christ—that God saves us freely by giving His Son to die for our sins—remains the province of Christian writers.

A good place to begin may be John Bunyan's *Pilgrim's Progress*. This pioneering work of fiction is not only delightful to read and astonishing in its spiritual insight, but it is also one of those books that can teach us how to read other books. Bunyan is not interested in "hidden meanings," so he clearly explains all of his rich and imaginative symbolism. On this allegorical journey to the Celestial City, we see Christian struggling with his guilt until his burden falls off at the foot of the cross and he squeezes through the narrow gate that leads to life. We see him sinking in depression—the Slough of Despond—until he slogs his way through the muddy swamp, pulled out by a friend's helping hand. We see Christian captured by the Giant Pride, mocked by the worldly sophisticates in Vanity Fair, and fortified by fellow believers and moments of spiritual illumination. Bunyan's story manages to be both a symbolic fantasy brilliantly told and a realistic rendition of human characters, landscapes, and emotions. Although not all fiction is so symbolic, this classic work of art gives the reader abundant practice in interpreting and applying literary meaning.

Other classics are steeped in the Christian worldview, from the plays of Shakespeare to the novels of Charles Dickens. Many modern writers too, as we will see later, are expressing their faith to a non-Christian age. Flannery O'Connor is a good example of a modern Christian novelist. She frankly admits that:

> I see from the standpoint of Christian orthodoxy. This means that for me the meaning of life is centered in our Redemption by Christ and that what I see in the world I see in its relation to that. I don't think that this is a position that can be taken halfway or one that is particularly easy in these times to make transparent in fiction.[17]

This does not mean that her Christian convictions limit her perceptions or what she feels free to write about. "I have heard it said that belief in Christian dogma is a hindrance to the writer," she writes, "but I myself have found nothing further from the truth. Actually it forces the storyteller to observe. It is not a set of rules which fixes what he sees in the world. It affects his writing primarily by guaranteeing his respect for mystery."[18]

And yet, writing in an unbelieving age poses certain difficulties for the Christian writer as O'Connor says:

> The novelist with Christian concerns will find in modern life distortions which are repugnant to him, and his problem will be to make these appear as distortions to an audience which is used to seeing them as natural; and he may well be forced to take ever more violent means to get his vision across to this hostile audience. When you can assume that your audience holds the same beliefs you do, you can relax a little and use more normal ways of talking to it; when you have to assume that it does not, then you have to make

your vision apparent by shock—to the hard of hearing you shout, and for the almost blind you draw large and startling figures.[19]

This she does. As Robert Drake observes, "Her overriding strategy is always to shock, embarrass, even outrage rationalist readers."[20]

O'Connor's stories are invariably set in the backwoods of the South and are filled with unforgettable characters that are both recognizable and grotesque. Her novels and short stories are populated with a whole cast of cripples, hypocrites, and eccentrics: a Bible salesman who steals a customer's wooden leg; an atheist who becomes an evangelist for a "Church Without Christ"; a complacent woman who is forced to acknowledge God as she is being gored by a bull. Such characters are comic, yet in a way that makes the reader uncomfortable. O'Connor is painting the picture of human sin in all of its inanity and ugliness. And yet, she always dramatizes in explicit terms the grace of God breaking into the hearts of sinful people and offering redemption through Jesus Christ.

Christians sometimes complain about "negativism" and ask for "positive stories" of good cheer and sunny optimism. There is a place for optimism, of course, but Christians need to remember that the Bible paints a negative picture of lost humanity. Stories filled with "good people" overcoming all odds may create the dangerous impression that human beings are, in fact, "good" and capable of saving themselves through their own moral actions. Such stories in their own way may be more spiritually dangerous than a blatantly immoral paperback. O'Connor, on the other hand, waters down nothing and makes no concessions to humanistic sensibilities. The result is that she forces us to laugh at human pretensions and to gain insights into the fathomless mystery of God's love.

When we read her short story "Temple of the Holy Ghost," we assume the point of view of a young girl who has the obnoxious but pervasive habit of scorning other human beings. We meet a number of more or less unattractive figures—some shallow teenagers, some ignorant country boys, a smelly obese driver with piglike ears—and the reader shares the girl's disdain. Then we encounter the most repulsive of all—a freak in a circus sideshow, a hermaphrodite. At this point in the story, both the girl and the reader are confronted by the doctrine that human beings are none other than temples of the Holy Ghost, that God's design for human beings gives them a dignity and a value that far transcends our human emphasis on appearance, intelligence, and physical perfection. The story ends by evoking the mystery of Christ's Incarnation into a world of suffering and imperfections. The reader, whose own reactions have been dramatically corrected, is left reeling.

In "The Displaced Person," O'Connor writes about a woman

who imports a World War II refugee to work on her farm. This displaced person "upsets the balance" and forces the woman—who insists, "I'm not theological. I'm practical!"—into confronting another displaced person: Jesus Christ. Sample O'Connor's narrative virtuosity, as she describes a priest, a peacock, and Mrs. McIntyre's spiritual blindness:

> The cock stopped suddenly and curving his neck backwards, he raised his tail and spread it with a shimmering timbrous noise. Tiers of small pregnant suns floated in a green-gold haze over his head. The priest stood transfixed, his jaw slack. Mrs. McIntyre wondered where she had ever seen such an idiotic old man. "Christ will come like that!" he said in a loud gay voice and wiped his hand over his mouth and stood there, gaping.
>
> Mrs. McIntyre's face assumed a set puritanical expression and she reddened. Christ in the conversation embarrassed her the way sex had her mother. "It is not my responsibility that Mr. Guizac has nowhere to go," she said. "I don't find myself responsible for all the extra people in the world."
>
> The old man didn't seem to hear her. His attention was fixed on the cock who was taking minute steps backward, his head against the spread tail. "The Transfiguration," he murmured.
>
> She had no idea what he was talking about. "Mr. Guizac didn't have to come here in the first place," she said, giving him a hard look.
>
> The cock lowered his tail and began to pick grass.
>
> "He didn't have to come in the first place," she repeated, emphasizing each word.
>
> The old man smiled absently. "He came to redeem us," he said. . . .[21]

POETRY:
The Art of Singing

Poetry is the most ancient and, apparently, the most natural form of literature. Prose fiction is a latecomer, and many societies never develop nonfiction, but all cultures have poetry. Many people today claim that they dislike poetry or do not understand it, yet as soon as they are by themselves, they turn on the radio or their stereo system to immerse themselves in songs. Certain songs are especially moving, stirring deep feelings and sometimes influencing the way people think about love or life or God. Song lyrics are poetry.

Originally all poetry was accompanied by music, from the epic strains of *Beowulf* to the love poems of Thomas Campion. (The term "lyric" poetry, the type of verse that expresses an emotion, comes from the name of the instrument which accompanied it—the lyre, precursor of the guitar. *Ode*, a poem which celebrates a person or an event, is the Greek word for "song.") Only after the invention of the printing press were poetry and music separated. Writers began writing for the printed page, although the rhythms, rhymes, and sounds of the verse created its own self-contained music. With the habit of reading silently, modern verse occasionally becomes less overtly musical. Contemporary poetry sometimes abandons the sound effects of traditional poetry—the regular rhythms and rhymes—for "free verse," although the essential elements of poetic form remain.

Today, the new electronic technology may be reuniting poetry and music—songs can be recorded and listened to over and over again. Rock 'n' Roll, contemporary Christian music, hymns used in worship, folk ballads, even the spontaneous street poetry of "rap," exert a powerful impact today, giving people both aesthetic pleasure and words to live by. Whether this impact is for good or for ill varies, but it demonstrates the continuing power of poetry.

Many people do not understand or appreciate poetry. They respond instinctively to a song lyric or a greeting card verse (which proves that the poetic impulse still lives), but they neglect the more difficult but more rewarding verse of the great poets, many of whom were devout Christians. Because poetry tends to address the whole person—the mind, the imagination, and the emotions—there may be no better way to cultivate a Christian sensibility and worldview (apart from reading Scripture itself) than to saturate oneself in Christian poetry.

And yet, most Christians have never heard of devotional poets such as George Herbert, who explores a personal relationship with Jesus Christ in poems of astonishing skill. Modern Christians are put off by the apparent strangeness of T. S. Eliot's verse, and thus neglect someone who could be one of their best allies in confronting the modern spiritual "wasteland" with the truth of Christian orthodoxy. By explaining how to read poetry and by focusing on the poetry of the Bible, of Herbert, and of Eliot, this chapter will attempt to help Christians enter the world of poetry.

POETIC FORM

Whereas the main unit of prose nonfiction is the paragraph, and the main unit of narrative (and drama) is the scene, the main unit of poetry is the line. Not all poetry has a regular pattern of rhythm or rhyme, but all verse, even the most experimental, will be arranged in lines. Each line often has a predetermined number of syllables or units of rhythm. Related lines are often organized together into stanzas.

Take out a hymnbook and notice the fine print that accompanies each song, giving the author, the composer, and musical information about the hymn. The numbers (10.10.10.10; 8.7.8.7; etc.) refer to the meter, the number of syllables in each line.

Consider the famous Christmas hymn "Angels We Have Heard on High." The metrical pattern is "7.7.7.7. and refrain." This means that each line has seven syllables and that there are four such lines in a stanza along with an irregular refrain ("Glo-o-o-o-o-oh-o-o-o-o-oh-o-o-o-o-or-ia"). The writer of the text worked with such a line length so that the words would fit the music (or the composer wrote the music so that it would fit the words). Interestingly, other poems with this meter will fit the same music. "Twinkle, Twinkle Little Star" also has four lines of seven syllables each and can be sung to the tune of "Angels We Have Heard on High." (Try it.) Conversely, the words of the hymn can be sung to the tune of the children's song. (Try that too.) This is why a text can be put to a number of different melodies, and a single tune can carry many different texts. (For example, the tune to "Twinkle, Twinkle Little Star" is also the tune for the alphabet song.)

Besides counting syllables, the poetic line can be determined by the number of repetitions of a rhythmic pattern. (English and other Germanic languages have a strong but variable rhythm, so a rhythmic meter fits well with our language. French and Japanese are less variable rhythmically, so their verse is nearly always syllabic. The poetic meter of ancient Greek and Latin was based on the alternation of long and short vowel sounds.) "Twinkle, twinkle little star/How I wonder what you are" features a pulsating rhythm of one loud syllable followed by a more quiet syllable, a pattern known as "trochaic": "Twínk-lĕ, twínk-lĕ lít-tlĕ stár." (Marking the "beats," known as scansion, is done by using an accent mark for a louder, stressed syllable and sometimes a "short" line for a quieter, unstressed syllable.) The English language has various rhythmic possibilities (iambic: ˘´, trochaic: ´˘, anapestic: ˘˘´, dactylic: ´˘˘, spondaic: ´´, pyrrhic: ˘˘). The number of "feet" refers to the number of such rhythmic units in each line (tetrameter has four; pentameter has five, etc.). The point is, the poetic line has a form and a music of its own.

These set patterns should not impose on poetry a monotonous sing-song or bind the poet in a straitjacket of rules. Rather, a good poet will *use* rhythm to establish an effect or meaning. Regular patterns can be varied, thus emphasizing the words that purposely violate the form. Notice how John Donne both follows the regular iambic rhythm required by the sonnet form and violates it to hammer home his meaning:

> Báttĕr mỹ héart, thrĕe-pérsonĕd Gód; fŏr yóu
> Aš yét bŭt knóck, bréathe, shíne, aňd séek tŏ ménd;
> Thăt Í măy riše, aňd stánd, o'ĕrthrów mĕ, aňd bénd
> Yoŭr fórce, tŏ bréak, blów, búrn, aňd máke mé néw.[1]

Using the image of a blacksmith repairing a metal implement, the poet asks God not to be so gentle with him. Knocking out the dents and applying a little polish is not enough to repair this sinner. He knows that he needs to be broken, thrown into the furnace, and totally remade. The rhythm is basically iambic, an unstressed syllable followed by an accent, but the pattern is varied to imitate the blows of the hammer. The alliterated words in line four are each accented, so that the hammer-blows of God's sanctifying power are punched into the reader's consciousness by the very rhythm of the line.

Lines may be connected and organized into related stanzas by rhyme, the repetition of final sounds. Besides adding to the inherent music of the poetic language, rhyme helps to mark off and define that main unit of poetry, the individual line. When we listen to a rhymed poem, we can hear the end of each line. ("Twinkle twinkle little *star*/How I wonder what you *are*.")

Predetermined rhyme schemes set lines into relationships with each other and have a bearing on the meaning of the poem. If the rhyme scheme requires three four-line stanzas, the reader can assume the poem will be divided into three units of meaning as well. The sonnet form used by Donne involves a complex rhyme scheme that has a direct bearing on the poem's meaning. The first eight lines often have only two rhyme sounds, the difficulty of the form paralleling the emotional difficulty that is the subject of most sonnets. The last six lines have an easier rhyme scheme, paralleling the solution to the difficulty or the emotional release that characterizes the end of most sonnets.

Modern verse which is written to be read silently on the page in a sense has no need of rhyme. The groupings and the relationships between the lines are conveyed visually on the page. Free verse lacks a predetermined rhythm and rhyme scheme, but it still has definite lines which need to be carefully crafted. Oral poetry, though, needs rhyme so that the listener can "hear" each line and how every line fits together into a larger stanza. This is why even the most experimental or wildly rebellious contemporary song will have a traditional rhyme scheme.

Prose hurries by so that we become caught up in the content of what is said rather than by the language itself; poetry, on the other hand, slows us down, calls attention to its language, and communicates in sharp, telegraphic bursts. Each line conveys an image or an idea that is orchestrated with the other lines in the stanza and in the poem as a whole. Moreover, because each line is so sharply defined, each word in the line is made to stand out. Every word is important in a poem and takes its place in a mosaic of meaning.

Another feature of poetry is that it generally operates with vivid, tangible images. That is, its words appeal to our senses, so that we must read it with our imaginations. Poetry is almost never abstract for long—abstractions, of course, are often easier for our intellects to comprehend, but poetry requires us to picture things in our minds and to respond to them in a personal way.

Continuing with the example of one of the first poems most of us ever learned, consider its imagery:

Twinkle, twinkle little star,
How I wonder what you are.
Up above the world so high,
Like a diamond in the sky.

The first line pictures the star in the sky; the word *twinkle* describes the way the light from a star flickers, and the repetition of the word calls attention to the way the light shimmers and changes from moment to moment. The star in the black sky is like a diamond in its appearance (its multi-faceted sparkling) and in its preciousness. The star seems so little because it is so distant, far above the whole world. (The altitude is emphasized by two references—"up above" and "so high"—in a single line.) With this description of the star in its remote, mysterious beauty, the second line conveys the universal human response of wonder, curiosity, and awe in the face of the vastness of the universe. The theme of this children's poem is similar to that of the psalmist: "When I consider your heavens, the work of your fingers, the moon and the stars, which you have set in place, what is man that you are mindful of him, the son of man that you care for him?" (Psalm 8:3, 4)

It may seem ridiculous to dwell so closely on a children's lyric, but this is how one must read poetry. We have heard this song over and over again, but our tendency has probably been to read it like prose, letting the words wash over us, or to let its sing-song lull us to sleep. Poetry, though, requires active reading. The reader must become involved more personally and actively than in other kinds of reading. The imagination must be fully engaged, the language must be taken in completely, and the feelings, associations, and ideas conjured up by the language must be allowed their full play.

This does not mean that reading poetry is hard work or that a poem is nothing more than a puzzle with a "hidden meaning" that must be deciphered. Much modern poetry, I admit, is overly obscure, and older poetry sometimes requires historical explanation of its language and its references. Most poetry in its essence, though, communicates freely and clearly. There is nothing hidden in the poem about the little star—everything is right on the surface. Readers of poetry simply need to allow the language of the poem to sink in. The form of the poem allows that to happen.

The demands of the poetic form also pull insight from the poet. Working with a difficult metrical system or rhyme scheme means that the poet cannot be content with the first words to come to mind. Rather, the poetic form challenges the poet to think more deeply, to grapple with the language and its meaning until words are found that both convey the experience and that mesh with the objective form. As a result, the poet, as well as the reader, is often surprised by what the finished poem reveals.

THE TRUTH OF METAPHORS

Because poetry is concrete, working with vivid sensory descriptions, even abstract ideas must be rendered through tangible imagery. In other words, poetry works through figures of speech and symbols. Consider a line from another children's poem: "Life is but a dream." Here the vast abstraction "life" is brought down to earth by a metaphor: the qualities of a dream which we all know from experience are applied to life as a whole. Both life and dreams are transitory, mysterious, and ephemeral.

What we have here is a metaphor, not a dogma. The poet is not asserting that all reality is an illusion, in the fashion of Eastern mysticism. Metaphors must be taken metaphorically, not literally. There is no real contradiction with the other poet who insisted that "Life is real! Life is earnest!"[2] Poets bring abstractions down to earth by writing about them in terms of sensory experience. Shakespeare compares his love to a summer's day; Donne speaks of death as a "short sleep"; Hopkins contemplates Christ as he watches a bird soar through the sky.

The use of figurative language does not mean that poems are only fanciful or subjective in their meaning, much less fictional. Metaphors are ways of speaking about truth. In fact, all language, not only that of poetry, is metaphorical. Consider a prosaic statement such as the following: "Many people have bouts of depression, but when they learn to reach out to others they find that life looks brighter." The term *depression* literally means a low point in the ground; it has become a metaphor for a mental condition, of feeling "low" (another metaphor). *Bout* refers to a round of fighting. The gesture of "reaching out" and the optical image of something becoming "brighter" are more obvious metaphors. The point is (notice the metaphor involved in that phrase), dull prose (another metaphor) is actually alive with unconscious metaphors. According to Emerson, "Every word was once a poem."[3] (Browse through a dictionary, noticing the origin of each word, the "etymology" provided in square brackets for each entry.) As Emerson observes, "The etymologist finds the deadest word to have been once a brilliant picture. Language is fossil poetry."[4]

The Bible too employs metaphors. How else could we creatures of flesh and blood comprehend spiritual realities unless they are explained in terms of flesh and blood? When Jesus says, "I am the door; if any one enters by me, he will be saved" (John 10:9 RSV), He is speaking metaphorically, but also truly. Our Lord is not saying that He is a wooden gate, but that He is the only means of salvation, that He is our only entrance point into Heaven. He really *is* our door, and that truth can be spoken in no clearer language.

The Bible's use of metaphors does not detract from the truth and inerrancy of Scripture. Mormons assert that God has a physical body, taking as evidence texts such as "The eyes of the Lord are on those who fear him" (Psalm 33:18) and "The Lord will lay bare his holy arm" (Isaiah 52:10). If we believe in the Scriptures, should we not then believe that God has physical eyes and a physical arm? Orthodox Christians, who interpret Scripture according to Scripture, interpret these texts according to the clear statement that God is spirit (John 4:24). To speak of God's eyes is to express God's omniscience and His intimate awareness of His people's problems. To speak of God's arm is to express God's omnipotence, His active power in judgment. Since God chose to reveal Himself to us by means of human language, He employs metaphors as the best way of communicating truth.

The authority of Scripture lies in the words and what they say and what they mean. The metaphors of Scripture are also authoritative and utterly true.[5] Some people assume that if a passage is not to be taken "literally," they are under no obligation to believe it at all. If they see a metaphorical passage in Scripture, then it is "only poetry" and can be ignored. This confusion of poetry with fiction is a curious legacy of nineteenth-century Biblical scholarship, surviving still among many liberal theologians and Bible scholars.[6] Actually, metaphor heightens and intensifies the truth it conveys.

Poetry is not the same thing as fiction, nor does poetic language signal a purely imaginary creation. Actually, poetry is probably closer to reality than other forms of literature. Nonfiction can be abstract, and fiction is wholly imaginary, but poetry tends to be written out of the intensity of lived experience. Poetic descriptions are nearly always direct and firsthand, whether the poet is writing about the grandeur of the Alps, romantic love, or ecstasy in the presence of God. The language of a poem is intense and complex because the reality that it seeks to evoke is intense and complex. Poetry has been called "a trap for meditation." When we read a poem about a little star or God battering the heart or a Grecian urn or the wrath of Achilles, the language and the form of the poem cause us to respond with our minds and feelings, concentrating and reflecting on some aspect of life. This sort of meditation can be a valuable discipline for a Christian.

Whereas Eastern meditation involves emptying the mind of all traces of the external world, often through repetition of some meaningless syllable, meditation in the Christian tradition involves focusing on external reality and is centered in language. "I meditate on all thy works," says the psalmist; "I muse on the work of thy hands" (Psalm 143:5 KJV). In the night watches, the psalmist meditates on God's Word (Psalm 119:148). When I read any poem, I find myself meditating on reality as established by God and on the human condition. Because a poem demands a personal response from the reader, I can only respond as a Christian, even when the poet lacks my faith. The meditation encouraged by poetry promotes concentrated thinking, heightened sensitivity, and an integrated Christian sensibility. That

Scripture itself often turns to poetry makes it especially worth our attention.

THE PSALMS

Whereas poetry based in the European languages and in the Greek and Roman aesthetic tradition is centered around rhyme schemes and metrical patterns, the ancient Hebrew poetic form is based upon parallelism. That is, the language is patterned by repetitions of meaning, by saying the same thing twice in different ways. As Ruth apRoberts has observed, parallelism may be the only poetic device that can be fully translated from one language to another.[7] Thus the Bible, translated into hundreds of languages, maintains its original poetic form and effects in every tongue, a linguistic curiosity that is clearly God's design.

Note the complex repetitions in Psalm 24 (RSV), here arranged and printed to highlight the parallel phrases:

> The _earth_ is the LORD'S, and _the fulness thereof;_
> The _world_, and _they that dwell therein._
>
> For he hath _founded it upon the seas_
> and _established it upon the floods._
>
> Who shall _ascend into the hill of the LORD?_
> or who shall _stand in his holy place?_
>
> He that hath _clean hands_
> and _a pure heart;_
>
> Who hath not _lifted up his soul unto vanity,_
>   nor _sworn deceitfully._
>
> He shall receive _the blessing_ from _the LORD,_
> and _righteousness_ from _the God of his salvation._
>
> This is the generation of them _that seek him,_
> _that seek thy face,_ O Jacob.
>
> _Lift up your heads,_ O _ye gates;_
> Even _lift them up_, _ye everlasting doors;_
>
>   and _the King of glory_ shall come in.
> Who is this _King of glory_?
>
> The _LORD of hosts,_
> He is _the King of glory._

Just as Western poetry repeats patterns of rhythm and sounds, Hebrew poetry repeats patterns of ideas. Sometimes the repetition is only formal (the last verses here repeat "King of Glory" in various configurations). Other times the parallelism sets up variations on a theme, extending and clarifying its meanings.[8]

For example, "blessing" in verse 5 is parallel to "righteousness." The blessing referred to is thus not a matter of temporal rewards but of inward righteousness. Conversely, we see that "righteousness" is understood not as human merit but as a "blessing" from the Lord. The verse speaks clearly in a vein usually associated with the New Testament of justification by grace. God is described as the sovereign LORD and also as "the God of his salvation." The psalm refers literally to pilgrims ascending the hill of Jerusalem to worship at the Temple. As such, the psalm is a meditation upon coming into the presence of a holy God. Metaphorically, it can apply to our coming into God's presence in Heaven, which we can only do through God's gift of salvation. The significance of this psalm for evangelicals is evident only by close attention to its poetic form.

A commonplace of Biblical theology is that "Scripture interprets Scripture." Parallelism is one means by which Scripture interprets itself. Thus, the one who ascends into the Holy place must have "clean hands and a pure heart." Does this mean that the hands had to be rinsed in a ceremonial way before a person would be allowed to enter the Temple? Perhaps, but the poetic form makes "clean hands" parallel to "a pure heart." Metaphorically, having clean hands—one's actions purged of guilt—is related to an inner purity. Conversely, inner purity manifests itself in pure actions ("clean hands"). On a larger plane, ritual actions, such as the ceremonial washings required for entrance into the Temple, must be parallel to spiritual reality, just as the ceremonial ascent to the Temple parallels the soul's ascent to God.

Parallelism is a formal property of all Hebrew literature, not just poetry. Throughout Scripture, incidents are repeated, with the same facts being shown from different but parallel perspectives. We read about the life of David in the books of Samuel (which bring out his sinfulness), and then read about his life again in 1 Chronicles (which stresses his greatness). We read about the various monarchs and the decadence of Israel and Judah in 1 and 2 Kings, and then read about them again in 1 and 2 Chronicles. In the New Testament, we read about the life of Christ in Matthew, then again in Mark, then again in Luke, and then again in John. This fourfold parallelism is not mere repetition. Rather, each Gospel contributes a special emphasis or perspective on this most important event of history. By presenting the life and teachings of our Lord from so many different angles, the Gospels present the Incarnation three-dimensionally.

Biblical scholars have yet to recognize the full implications of Hebraic literary form. When they notice "two creation stories," or two accounts of Noah and the ark, or repetitions of incidents or parables in the Gospels, scholars often conclude that the Biblical text lacks unity. They assume that various traditions composed by different authors have been combined by an editor who randomly cut and pasted varying accounts together. Such conclusions are often used to cast doubt on the authority of Scripture. Actually, parallel repetitions in Hebraic literature are evidence for the *unity* of the text. The Biblical writers employed parallelism as their way of organizing and fully exploring their subjects.

The imagery of Biblical poetry is also different from what we are used to in Western, classically influenced verse. Our imaginations, like those of the ancient Greeks, are largely visual. We orient ourselves to our environment and to other people by the sense of sight, so we expect our literature to tell us what the characters look like and to enable us to "visualize" the setting. The ancient Hebrews, on the other hand, were leery of visual images. Their pagan neighbors could see their gods, who supposedly manifested themselves by means of "graven images." The God of Abraham and Isaac, however, reveals Himself not by sight but through hearing, by the proclamation and reading of His Word. The Hebrew prohibition of images manifests itself throughout their language and art. The Bible never describes, for instance, what Jesus or any other Biblical characters looked like. The writings of the ancient Greeks, on the other hand, are full of visual descriptions of the characters and their settings, and our Western literature follows them in insisting upon a panorama of visual detail. The Bible often employs imagery, but instead of being visual, it draws on the other senses and the whole range of associations the image suggests.

Consider the lush poetry of the Song of Solomon:

Behold, you are beautiful, my love, behold, you are beautiful!
Your eyes are doves behind your veil.
Your hair is like a flock of goats, moving down the slopes of
    Gilead.
Your teeth are like a flock of shorn ewes that have come up
    from the washing, all of which bear twins, and not one
    among them is bereaved.
Your lips are like a scarlet thread, and your mouth is lovely.
Your cheeks are like halves of a pomegranate behind your veil.
Your neck is like the tower of David, built for an arsenal,
    whereon hang a thousand bucklers, all of them shields of
    warriors.
Your two breasts are like two fawns, twins of a gazelle, that
    feed among the lilies. (4:1-5 RSV)

What are we to make of these images? Cheeks like pomegranates, a fruit with hundreds of seeds imbedded in little red cells? Does this mean that the Shulamite had acne? Breasts like two deer? Hair like goats? Neck like a tower with shields all over it? What do these mean? How are we supposed to picture her?

The difficulties disappear and the greatness of the poetry emerges when we stop trying to interpret these images *visually* and interpret them according to our other senses. The woman's cheeks do not *look* like pomegranates; this is a description of their fragrance and perhaps, even more sensuously, of their taste. The image of her breasts being like two fawns is not visual but *tactile*. Hebrew imagery is also associative, drawing on the various connotations of the image. Thus, the hair like goats is another tactile image (think of the heaviness and texture of a goat's fleece). It also conjures up images of prosperity and well-being for a culture of shepherds. The description of her neck like a tower with shields refers to the way she stands—tall and imperious, but also inaccessible, shielded, an allusion to her chastity.[9] The other images can be similarly re-imagined. The result is to experience a poem of the very highest order, a love poem astonishing in its sensuality and emotional intensity.

Is the Song of Solomon a celebration of married love or an allegory of Christ and the church? I would say on the basis of Ephesians 5:31, 32, which teaches that human marriage is symbolic of the relationship between Christ and the church, that it can hardly be one without the other. At any rate, the inclusion of the Song of Solomon in the canon of Holy Scripture proves beyond any doubt that God approves of poetry.

GEORGE HERBERT

A poet whose work exemplifies the classic traditions of English verse is George Herbert, a seventeenth-century English pastor recognized as one of the greatest lyric poets of our language. Herbert is especially significant for Christian readers; there is no writer more evangelical, more saturated with Scripture, more honest and more profound in his depiction of a personal relationship with Jesus Christ, a topic which engages all of his poetic power.[10] Or, as he puts it:

> *Philosophers have measured mountains,*
> *Fathomed the depths of seas, of states, and kings,*
> *Walked with a staff to heaven, and traced fountains:*
>   *But there are two vast, spacious things,*
> *The which to measure it doth more behove:*
> *Yet few there be that sound them; Sin and Love.*
>   ("The Agony," ll. 1-6)[11]

Human beings are fond of probing and measuring the physical world and the complexities of social and political life. In the sort of startling anachronism one becomes accustomed to in reading great poets, we have even "walked with a staff to heaven," a metaphor suggesting for twentieth-century readers the ease of air travel and space exploration. The mysteries of human sin and the love of God, however, are "vast, spacious things"—taller than mountains, deeper than oceans, more complex than politics and statecraft. "Few there be that sound them," but Herbert does. Throughout his poetry, he explores the psychological complexity of human sinfulness countered by the unconditional grace of God, who breaks into our sinful condition with the good news of free salvation. Both sin and love come together in the passion of Jesus Christ.

The rest of the poem describes Christ's agony in the garden, His death on the cross, and the personal significance of that suffering for the sinner who accepts it:

> *Who would know Sin, let him repair*
> *Unto Mount Olivet; there shall he see*
> *A man so wrung with pains, that all his hair,*
> *   His skin, his garments bloody be.*
> *Sin is that press and vice, which forceth pain*
> *To hunt his cruel food through every vein.*
>
> *   Who knows not Love, let him assay*
> *And taste that juice, which on the cross a pike*
> *Did set again abroach; then let him say*
> *   If ever he did taste the like.*
> *Love is that liquor sweet and most divine,*
> *Which my God feels as blood, but I, as wine.*

To know the full magnitude of sin, we must confront the suffering of Christ. The weight of human sin is what tormented our Lord when He took the sins of the whole world upon Himself. His suffering was not only physical; it was also spiritual, as He who knew no sin was made sin for us (2 Corinthians 5:21) and suffered all of its penalty. Sin was "the press and vice" that squeezed and crushed our Lord and that made Christ sweat blood.

To know the full magnitude of love, one must also confront the suffering of Christ. Christ's body was pierced by a spear ("a pike"), and His blood shed for sinners is the ultimate measure of His unfathomable love for us. All that we have to do is receive the benefits of His suffering to taste the sweetness of what He has done for us. What God experiences as blood, we experience as wine (a sacramental image). The suffering is His; the benefits are ours. The conflict between our sin and God's love is overwhelmed on the cross when Christ takes our sin upon himself and freely pours out His love in His saving blood.[12]

What makes Herbert a great poet is not his evangelical subject matter, but his mastery of poetic form. Specifically, Herbert integrates form and content, using the poetic form to amplify and establish his poetic meaning.

One of Herbert's most famous poems, "The Collar," is about a moment of rebellion when the speaker wants to throw away his ministry, the restrictions of the Christian life, and all of the burdens of faith:

> *I struck the board, and cried, No more.*
> *I will abroad.*
> *What? shall I ever sigh and pine?*
> *My lines and life are free; free as the road,*
> *Loose as the wind, as large as store.* (ll. 1-5)

The human will desires autonomy and freedom. The constraints of a life devoted to the moral and religious life have become unbearable. The poet wants to run away from God and from his responsibilities, to be "free as the road/Loose as the wind." He goes on to doubt, to raise the possibility that his religious impulses have come not from an external God, but from himself:

> *Recover all thy sigh-blown age*
> *On double pleasures: leave thy cold dispute*
> *Of what is fit, and not. Forsake thy cage,*
> *Thy rope of sands,*
> *Which petty thoughts have made, and made to thee*
> *Good cable, to enforce and draw*
> *And be thy law,*
> *While thou didst wink and wouldst not see.* (ll. 19-26)

He desires pleasure; he wants to stop debating rights and wrongs, to leave behind the restrictions "which petty thoughts have made." The moral law which binds him, he is beginning to think, has no reality in itself—it is nothing more than a rope of sand, but he has shut his eyes to this truth and now wants to make up his wasted self-denial in "double pleasures."

The poem continues in this vein for some thirty lines. At the very end of the poem, at the very point of ultimate denial, another voice breaks through:

> *He that forbears*
> *To suit and serve his need,*
> *Deserves his load.*
> *But as I raved and grew more fierce and wild*
> *At every word,*
> *Me thoughts I heard one calling,* Child!
> *And I replied,* My Lord. (ll. 30-36)

In the midst of this rebellion, God calls out to the sinner in a voice of love: "Child!" God still loves the rebel despite his sin and breaks into his chaotic heart by means of a Word. The rebellion melts away as the speaker reexperiences the reality of his Heavenly Father and the personal relationship at the root of the religious life. The speaker not only hears the Word of God, but he replies with a submission and acknowledgment that reestablishes the relationship: "My Lord."[13]

Herbert is exploring the psychology of sin, describing honestly those feelings which continue to tempt Christians today, leading them into sin and then, to justify their desires, to unbelief. He also explores the dynamics of divine grace as God "calls" the sinful human being to Himself.

What makes this a good poem as well as good theology is that the meaning is conveyed in the very form of the poem. The lines describing the sinner's spiritual chaos are themselves chaotic—the rhythm is irregular, lines vary in length, and the rhyme scheme is wildly disordered. When God breaks in, however, order is restored. The lines assume a regular rhythm ("Bŭt ás Ĭ ráved aňd gréw mŏre fíerce aňd wíld"). The lines rhyme (wild, word, child, Lord). The new spiritual harmony is signaled by the restoration of the poetic harmony.

Herbert's multi-leveled language comments upon the rebellion and suggests the reality of God's grace throughout the poem. The speaker hears God's calling "at every word." The very terms of his complaints ironically point to their answers: The desire to be "free as the road" can be seen as a pun upon "rood," the old English term for cross. The speaker has freedom all along, the freedom of the cross. The desire to be "loose as the wind" recalls the Biblical image for the Holy Spirit, and so on throughout his complaints. The title of the poem, "The Collar," exemplifies Herbert's characteristically brilliant word play: it can refer to his clerical collar, to the collar as a restrictive yoke, to "the Caller" of the last four lines, and thus to the call of faith and to the calling of a pastor.[14]

The speaker of the poem may think that "My lines . . . are free," but they are actually ordered, although their order is not apparent until the climactic four lines. That final stanza consists of four rhymed lines of five, two, four, and three metrical feet. Going back to the "fierce and wild" lines, we see that they too, for all of their seeming lack of order, actually contain five, two, four, or three feet. All of the lines, even the disordered ones, do eventually rhyme. The point is, there was an order even in the chaos; God's plan of salvation was operative even though His "child" was blind to the way God was working in his life. God was holding onto him even in the midst of his rebellion, and He refused to let go.[15]

This unity of form and meaning is characteristic of Herbert's verse. He writes poems about sacrifice that assume the shape of altars; he writes Easter poems in the shape of wings; "The Agony" quoted above is in the shape of a winepress.[16] Over and over again, the human words are resolved by a divine Word which intervenes to "mend my rhyme" ("Denial") and to save the sinner from himself.

Herbert arranges the very sequence of his poetry to explore the spiritual life. His single volume, *The Temple,* begins with a poem on the Law and ushers us into a section titled "The Church." A long poem depicting Christ on the cross, entitled "The Sacrifice," is followed by poems of response, interspersed by poems on the resurrection. Having thus portrayed the process of justification by faith, Herbert follows with a number of poems on sanctification—the ups and downs, the victories and defeats, of the Christian life, climaxing in a series of unforgettable poems on death and the soul's reception into eternal life.

The final poem in "The Church" portrays that reception not in terms of pearly gates and harps, but in terms of a traveler—hesitant, dusty, and feeling guilty—being welcomed into an inn, finally being forced into acceptance of God's all-providing Love:[17]

> *Love bade me welcome: yet my soul drew back,*
> *   Guilty of dust and sin.*
> *But quick-eyed Love, observing me grow slack*
> *   From my first entrance in,*
> *Drew nearer to me, sweetly questioning,*
> *   If I lacked anything.*
> *A guest, I answered, worthy to be here:*
> *   Love said, You shall be he.*
> *I, the unkind, ungrateful? Ah, my dear,*
> *   I cannot look on thee.*
> *Love took my hand, and smiling did reply,*
> *   Who made the eyes but I?*
> *Truth, Lord, but I have marred them: let my shame*
> *   Go where it doth deserve.*
> *And know you not, says Love, who bore the blame?*
> *   My dear, then I will serve.*
> *You must sit down, says Love, and taste my meat:*
> *   So I did sit and eat. ("Love [III]")*

Simone Weil, the French intellectual, said that while contemplating this poem, the meaning of the gospel suddenly came to her, and that Christ came into her heart.[18]

T. S. ELIOT

George Herbert is important both for his place in English literature and for his spiritual insight, and yet many Christians have never read his verse. The same is true for T. S. Eliot, perhaps the greatest modern poet, who was converted to Christianity and who confronted modern culture with the truth of the Christian faith for the rest of his life. Eliot single-handedly changed the course of modern poetry—it has become more fragmented, less "pretty," and more difficult. Many Christians, preferring the orderly harmonies of the age of faith, cannot forgive him for his Modernist style. Nevertheless, as a conservative, orthodox Christian, Eliot confronted the spiritual failures of the modern world in a bold, original, and profound way. He is a valuable ally for evangelical Christians, especially for those interested in understanding the modern spiritual condition and its relationship to Christian truth.

In his early verse before his conversion, Eliot was already indicting the spiritual emptiness of the twentieth century. There is no harmony and order in modern life, he reasoned. How can poetry about that life be harmonious and orderly? (This relating of form to content, of course, recalls Herbert.) In "The Love Song of J. Alfred Prufrock," Eliot describes the shallowness of modern relationships and the inability of the modern mind to comprehend what love is. He portrays unforgettably the insecurity, self-consciousness, and superficiality that characterize modern life. At a party, Prufrock realizes that he and everyone else are merely playing roles—you must "prepare a face to meet the faces that you meet" (l. 27).[19] But he is too self-conscious to reach out to the woman he cares about, and she is too self-absorbed to reach out to him. Prufrock feels that he is being led to "an overwhelming question" (l. 10, 93), but he is afraid to ask it.

In "Gerontion," it seems that Eliot can already sense the reality of Christ, prowling on the outskirts of his mind:

> . . . *In the juvescence of the year,*
> *Came Christ the tiger,*
> *In depraved May, dogwood and chestnut, flowering judas,*
> *To be eaten, to be divided, to be drunk*
> *Among whispers. . . .*
> . . . . . .
> *The tiger springs in the new year. Us he devours. Think at last*
> *We have not reached conclusion, when I*
> *Stiffen in a rented house.* (ll. 19-23, 49-51)

This poem is a good example of Eliot's style. He often writes in free verse (although not exclusively), but the language is still intense, rhythmical, and carefully chosen. He writes in seemingly disconnected images, which are sometimes startling and demand interpretation, and yet they are connected.

How is Christ like a tiger? Certainly Christ is a threat and a danger to sinful human beings, and Eliot deftly avoids cliché and sentimentality by surprising us with this image of the ferocity of a holy God. Eliot's verse is also highly allusive, subtly quoting and referring to other texts and drawing their implications into his own poetry. Here Eliot is probably alluding to Blake's poem "The Tiger," which, with its companion piece "The Lamb," suggests the sublimity as well as the gentleness of God. Instead of the tiger eating us, however, as we expect, this tiger gives Himself to be eaten. "Came Christ the tiger . . . /To be eaten, to be divided, to be drunk/Among whispers." The description of Christ, menacing in His holiness, coming in judgment, shifts abruptly to that of a Communion service, to a picture of Christ's giving of Himself ("This is my body given for you; do this in remembrance of me" [Luke 22:19]). The mood of the poem changes to the peace of the Gospel. Eliot's images are often bleak—dying alone is referred to graphically as "stiffening in a rented house"—but they can trap their readers into valuable meditations.

Eliot's greatest and most famous poem is "The Waste Land," written shortly before his conversion. The controlling reference throughout the poem is to the Legend of the Holy Grail. According to this ancient legend, which exists in many forms, the cup used by Christ at the Last Supper was brought to a chapel where it brought life and fruitfulness to the land. A sacrilege was committed, however, and the Grail vanished. Immediately, the fruitful land became a barren wasteland. The greatest knights then go on a quest to find the Grail, a spiritual journey that can be fulfilled only if they find the wounded fisher-king and ask him the right question. Eliot uses this medieval legend as a way to explore the modern spiritual condition: Something holy has been lost; as a result, we live in a spiritual wasteland.

"The Waste Land" is a complex symphony of myth, literary allusion, and popular culture. Eliot goes so far as to supply footnotes to his poem, explaining some of his more obscure allusions. The difficulty of his work, and that of modern poetry in general, makes it less accessible than earlier poetry, but Eliot's verse is worth the effort. He interweaves and superimposes scenes of modern life with scenes drawn from ancient literature. For example, he describes London commuters streaming into the city to get to work by 9:00 a.m. with the language Dante uses to describe the hosts of souls in the first circle of Hell—those neither evil nor good, the "lukewarm" whom Christ spews out of his mouth (Revelation 3:15):

Under the brown fog of a winter dawn,
A crowd flowed over London Bridge, so many,
I had not thought death had undone so many.
Sighs, short and infrequent, were exhaled,
And each man fixed his eyes before his feet. (ll. 61-65)

The barrenness and sterility of the modern wasteland are evident in the lovelessness of casual sex (ll. 220-256) and in the nonchalant acceptance of abortion:

You ought to be ashamed, I said, to look so antique.
(And her only thirty-one.)
I can't help it, she said, pulling a long face,
It's them pills I took, to bring it off, she said.
(She's had five already, and nearly died of young George.)
The chemist said it would be all right, but I've never been the
same. (ll. 156-161)

The poem ends with a knight stumbling in the desert, dying of thirst. But then it begins to thunder. The healing, life-giving water is foreshadowed, but it never comes in "The Waste Land."

It came for Eliot shortly afterwards when he accepted Christ. Soon thereafter he wrote "Ash Wednesday," a poem of repentance. Some of the imagery and much of the style of the earlier poems are present here as well. Again we see a desert and some ferocious cats, but the tone is remarkably different:

Lady, three white leopards sat under a juniper tree
In the cool of the day, having fed to satiety
On my legs my heart my liver and that which had been
*   contained*
In the hollow round of my skull. And God said
Shall these bones live?
. . . . . .
Under a juniper-tree the bones sang, scattered and shining
We are glad to be scattered, we did little good to each other,
Under a tree in the cool of the day, with the blessing of sand,
Forgetting themselves and each other, united
In the quiet of the desert. This is the land which ye
Shall divide by lot. And neither division nor unity
Matters. This is the land. We have our inheritance.
                                    (Section II, ll. 1-5, 48-54)

The lady is a symbol of the Christian church; the leopards are apparently an allusion to a poem by Dryden who used the panther as a symbol for the Anglican church which Eliot had just joined. The leopards also recall "Christ the Tiger" of Eliot's earlier poem. Although the descriptions are comically gruesome, the tone is joyful. The bones are "glad to be scattered"—in their old life of sin, they "did little good to each other." The description of leopards munching on his bones gives way to a direct quotation from Ezekiel 37, which describes the valley of dry bones. At God's word, these scattered bones fly together, take on flesh, and are resurrected. Eliot's poem is thus describing the death of the old self which precedes the new life in Christ.

Later in this complex poem, Eliot describes Christ, the Word of God, as the center of all of existence:

> *If the lost word is lost, if the spent word is spent*
> *If the unheard, unspoken*
> *Word is unspoken, unheard;*
> *Still is the unspoken word, the Word unheard,*
> *The Word without a word, the Word within*
> *The world and for the world;*
> *And the light shone in darkness and*
> *Against the Word the unstilled world still whirled*
> *About the centre of the silent Word.*
>
> (Section V, ll. 1-9)

Notice how Eliot's poetic form, like that of Herbert, conveys his meaning: the lines running together, the repetitions, and the alliterations create the sensation of a whirling motion, reinforcing the meaning that all of creation "whirls" around the Word of God.

The passage makes clear that the Word is still the center even though the modern world refuses to hear it. "Where shall the word be found, where will the word/Resound? Not here, there is not enough silence" (Section V, ll. 11-12). Nevertheless, the scattered bones are told to "prophesy" (Section II, l. 22). Eliot throughout his career was attempting to forge new ways of breaking through to the modern imagination with the Word of God. His radical verse, for all of its fragmentation reflecting the fragmentation of his age, was attempting to translate the truths of the Christian faith into the language of modernism. Or, as he put it in "Ash Wednesday," "restoring/With a new verse the ancient rhyme" (Section IV, ll. 16-17).

Modern poetry as well as classic poetry and Biblical poetry deserve the attention of contemporary Christians. If poets are the unacknowledged legislators of the world as Shelley says,[20] then Christians dare not surrender poetry's influence on the whole mind to the rock musicians or to avant garde nihilists. Christians should think of poetry as well as music when they are enjoined to "speak to one another with psalms, hymns and spiritual songs" (Ephesians 5:19).

THE MODES OF LITERATURE

This section examines four well-known literary types: tragedy, comedy, realism, and fantasy. These modes of literature (for lack of a better term) cut across distinctions of genre. They involve not only what literature is, but also what it can do.

Tragedy and comedy can be distinguished according to the effect a work has on its readers. Both modes invoke the extremes of human emotions: suffering and joy. The difference between tragedy and comedy is how these two emotions are related to each other, and which is ultimate.

Realism and fantasy involve the relationship of the work to the world outside of the text. Some writing attempts a close correspondence with reality. Other writing attempts to project a purely imaginary world. Like tragedy and comedy, these modes are opposite, but they are also related. The most rigorous realism bears the marks of imaginative invention. The most outlandish fantasy is bound to certain elements of the objective world.

These modes have precedents in the classical tradition that began with the ancient Greeks. They have also acquired significant Christian variations. The impact of Christianity upon Western culture is evident in the way these modes were redefined and practiced by the great Christian authors. Tragedy and comedy, fantasy and realism can lead readers to the intersections between literature and faith.

TRAGEDY AND COMEDY:
The Literature of Damnation and Salvation

Some works of literature can make us cry; others can make us laugh. That much is obvious, but the range of emotions awakened by literature raises some puzzling questions. I remember overhearing a student urging her friends to see a certain movie. "It was so good," she said, "that it made me cry and cry and cry." How is it that we can enjoy stories that make us sad? We do not enjoy crying in real life, and yet a work of literature that brings tears to our eyes can seem especially satisfying. Why do other stories strike us as funny? How can we explain that sensation of hilarity, that sharp stab of joy we feel when we encounter absurdities? We agonize over the problem of pain, why God allows us to suffer and what its meaning is for our lives. I wonder too about the problem of laughter, why God allows us to experience joy and what its meaning is for our lives.

Comedy and tragedy can be found in any of the major genres. A true story (nonfiction), a made-up joke (fiction), or a limerick (poetry) can make us laugh and so can be thought of as comic. By the same token, each type of literature can fill us with sorrow and so can be thought of as tragic. The terms comedy and tragedy, however, come from drama—which itself is a combination of the real (actual actors onstage), the fictional (the story), and sometimes the poetic (the language). Whichever genre they manifest themselves in, comedy and tragedy have formal characteristics which point beyond themselves to spiritual dimensions—to the meaning of life, the significance of suffering, the ultimate destiny of the soul in Hell or Heaven.

DANTE'S DEFINITIONS

A tragedy, according to Dante, is a story that begins in joy but ends in pain. A comedy, on the other hand, is a story that begins in pain, but ends in joy.[1] Such definitions, echoed by other medieval writers, might seem to miss the point. Dante defines the two in terms of how they begin and how they end—his definition of tragedy has none of the complicated analysis given by Aristotle and other critics; his definition of comedy says nothing about humor. It does explain why his masterpiece is entitled "The Divine Comedy"—the story begins in pain (Hell) and ends in joy (Heaven)—but otherwise it seems a quaint medieval oversimplification. And yet Dante was one of the greatest literary geniuses in the Christian faith, and we neglect his insights at our peril.

Consider the stock gag, immortalized in slapstick comedies: A stout, well-dressed gentleman, nose in the air and the personification of dignity, is out for a stroll. A fellow in a baggy plaid suit is eating a banana and casually tosses the peel on the sidewalk. The dignified gentleman steps on the banana peel and falls on his ample posterior. We cannot help but laugh even if we think ourselves too sophisticated for slapstick humor, especially when we see the look on his face, his pomposity deflated by a banana peel.

Imagine the scene again. The dignified gentleman slips, but this time his head hits the pavement. He does not get up. Blood pools on the sidewalk. He is dead. This time we would not laugh. We would have witnessed a "tragic" accident.

The difference is the ending. In the case of the vaudeville pratfall, we know that the man is not really going to be harmed. He will lose his dignity and composure, but we know in advance nothing serious will happen to him. The assurance of a happy ending frees us to laugh at the pain that he does experience at the moment. His suffering, momentary and inconsequential as it is, is a result of his sense of overblown importance, and we enjoy the spectacle of pride cast down. On the other hand, if the ending is sad, the self-assuredness and smug happiness of the gentleman would seem painfully ironic, compounding the horror of the tragedy.

Dante is right—comedies do begin in some kind of misery or trouble. "I Love Lucy" reruns depict enough marital strife to fill the divorce courts, but the inevitable happy ending changes our perception of them. For all of the hopeless messes Lucy gets into, Ricky always loves her, and in the end they are always reconciled. Knowing this, we can actually enjoy her troubles, the spectacle of human absurdities. The misunderstandings, desperate measures, deceptions, and foiled ambitions (exaggerated but recognizable enough in our own lives) are transformed into something funny.[2] Human suffering of one kind or another constitutes the material of comedy, from the casual joke to the high art of the theater. Shakespeare's comedies often open with a death sentence.

Tragedies, conversely, usually begin with their heroes at the pinnacle of success and happiness. Again, this seems to be true of both popular "tear-jerkers" and high art. The couple fall blissfully in love, and then they discover her fatal disease. *Old Yeller* shows the idyllic relationship between a boy and his dog—until the dog develops rabies and the boy must "put him out of his misery."[3] Oedipus has solved the riddle of the Sphinx and has been made King of Thebes. Macbeth has just won a great victory and is being acclaimed as a hero. The greater the height, the more devastating the fall.

Both comedy and tragedy deal with the extremes of human experience, and both put suffering and joy in relationship to each other. In comedy, the pain is transformed by the ultimate joy. This comic perspective allows the audience to experience delight all the way through the story as they witness the characters obliviously moving from suffering to the joy that awaits them. In tragedy, the joy is transformed by the ultimate pain. The audience is chastened even by the characters' initial happiness, which from the tragic perspective becomes an ironic compounding of their doom.

THE TRAGIC SENSE OF LIFE AND THE COMIC SENSE OF LIFE

Dante's definitions might also be applied to the story of human life itself. Is life ultimately tragic or comic? The answer to that question depends upon one's worldview and upon one's faith.

Those who expect life to end in the nothingness of death are assuming a tragic ending. Those who hold to a tragic sense of life will expect pleasure here and now. "You only go around once in life; you have to grab for all of the gusto you can." That television commercial—more philosophical than most—expresses a tragic sense of life. In poetry, the recurring theme of *carpe diem* (seize the day) makes the same point. Time is fleeting; we will not be young forever; death awaits; we must seize our pleasures now while there is still time. For all of their hedonism, such poems are essentially tragic.

Those who expect life to end in the bliss of Heaven are assuming a joyous ending. Life is a comedy. Those with a comic sense of life can view their present suffering, which does not at all surprise them, from a different perspective. Pain is not ultimate. "All will be well," as Dame Julian of Norwich insisted, "and every kind of thing will be well."[4] The happy ending promised for Christians means that God will wipe away every tear (Revelation 7:17)—that the sufferings we have experienced in this life will somehow be undone. "The ransomed of the LORD will return. They will enter Zion with singing; everlasting joy will crown their heads. Gladness and joy will overtake them, and sorrow and sighing will flee away" (Isaiah 35:10). Those with a comic sense of life may expect suffering now, but they will not take it (or themselves) quite so seriously.

Certainly, when life is seen as a comedy, the pain is still painful. Lucy is not enjoying herself when the assembly line in the bonbon factory starts coming at her faster and faster. Slipping on a banana peel or getting a pie in the face or finding yourself engaged to someone you do not love or fighting with one's spouse or being condemned to death (all familiar comic openings) are horrible for the characters as they are happening. Yet because of the larger framework of joy which safeguards and transforms those painful moments, the troubles are seen in a different way. What proves to be funny from the perspective of the happy ending is not the trouble as such but the human frailties they unmask. The naive egotism, the grandiose scheming, the pettiness and the stubbornness are all revealed to be ridiculous and therefore very funny. Usually what we are laughing at in comedies is human pride running smack up against human limits.

This is not to say that actual human suffering is funny. We need to experience sorrow at our sins and at the suffering of others (James 4:9). Our troubles here, however, are indeed proof of our limits—our failures to be the perfect parent or employee, our struggles with the consequences of sin, our inability to control our own lives. We are mortal. We are human. We are not gods. And yet in our mortal imperfection, God offers us the free gift of eternal life purchased by Jesus Christ, a fact that can make all the difference as we struggle through life on earth. "Those who sow in tears will reap with songs of joy," promises the psalmist. Because "the LORD has done great things for us," "our mouths were filled with laughter" (Psalm 126: 5, 3, 2).

From the point of view of Heaven, there will no doubt be much to laugh at. Dante describes a character in Heaven, Pope Gregory, who on earth wrote extensive theological discourses about angels. When he arrives in Heaven—when he actually gets to *meet* some angels—he sees that he was absolutely wrong. The scholarly work he had labored on for so many years and which had seemed so important at the time, all of his confident theological speculation, was for nothing. Instead of getting angry, instead of pouting, instead of lamenting his wasted efforts, now that he is in Heaven and looking at everything from this vantage point, he smiles.[5]

Whereas the souls in Dante's Hell are still obsessed with their lives on earth, still rehashing their old feuds and nourishing their old hatreds, the souls in Heaven see their former lives with a sense of amused detachment. Dante describes himself having transcended all of creation and at the highest reaches of Heaven. He then looks down at the earth, which from this height seems so small, so insignificant compared to the vast universe of God's eternal love, and all he can do is smile.[6] The Christian worldview encourages a comic sense of life.

On the other hand, life can be tragic. Christianity teaches that life can end in Hell. Those committed to a tragic sense of life will have what they choose. A person who insists upon pleasure in the here and now with no restraints, whose pride accepts no limits and no law, must face the tragic ending that is Hell.

If Dante provides the model for Christian comedy, Marlowe's *Dr. Faustus* provides the model for Christian tragedy. Faustus bargains away his eternal soul for twenty-four years of pleasure and power. As the play progresses, Faustus realizes that he is running out of time. At several points in the play, Faustus has the opportunity to repent (a pact with the devil is not binding, the play makes clear, since your soul does not really belong to you but to God), but he refuses to turn to Christ. Whenever Faustus is at the knife-edge of repentance, the demon Mephistopheles immediately assaults him with distracting pleasures or threatens him with momentary pain. Faustus is so afraid of suffering in the here and now and so demanding of pleasure in the present moment that he is willing to trade off eternal pleasure for eternal suffering, seeing them both as safely in the future. As his time runs out, Faustus despairs—wracked by the misery of a wasted life, still unwilling to trade momentary pleasures for the infinite joys of eternity and placing all of his faith in Mephistopheles. Faustus is damned.

Those with a tragic sense of life do not expect suffering *now*. They require pleasure and do not know what to do when they do not get it. The human comedy is such that human beings do experience pain. Without a larger perspective that offers hope in the midst of suffering, human beings—like Faustus—can despair. Many become self-pitying and cynical. Life becomes "a cruel joke." Life is a joke, of course, but those who see themselves as tragic heroes do not "get it." They do not understand life, and therefore they cannot find it amusing. Unless their disillusionment drives them to Christ, they will meet the tragic ending they expect, an eternity of self-pity, existential malaise, and actual suffering known as Hell.

TRAGEDY

The Greeks, in Dante's terms, had a tragic sense of life grounded in their worldview. After death, all souls, whether good or evil, go to the shadowy realm of Hades. (The Greek word *Hades* is used also in the New Testament, translated in English Bibles as Hell.)[7] It is little wonder that they so excelled in the theory and practice of tragedy. Tragedy as a literary form, as opposed to a philosophy of life, can have a powerful aesthetic and moral impact on its audiences.

Aristotle defined tragedy as the depiction of the downfall of a noble human being.[8] This tragic hero cannot be completely evil—a villain's downfall is not tragic; rather, the defeat of evil always gives us joy. Nor can the tragic hero be completely good—the undeserving downfall of a good person fills us with frustration and a sense of the injustice of life. For Aristotle, tragedy is the highest, the most moral, and the most satisfying form of literature. The ending must seem fair. Somehow, the tragic hero must be good enough to win our admiration and sympathy, yet evil enough to deserve whatever happens. The tragic hero must bring the disaster upon himself because of some flaw in an otherwise noble personality.

Aristotle's concept of "the tragic flaw" has been very influential among critics. Few seem to have recognized that the Greek word so translated is *hamartia*, the word the Greek New Testament translates as sin.[9] To use Christian terminology, the tragic hero falls because of sin. Conversely, sin is not merely an action or an attitude, but a "tragic flaw" that exists deep in our personalities and in our fallen human nature.

The *hamartia* most prevalent in "noble" human beings and thus in the heroes of Greek tragedies is the sin of pride. The Greek word is *hubris*, a term that means exalting oneself. A human being may be great, but the temptation of greatness is to exalt oneself beyond human limits, to think of oneself as a god. Mortals who dare compete with the gods risk being struck down for their rashness. In Christian terms, pride is that selfishness and egotism that puts me above my neighbors and that shuts out my need for God. The Serpent in Eden told Adam and Eve that "You will be like God" (Genesis 3:5), and this self-worship is at the root of sin after sin.

In the course of the tragic plot, the hero brings the disaster upon himself and so discovers what it means to be human. Oedipus, trying to evade the gods' prophecy, finds that he unwittingly caused it to happen by arrogantly refusing to step aside for someone else on a road. His self-discovery is one of the most wrenching in all of literature. Creon, in *Antigone*, refuses to bury Antigone's brother, believing that the soul of the unburied corpse will wander in torment forever. In so violating the religious law, Creon is taking upon himself the gods' prerogative to judge the dead. By presuming to play god, Creon destroys his whole family, whereupon he realizes that he is only a mortal.

At the end of a good tragedy, we feel emotionally drained. The wrenching emotions we have experienced leave us exhausted, yet satisfied and oddly exhilarated at the aesthetic experience. Milton describes the audience's feelings at the end of a tragedy as a "calm of mind, all passion spent."[10] Aristotle analyzes the audience's response at the final undoing of the tragic hero as a *catharsis*—an emotional cleansing—that comes from the release of pity and fear.

Tragedy causes us to feel pity. This is true in life as well as in art. When we witness the suffering of a friend or when we see photographs of starving children with their sticklike arms and swollen bellies, we pity them. This feeling is a manifestation of love. The Bible says that we are to love our neighbors as ourselves and even to love our enemies (Matthew 5:44, 22:39). Love is the opposite of pride and so works against the isolating *hubris* that shuts out others. Such is our sinfulness that we usually fail to love others as we should. And yet when we see someone hurting, that pang of pity we feel is a manifestation of love, a faint intimation of what God feels for the world.

Love is the most sought-after human emotion, although no one seeks after the suffering that often gives it birth. No wonder tragedies are prized so highly, even though they fill us with sorrow. They can awaken in us a tender, human feeling that is cleansing indeed because it is the highest and noblest of all human emotions. Such is the hardness of our hearts that we sometimes feel more compassion for fictional characters than we do for the real people around us, but properly considered, tragedy can train us in the disciplines of pity.

Pity cleanses the emotions, said Aristotle, and so does fear. Great tragedy confronts universal issues, so that the members of the audience recognize their own condition in the hero's catastrophe. The spectacle of Oedipus's unknowing guilt makes us shudder at our own blindness, at the unknown consequences of our unrecognized sinfulness. The pathetic end of Willie Loman in Arthur Miller's *Death of a Salesman* makes us wonder if our lives are likewise wasted, and we are filled with fear at what we may have done to our own families.

Fear, by definition, is unpleasant, but mediated through vicarious experience, it becomes cleansing. The reason is that we need to face our humanness. We need to be reminded of our mortality: that we are not gods, that our pride has no foundation, that despite our accomplishments we are weak, that we have insurmountable limits. Aristotle suggests that such a revelation, though unwelcome, is nevertheless cathartic and somehow satisfying. This is probably because we have an urgent need to realize the truth of our human condition. When we do, we perhaps for a moment let go of our *hubris*. Only when we stop trying to be gods and allow God to be God, accepting our more natural place as creatures utterly dependent upon Him, can we know the peace for which we were made.

Classical tragedy, as defined by Aristotle, corresponds profoundly with the Christian worldview. This tradition still lives—consider the tragic heroes in a novel such as *Moby Dick* or a film such as *Citizen Kane*, both of whom show aspects of greatness yet are flawed in their sinfulness. On the other hand, although stories with sad endings abound, Aristotle would not necessarily consider them tragedies.

In the disease-of-the-week plots that dominate television mini-series, we typically meet a likeable character surrounded by loving friends and family. Filled with happiness, energy, and potential, the character is diagnosed as having a fatal disease. After a brave struggle, false hopes, and deepened relationships, the character poignantly dies.

In a tear-jerker ballad, we might be introduced to teenage lovers whose car becomes stalled on a railroad track as a train is coming. After the boyfriend heroically pulls out his beloved, she rushes back into the car just as the train smashes into it. When they recover her body, they find clutched in her lifeless hands the precious token that she gave her life to recover: the boyfriend's class ring.

In more sophisticated modern works of literature, we encounter characters who become embittered because someone they love has met with a senseless, meaningless death. The characters are victimized by unpredictable diseases, arbitrary acts of violence, and grotesque accidents totally out of anyone's control. The very randomness of such calamities is a manifestation of the absurdity of life.

Dante would consider such melodramas, sentimental songs, and absurdist literature to be tragedies, inasmuch as they have happy beginnings and sad endings, but Aristotle would not. For him, the catastrophe must be caused by character, not by accident. The tragic hero's choices and actions must trigger the catastrophe, making the hero personally responsible for everything that happens. In fact, the hero's complicity in the disaster and the guilt that overwhelms him is a large part of why we feel so much pity and fear. If the hero is purely a passive victim of circumstances beyond his control, there is no true tragedy.[11]

To have Oedipus go blind because of glaucoma would not be a meaningful tragic ending. If the catastrophe is unmotivated and arbitrary, unrelated to the nobility and flaws of the hero's personality, there can be no true catharsis. The audience is disappointed and frustrated. Classical tragedy leaves the audience fulfilled and even, paradoxically, uplifted. The audience may be chastened by the hero's downfall, but still exalted by the spectacle of justice satisfied and the grandeur of the human spirit.

Ironically, our secular humanist age has a far lower view of mankind than the ancients, who stressed human limits under a supernatural order. Our literature reveals our sense of helplessness. Human beings do not have control over their lives, but are at the mercy of nature and society. People are not responsible for their fate, but are passive victims of their environment. In comparing the literature of the past with that of the present, one is struck by how much the heroes have diminished. Compare Oedipus, Faustus, and Lear in the magnitude of their personalities to Willie Loman in *Death of a Salesman*, Laura in *The Glass Menagerie*, and the tramps in *Waiting for Godot*. Today, the very word *hero* seems anachronistic; ours is the age of the "anti-hero." The classical hero is essentially noble but afflicted with a tragic flaw; the anti-hero is essentially flawed but afflicted with a streak of nobility. The ancients, whose worldview minimized humanity, managed to portray human greatness. The modern worldview glorifies humanity, and yet manages only to portray its impotence.

Aristotle would deny that there can be a "tragic accident." Accidents, when they happen, are lamentable; but only those for which we are responsible are tragic. When someone is killed because a car's brakes failed, we are shocked at the seeming haphazardness of life and death, but Aristotle would not consider this tragic. When someone is killed because of a drunken driver, that would be tragic, precisely because it could have been avoided so easily were it not for a moral failure. The death of a soldier in battle may fill us with sorrow, but such a death, marked by courageous devotion to a noble cause, Aristotle might even consider glorious. The death of the soldiers described in Tennyson's "Charge of the Light Brigade," who were sent to certain death by the blunder of their commanding officer, might be considered tragic. Death is not in itself tragic. In Greek drama, the tragic hero is almost always the one who survives.

Dante's Christian vision of tragedy is broader, less severe, and more sympathetic to the modern tales of futility and desperation. Modern tragedies with their powerless heroes do accord with classical tragedy's revelation of human limits. Aristotle's moralism, like the religious system of the ancient Greeks, speaks to us of law, but offers no hope to someone rightfully condemned by that law. The unremitting, hopeless burden of guilt lies at the essence of the tragic anguish. Christianity affirms the moral law and so agrees with the tragic vision, but goes on to offer the atonement of Christ.

Aristotle's artistic, rather than theological, analysis is nevertheless helpful in showing how tragedies as works of literature can go wrong. For a work of fiction to succeed aesthetically, there must be a sense of connection from incident to incident. That is, there must be a coherent plot rather than a series of random actions. By showing how the tragic action must be related to the personality of the tragic hero, Aristotle brilliantly integrates the two major elements of fiction: plot and character.

The disease-of-the-week mini-series and the tear-jerking ballads are aesthetically bad because there is generally little connection between the characters and what happens to them. (A program about the downfall of an AIDS victim whose actions did bring about his disease could conceivably be tragic in the classical sense. Ironically, contemporary dramas on this subject deliberately avoid portraying the hero as responsible for the disease and so miss the opportunity for high tragedy.) Sensationalistic TV shows and sentimental songs may still be effective in generating an emotional response from their audiences. Their artistic and philosophical disjointedness, however, makes them incapable of carrying a coherent meaning.

The sentimental ballad can make its listeners misty-eyed for a few moments, but then what else have they gained from the song? Have they learned not to rush back into a car stalled on the railroad track to get a class ring? Didn't they already know that? To value the symbol (the ring) more than the relationship it symbolizes (two people alive and in love) is patently ludicrous, and yet it is the cathartic moment of the ballad. Such an ending can manipulate its listeners into an emotional response, but the story can bear no examination or reflection, and it imparts no understanding. Emotional stories that fall short of tragedy are properly termed "melodramas."

Well-crafted dramas that integrate plot and character can pass the deeper test implied by Aristotle's dictum even though they portray weak or passive characters. Willie Loman does bring about his own downfall through his materialism, pride, and neglect of his family. Laura in *The Glass Menagerie,* one of the frailest personalities in literature, is perfectly integrated with the action and the meaning of the play.

Christians with Dante in mind will see in tragedy intimations of · what it means to be damned. Because good tragedy awakens our pity, it does not allow us to be judgmental. Rather, we witness human pride with its other sinful manifestations bringing judgment upon itself. This is true whether the tragedy presents the moral deterioration of a sympathetic human being (such as *Macbeth*) or the horrible Hell-like isolation of being unwilling to love (*Citizen Kane*). This does not mean that tragic heroes never find spiritual salvation. Christian writers such as Milton and Graham Greene write of tragic heroes who are saved, not by their flawed personalities or by their carefully planned but futile actions, but only by grace.[12]

Tragedy forces us to consider our own flawed, *hubris*-ridden lives, centered around our own pleasures and our pride. It confronts us with our mortality, our limitations, and our human condition under the curse of God's righteous judgment. Gazing upon this truth, oddly enough, can awaken in us feelings of compassion for others and humility for ourselves. We come away from a tragedy feeling chastened, emotionally drained, and yet not depressed (as we may be by the meaningless suffering of melodrama). In tragedy we sense that life, despite its sufferings, is profoundly and mysteriously meaningful and, in an austere yet compelling way, beautiful.

COMEDY

If tragedy forces its audience to confront the limitations of the human condition, so does comedy, although in a very different way. Whereas tragedy involves the audience in the hero's suffering (provoking pity and fear), comedy creates a sense of detachment (provoking laughter and joy).

As with tragedy, Dante's Christian concept of comedy can be supplemented by that of the ancient Greeks.[13] The purpose of comedy, according to the classical theorists, is to ridicule vice. Although many of the classical comedies seem rather risqué, they were understood to be explicitly moral, even didactic. As Sir Philip Sidney puts it, "Comedy is an imitation of the common errors of our life, which [the dramatist] representeth in the most ridiculous and scornful sort that may be, so as it is impossible that any beholder can be content to be such a one."[14] Comedy teaches the audience to hold moral faults in contempt.

Just as tragedies would portray "noble" characters (in the sense of both social standing and personality), comedies would portray "ignoble" characters. Instead of kings and heroes, classical comedies portray shepherds, braggart soldiers, and conniving slaves. The audience looks up in awe at the tragic hero, but looks down in derision at the comic protagonists. (No one wants to be like the Three Stooges.)

The classical "rules" point to an underlying aesthetic truth; in this case, the audience must be distanced from the characters for the effect to be comic. The tragic heroes may be distant from the audience in their greatness, but pity and fear create a powerful emotional identification. In a comedy, the audience may identify with characters to a certain extent, but intense feelings of pity or fear would make laughter impossible.

Classical comedy often seems somewhat harsh. In Ben Jonson's *Volpone*, a slick con man turns the characters' own vices against them until his own schemes collapse around his head. Nearly everyone is revealed to be a fool. Jonson is unmerciful in picking apart his characters' immorality. The rigorous objectivity of classical comedy means that human weakness and foibles are judged with clear-eyed thoroughness.

An important variation of this tradition is satire: the technique of attacking social and moral evils by means of humor. The greatest master of satire in our language is the conservative Christian clergyman Jonathan Swift. His *Gulliver's Travels* and other writings devastatingly deflate the rational humanism of the Enlightenment. All satire presupposes the existence of objective moral standards against which the targets are measured and found wanting. Humor can be a potent weapon in the clash of ideas. If people can be made to laugh at something, they can no longer (as we say) take it seriously.

Contemporary Christian writers might consider laughter as an offensive weapon against the falsehoods and absurdities of our own age. Poking fun at something may be a more effective way of refuting an idea or smashing a cultural icon than intellectual analysis alone. (Read Walker Percy's "The Last Donahue Show" and notice how you react ever after to TV interview shows.[15] Watch Rob Reiner's film *This Is Spinal Tap* and notice what it does to your perception of rock musicians.)

Just as a sad story may violate the principles of classical tragedy, a humorous story may not measure up to the demands of classical comedy. Mere mockery is not satire. Making fun of virtue would be a violation of the comic spirit. I suspect that Aristotle would also be unamused by "sick humor," such as the scurrilous "dead baby jokes." Laughing at what should provoke pity is cruel and unnatural. The atmosphere of comedy, despite its moral severity, must be festive, light-hearted, and joyful. No one is ever seriously hurt. One convention of traditional comedy is that no one ever dies. This celebratory framework helps create the comic detachment which lifts the audience above the sufferings of ordinary life, freeing them to laugh at the characters' predicaments, which always turn out to be minor. Discordant cruelties are thus excluded from true comedy. Everything must be resolved by a truly happy ending.

The importance of the happy ending takes us back to Dante. The principles of classical comedy, like those of classical tragedy, can help us to understand the technique and the effect of these forms, but Dante's distinctly Christian theories help us to see them from a different height. If tragedy is an image of damnation (although it arouses pity), comedy is an image of salvation (although it arouses judgment). Greek paganism, despite its moral lapses, was a religion of law, harsh in its moralism and offering no forgiveness and no grace from the gods. Thus, both its sense of tragedy and its sense of comedy are colored by its hopelessness.

Although the classical understanding of comedy has been influential in our literature, Dante's version of Christian comedy has also left its mark. Chaucer is perhaps the greatest comic writer in the English language. His *Canterbury Tales* make up a variegated tapestry of Medieval literature. Most of the tales are Dantean in their comedy and in their meaning. They begin in suffering, but end in joy—and in between are depictions of human foibles, although presented with an affectionate hilarity rather than with the sternness of classical comedy. "The Nun's Priest's Tale" opens with nightmares and predictions of doom so dire that we almost forget that the main characters are chickens. The rooster's escape from the fox, presented with mock-epic elevation, provides the happy ending so the comedy is complete. "The Franklin's Tale" begins with a wife's Job-like lament at life's cruelty and an extortion scheme wherein to save her husband's life the wife must be unfaithful to him. The impossible dilemma is resolved by a device rarely used in fiction: the wife tells her husband the truth. The story ends not in the villain's death but in his repentance. The ending is one of forgiveness and mutual love between the husband and the wife. "The Wife of Bath's Tale" begins with a knight being sentenced to death for rape; it ends with repentance, forgiveness, and a marriage based on love and respect for women.

Medieval drama, which began as dramatizations of Biblical stories, is also profoundly comic. "The Second Shepherd's Play" begins by presenting the misery and degradation of the shepherds shortly before the first Christmas. They are shivering in the cold; they are hungry; they are oppressed by the nobility; they can scarcely feed their families. Then ensues a slapstick plot about sheep stealing (the offender and his wife disguise the stolen lamb as a baby), which turns into a startling symbol of Christ, the Lamb of God who substitutes Himself for sinners. At the end of the play, angels intervene, announcing the birth of the Christ child, who also turns out to be cold and poverty-stricken, offering these sinful and comical shepherds the happy ending of eternal life.

The medieval understanding of comedy did not require humor as such, although laughter often accompanied the transformation from suffering to joy. The Middle Ages gave birth to another literary form, which is also related to Dantean comedy: the romance. The romance was a tale of adventure, love, and wonders. The King Arthur stories were collections of romances. Although a romance could be tragic (as with the love triangle of King Arthur, Lancelot, and Guinevere or the doomed love affair of Tristan and Iseult), the romance was essentially a serious story with a happy ending. Some of these ancient stories have survived as fairy tales, which may at the beginning engage our deepest fears, but which end with the apocalyptic promise that "they lived happily ever after."

The Renaissance adapted the romance into a hybrid form of drama known as the "tragi-comedy." These stories were not light-hearted; people could be killed. And yet, everything is resolved in the happy ending. The villains are punished; the mysteries are solved; the hero marries the heroine. This tradition of serious stories with a happy ending has flourished in the stories of adventure and love found throughout our literature, from the most serious novels to the popular fiction of the paperback racks and the television series.

While other Renaissance playwrights such as Ben Jonson were exploring the implications of classical comedy, Shakespeare was drawing on the Medieval traditions of romance and comedy to craft his unforgettable "romantic comedies." These begin in pain: a family torn apart, a shipwreck, a death sentence. They end not only in joy, but with specific images of love, reconciliation, and forgiveness: the villains are pardoned; the community is restored; a marriage is celebrated.

Midsummer Night's Dream begins with a father condemning his own daughter to death if she does not marry the young man he chooses for her. She runs away into the woods, along with a number of other people unfortunately in love with the wrong people. In the course of the play, amidst a bewildering array of mix-ups and love potions gone awry, order is restored by true love, the families are restored, and everyone lives happily ever after. *The Tempest* depicts brothers at each other's throats, natural disasters, frustrated love—all part of a larger design that ends in forgiveness. In *The Winter's Tale* and *Cymbeline*, extreme grief melts into extreme joy as those who are thought to be dead are restored to life. Shakespeare's more serious and less romantic "dark comedies" or "problem plays" (such as *Measure for Measure* and *The Merchant of Venice*) are almost unsettling in the way he depicts justice being overcome by mercy.

As You Like It begins with discord in the most basic human community: the family. A usurping duke has stolen the throne from his brother, the rightful ruler. Another man plots the murder of his brother. The ensuing love story in the enchanting Forest of Arden culminates when the would-be murder victim saves his evil brother's life, and the two are reconciled. The evil duke suddenly abandons his throne and his military operation against his brother because he is converted:

> *[The duke] meeting with an old religious man,*
> *After some question with him, was converted*
> *Both from his enterprise and from the world. (5.4.154-156)*

Literary purists, such as Ben Jonson, would criticize the construction of such a plot. The villain's sudden conversion may be a sign that the author has written himself into a corner and can only get out of it by resorting to an unmotivated miracle. Such a trick is called a *deus ex machina,* from the old device in certain classical dramas of having a character dressed up like a god be let down from a rope to untangle the characters' dilemmas. And yet Christians, especially those schooled by the Reformation, would insist that in real life we are saved by a *deus ex machina*—our lives are hopelessly tangled and filled with sin until God intervenes by His grace. Christ is a God let down from Heaven; the Holy Spirit does break into our lives. The pattern in

Shakespeare's comedies of sin/death resolved by gratuitous forgiveness/marriage is analogous to what the Bible says about the life of the Christian. We are in a state of sin which wrecks our relationships and puts us under judgment. Nevertheless, we can find forgiveness and experience the love and reconciliation of Heaven, described in Scripture as the marriage of Christ with the church (Revelation 19:7). Shakespeare's comedies seem relatively secular in their overt content, but their themes are symbolic of the gospel itself. His comedies can be seen as Reformation reworkings of Dante's cosmic comedy.[16]

MERLIN'S LAUGH

Although seemingly opposites, comedy and tragedy are closely related.[17] Both evoke the extreme and opposite human emotions—suffering and pleasure—and place them in relationship to each other. Both reveal human limits. Tragedy corrects human pride by exalting its hero to the skies, only to show him come crashing down to earth. Comedy corrects human pride by squelching its heroes, reinterpreting pride as a comical pretension.

Tragedy has a special importance for Christians because it can train us in the disciplines of compassion. Although we may have a comic sense of life, much of the hilarity must be reserved for the happy ending in Heaven. For now, we still need to cultivate the involvement with others taught by tragedy. Comic detachment to a human being in need will not be amusing to our Heavenly Father.

Much of our pity must be felt for those who see life as a tragedy: the existentialist lamenting the meaninglessness of life and the nothingness of death; the humanist whose utopian ideals are coming to nothing; the hedonist whose body is wracked by disease; the nihilist for whom life is not even worth living. Their bitterness and hopelessness should fill us with pity and fear, even more so as we consider that their self-chosen tragic ending will, apart from Christ, last forever. Christians, on the other hand, are given a hope which can translate into a comic ending.

Robinson Davies tells of an old legend about Merlin, King Arthur's wizard:

> The magician Merlin had a strange laugh, and it was heard when nobody else was laughing. He laughed at the beggar who was bewailing his fate as he lay stretched on a dunghill; he laughed at the foppish young man who was making a great fuss about choosing a pair of shoes. He laughed because he knew that deep in the dunghill was a golden cup that would have made the beggar a rich man; he laughed because he knew that the pernickety young man

would be stabbed in a quarrel before the soles of his new shoes were soiled. He laughed because he knew what was coming next.[18]

Merlin's knowledge of the future enabled him to laugh when no one else could. In Davies's examples, Merlin laughs at the bitter ironies of life; but if he could foresee the beggar finding the gold cup, Merlin's laugh would be truly comic. The point of the legend is that whether something is comic or tragic depends upon one's perspective, knowledge, and awareness of whatever is ultimate. Christians, insofar as they know what is coming next and remember how to pity and fear, can emulate Merlin's laugh.

REALISM:
Literature as a Mirror

*I*s the mind a mirror or a lamp? If the mind is like a mirror, its purpose—and that of the imagination and the art it engenders—is to
reflect the external world. This view of the mind corresponds to the
belief that art should imitate the external world. Such is the assumption
of classical philosophy going back to the ancient Greeks, manifesting
itself in the traditions of representational art and realistic fiction.

If the mind is like a lamp, then the imagination is a source, not
merely a reflector. The mind is a creative power, generating new light
and new creations. Art is seen as a creation, a fabrication of something
new which does not exist already in the external world. Such is the
assumption of romanticism, although it had earlier precedents in the
traditions of nonrepresentational and expressive art and in fantasy
fiction.

The metaphors of the mirror and the lamp as a way of summarizing two contrasting assumptions about the mind and about art were
first suggested by M. H. Abrams.[1] (Notice how a "poetic" device such
as metaphor can crystallize complex ideas and thus be an important
tool for thinking.) Abrams has shown how vacillation between these
two notions of the mind can account for shifts in the way people have
thought about aesthetics, ethics, science, and even theology.

Which notion is closer to the Biblical view? Human theories generally turn out to be partial and simplistic when measured by the com-
prehensiveness of Christian revelation. The doctrine of the Creation
means that Christians must never minimize the existence and value of
the world outside themselves, which is celebrated as God's handiwork.
This orientation to God's creation might favor the mirror metaphor:

the human mind is to take in what God has made and reflect it back in praise.

On the other hand, the Bible makes clear that God created human beings to be distinct from the rest of creation. Adam and Eve were created in the image of God and given dominion over nature. Human beings therefore bear traces of God's creativity in themselves and are enjoined to act upon creation—ruling, subduing, and naming what God has made (Genesis 1:28, 2:19-20). This orientation to the divine image in human beings (obscured though it is by sin) might favor the lamp metaphor: the human mind is to emulate its creator in creations of its own.

The mirror metaphor taken to an extreme reduces the mind to a blank slate totally dominated by the environment and by impersonal forces (as in behaviorist psychology). The lamp metaphor taken to an extreme implies that the mind creates its own reality, that the self is the source of all truth (as in humanistic psychology). Christians can draw on both understandings of the mind as long as each is balanced with the other.[2]

The mind is like a mirror in its capacity to learn about the objective world, as evidenced in the fields of science. The mind is like a lamp in its capacity to act creatively, as in the fields of technology, in which scientific knowledge is applied creatively in new inventions. Television sets and microwave ovens do not exist in nature, although knowledge of nature is essential in their invention.

Literature as a mirror reflects truth as it is. As such, it can be a way of learning about the world—about history, about society, about how people behave, about "real life" in all of its complexity. Mirrors, for all of their objectivity, also are a way of looking at ourselves, and so it is with literature as a mirror. We can never look directly at our own face. We are too close to ourselves; we lack a vantage point from which to see ourselves objectively. A mirror creates such a vantage point. Even fantasy can function as a mirror, perhaps a fun-house mirror, whose exaggerations can help us notice what we normally would ignore.

Literature as a lamp projects what is in the mind into tangible forms. A lamp is outward-looking, shedding its light throughout the room, illuminating dark corners. When a lamp gives off light, it enables people to see not only itself but the external objects around it. Good fantasy does the same. While projecting inner longings and fears, it also sheds a hard, objective light on the human condition. Even realistic fiction as a human expression and an active interpreter of the world it comments upon can serve as a lamp.[3]

Any given work of art is both an imitation and a creation: the author or the painter begins with something given (colors and shapes, the physical properties of the material, the language, the subject matter) and then actively shapes it according to a creative design (selecting details, establishing emphasis, conveying emotion, planning aesthetic effects). Some works of literature are in a realistic mode—although the reader should be alert to the mind of the writer behind the shaping. Some works of literature are in a fantasy mode—although the reader should be alert to the reality that can be disclosed in the play of the writer's imagination. Realism and fantasy represent distinct literary approaches, both of which are congenial to Christianity.

BLURRING THE DISTINCTION

Before treating realism and fantasy separately, it might be helpful to blur the distinctions. Fantasy writers, no less than realistic writers, are bound to God's creation. Writers of fantasy are often said to be "creating" what does not in reality exist. "Creation" is a useful antonym for "imitation" in describing a facet of the artistic process, but, strictly speaking, only God creates. The most outrageous monster conceivable is only a new combination of what already exists. A dragon is simply a giant reptile, with perhaps the wings of a bat and the fire of a blast furnace added on. The Sphinxes, Griffins, Gorgons and other nightmares from classical legends are always described as combinations of familiar creatures (in the case of the Sphinx, the body of a lion, the wings of an eagle, the head of a woman). Try to imagine a monster that owes nothing to what is real. Does it have tentacles (like an octopus) or sharp teeth (like a tiger)? Is it slimy (like a slug) or hairy (like a bear)? Is it shapeless (like a jellyfish or a paramecium)? Is it recognizable as belonging to one of the existing animal kingdoms—an insect, a mammal, a reptile, a human? Try to imagine a new shape or a new emotion. Try to imagine a new color. The mind must work in terms of the existing created order, of which it is a part.

Human beings do fantasize, both in their dreams and in their art, combining elements of reality into new patterns and suspending ordinary physical laws. This capacity of the imagination is not quite creation, but it is a sort of "sub-creation." (The term is J. R. R. Tolkien's, who worked to reconcile his fantasy and his faith.)[4] Fantasy is tied to reality, both to the physical world that is rearranged and to the spiritual reality of the human mind that does the rearranging.

If fantasy can be realistic, it is also true that the real world can be fantastic. The wonders of the real world can outdo our wildest imaginations. The giant squid or the preying mantis or the denizens of the ocean floor with their exaggerated teeth and their incandescent flesh are more monstrous than anything in a fairy tale or in a nightmare. Black holes and the behavior of sub-atomic particles are more outlandish than the most speculative of science fiction. Real people and real events can be more astonishing than those we could dream up in our fantasies. Marvels are all around us, although we take for granted our strange, enchanted, and adventure-filled world. The impulse toward realism in literature can be a tribute to Creation, a salute to the staggering imagination of God.

Realism, no less than fantasy, involves the writer's active imagination. Details from the external world must be selected (according to principles from the author's mind, worldview, and aesthetic purpose). These details must be emphasized and orchestrated together into a coherent pattern. The realistic writer, no less than the fantasy writer, is expressing an inner vision and must project it in carefully chosen language. The process of writing—the narrative techniques, the elements of plot and character, the manipulations of language and style—is the same whether the author is writing realism or fantasy.

The main difference is that the realistic writer's primary material is taken from the external world. The realistic writer is gazing outward in an attempt to reflect the world outside of the self. The fantasy writer's primary material is taken from the inner world. The fantasy writer is gazing inward, bringing to the surface longings, dreams, and ideals and expressing them in tangible forms. The spiritual realm includes both the outer and the inner worlds. For this reason, both realistic fiction and fantasy fiction have always been of interest to Christian readers and Christian writers.

IMITATION

The Greeks believed that the essence of all art, including literature, is imitation. Literature is an imitation of some action. Although the characters and situations in a story may be fictional, they emulate the way people act in the real world. A good story is believable, not only on its own terms, but also in its faithfulness to the reality it depicts.

Part of the pleasure of reading a realistic story comes from the thrill of recognition. We read about a character, and we suddenly realize that we know someone like that. The setting calls to mind places we have been and things we have seen. We recognize our own experiences in the problems and struggles of the characters. We are usually so immersed in our environment and in our thoughts that we lack the perspective we need to truly think about our lives. While reading a book, we are distanced from the fictional lives of the characters, enabling us to see our own condition, mirrored in the plot, more clearly.

Realistic novels have a social dimension as well. Fiction can open our eyes to cultural pressures and social evils. A nation that had tolerated slavery was jolted by Harriet Beecher Stowe's *Uncle Tom's Cabin*. Dickens's novels mobilized the British public to abolish the work houses and to pass child labor laws. More recently, Tom Wolfe's *Bonfire of the Vanities* has dissected with a satirical scalpel the urban culture of New York City, with its social hierarchies, tangled racial relations, Wall Street materialism, and skewed legal system. Realistic fiction forces people to recognize and reflect upon what is before their eyes, and as such it can have a powerful moral impact. (We need Christian novelists to awake the public to the evils of abortion, sexual depravity, materialism, and other symptoms of contemporary moral decadence.)

Realistic literature operates by "defamiliarizing" experience.[5] It is often said that familiarity breeds contempt; it is probably more accurate to say that familiarity breeds blindness. When we become used to something, we stop noticing it. Driving a car for the first time was exhilarating; after awhile, the complexities of driving become automatic and routine. I remember moving to an apartment which had a magnificent view. From the balcony one could see for miles—the city, farmland and forests, a mountain in the distance. At first, I would stare out at the beauty. After awhile, I became used to it. I no longer stopped to admire the view; in effect, I stopped even seeing it.

Such is the perversity of human nature that what we have in abundance—our work, our possessions, and the beauty of our surroundings—we take for granted and learn to ignore, so that we are often paralyzed by boredom, indifference, and ingratitude. Unless we are very careful, even relationships can fall prey to this same deadening insensitivity. Our spouses, our children, our friends can likewise be ignored because they have become so familiar that they fade into the background.

Literature "defamiliarizes" experience by causing us to take notice of realities that we have come to ignore. A realistic novel about ordinary life can open our eyes to the rich texture of our own "ordinary" life—to its problems and dramas, to the complexity of relationships, to the preciousness of the common cycle of life (growing up, falling in love, raising a family, working, dying). The aesthetic distancing, the way the writer makes us imagine the significant details, the complexity of the form (which demands close attention and reflection)—such literary devices can awaken us to what we have taken for granted, the unseen and unfelt all around us. A novel about love, marriage, and children can enable us to appreciate our own families. A play such as Thornton Wilder's *Our Town* or the poetry of Walt Whitman or the essays of G. K. Chesterton are good cures for ingratitude.

Literature increases our perception, and this is why it can enrich our lives. The discipline of reading can help us to be more aware of our surroundings, more sensitive to the people and events we encounter, and more alert to their significance and value. Nineteenth-century Londoners saw poor children every day swarming through the streets, but most never gave them a second thought. When they read Charles Dickens's *Oliver Twist,* however, they noticed those children, and they were moved to compassion and to action.

Dickens heightened his descriptions of London orphans in order to increase the emotional impact—this was a function of his creativity. A novelist is always more than a passive transcriber of details. Yet realistic novelists of whatever kind draw on the external world. Whether trying to recreate a historical setting or to render accurately a modern problem, such novelists will generally make every effort to have their work ring true to the facts even though it is fiction.

A good historical novel (such as Mary Renault's novels of ancient Greece) can give readers an access to the past that goes beyond knowledge of historical facts. Fiction helps readers imagine from the inside what it might feel like to live in another time. Realistic novels with roots in science, psychology, anthropology, or current events can be more informative than abstract articles on the subject because fiction gives facts a human context. The classic novels of Fielding, Austen, Thackeray, and James are realistic both in the way they depict their times and in their analysis of the human condition, which remains the same for every age.

Of course, there are realistic writers who draw our attention to ugliness rather than beauty. This can have its place in puncturing worldly complacency. The sordid aspects of life also need to be defamiliarized. And yet many contemporary realistic writers project a loathing for existence. Their realism is heavy, oppressive, and void of affirmation.

In reviewing one such novel, David Ruenzel describes the unrelenting dreariness of much contemporary realism: "On certain gloomy days, when we're a bit tired and out of sorts, we're likely to discover a cavity with the tongue, a clump of hair stopped in the basin, an unpaid bill in the bottom of a drawer." This novel, he says, "takes this ordinary drabness and intensifies it chapter after chapter."

> But while the aura of emptiness is convincing enough, it also seems—after so many dreary novels with so many dreary characters in so many dreary places—something of a "dressed-up" existential cliche. Emptiness, true enough, is a universal emotion, but not always a particularly compelling one. It's all too easy to represent (or misrepresent) bleakness as truth. One begins to wonder if emptiness isn't most hospitable to the writer who lacks the vision to create alternatives.

One problem endemic to the new breed of "minimalist" realists is their condescension and contempt for ordinary people, a pose sometimes referred to as a "hipper than thou" attitude (more insufferable than any "holier than thou" attitude). Ruenzel notices that in the novel under review "a subtle class snobbery pervades the book":

> Only Mel (an administrator at an art gallery) and Jody, educated people with artistic interests, have a chance to rise above the pervading despair; blue-collar folk seem doomed to live out random, hollow lives in rooms stocked with bad furnishings. . . . The general air of despair lacks sufficient cause. Perversely, one almost wishes for a real catastrophe, a death, to lend despair weight. Suffering, so unrooted, begins to feel like a gross self-indulgence, a yuppie extravaganza.[6]

Whether such writers are striking a Bohemian pose or whether they sincerely believe that existence is hell, they labor under a deadening worldview.

WHAT IS REAL?

The novelist of yuppie despair and Charles Dickens are both realistic writers. If both are holding up a mirror to the world, why are their works so different? Mel the art administrator, doomed to a universe of bad furnishings, lives in a narrower and less lively world than the least of Dickens's characters. One would think that two authors trying to describe the objective world would come up with something similar. Obviously, there are different opinions about what is real. Therefore, there are different kinds of realism.

It is not possible for an author to simply transcribe the objective world in a purely passive way. The author's beliefs and assumptions keep intruding themselves, actively shaping perceptions and how they are conveyed. A writer may try to be a mirror, but cannot help also being a lamp. If a writer claims to be a realist, we must ask what that writer considers to be real. The rise of Darwinism in the nineteenth century led to a literary movement known as naturalism. According to this view, only nature and nature's laws are real. The theory of evolution taught that human beings were nothing more than animals, that human life is determined by physical laws outside of the control of the individual, and that life consists of conflict in which only the fittest will survive. This brand of realism, exemplified by Emile Zola, Stephen Crane, and Jack London, was often brilliant in its vivid descriptions, its lifelike evocations of the natural world, and its penetrating language. The atmosphere of their works is generally bleak and hopeless; the characters are swept up by deterministic forces outside their control. Although the naturalistic writers accepted a materialistic worldview, their spirits often rebelled against its implications, resulting in works of enraged despair at such an empty universe.

A related view of reality was that of Karl Marx, who stressed a determinism based not so much on nature but on social forces. This helped inspire another group of writers whom we could call social realists. At their best, these writers portrayed the dynamics of social life with penetrating insight or exposed social injustice. Sinclair Lewis savaged small town America in novels such as *Babbitt* (the story of a businessman's attempted rebellion against his drab middle class life) and *Elmer Gantry* (the story of a hypocritical evangelist who is ruined by his affair with a church secretary—notice how life sometimes imitates art). Upton Sinclair's *The Jungle,* a story of the brutal conditions faced by immigrants in the meatpacking plants of Chicago, led to legislation regulating the food industry (although Sinclair's purpose was to promote socialist political reform).

At their worst, however, the social realists' ideology stood in their way of writing good fiction. If human beings are nothing more than victims or products of their social and economic environments, then characterization must suffer. Their worldview excluded complicated, active characters with an inner life and responsibility for their actions. Instead, characters in many works of social realism tend to be stereotyped representatives of their social class rather than unique individuals. Since social realism assumes individuals have little control over their destinies, the plots often hinge upon accidents and vast impersonal forces rather than upon the motivated actions of the characters.

An extreme version of social realism is the overtly Marxist social*ist* realism. Communist regimes prescribed socialist realism as the only permissible literary style, and they enforced this artistic orthodoxy by censorship and arrest. In this style (required too of painting and film), muscular workers unite against the capitalist bosses with their fat bellies and derby hats. A hero of the masses emerges, looking like all other members of the masses, to urge the selfless labor necessary for the victory of the classless state.

Character, plot, setting, and theme all must conform to the ideological canons of socialist realism. The very concept of individualism is condemned by Marxism as a bourgeois trait. Only social classes and collective humanity are significant, according to Marxism. A good novelist, however, *must* believe that the individual is significant, with uniqueness and value, in order to create multi-dimensional characters acting in a purposeful story. Because Marxism reduces reality to matters of economics, purely aesthetic interests fall under suspicion. The imaginative "escape" of fantasy and the pursuit of beauty for its own sake are condemned for being anti-social, a remnant of that self-absorbed individualism fostered by the decadent middle class. Under Marxist regimes, therefore, the author's own individualism and creativity are inherently shackled.

Marxist writers in the Western democracies create some striking effects by criticizing their societies. When strict Marxists rule, however, they allow no social criticism. The writers have to celebrate the socialist state. Their writings must have a clear didactic lesson that supports the status quo. Writers must be socially useful. They are valued as propagandists, but persecuted as artists.

Although Christians are sometimes tempted to similarly stifle literature in the name of ideology, insisting on bland stereotypes and uplifting didacticism, the Christian faith actually encourages literature of a greater magnitude. The Soviet literary establishment with its stifling socialist realism has produced nothing of the distinction of Tolstoy and Dostoyevsky with their profound Christian consciousness. Christianity can inspire great art in a way that dialectical materialism cannot.

Communism, in effect, forbids good writing and requires mediocrity. Writers who refuse official literary standards, and any good writer would *have* to refuse them, become dissidents and face expulsion from the writer's union (which means no publication), admission to mental hospitals, incarceration for decades in prison camps, or worse. Their works, though, often have been photocopied or copied by hand and eagerly passed in secret from friend to friend, each of whom would make new copies, thereby circulating the works throughout the population. This process, known as "samizdvat" (i.e., self-publishing), is a model for the dissemination of literature out of favor with the ruling elite who control the printing presses. (Christians facing persecution or writers who cannot get their works published might also experiment with this underground approach to publication.)

Dissident writers, whose mastery of the language has enabled them to cut through totalitarian lies, have in fact been largely responsible for the popular upheavals that have recently shaken Communist orthodoxy to its core. The Pro-Democracy movements of the Soviet Union, China, and Eastern Europe have all been led by writers. Alexander Solzhenitsyn, imprisoned for eleven years but never silenced, looms as a giant among contemporary Christian writers. It was he, not Gorbachev, who first called for the policies of openness known as "glasnost."[7] Irina Ratushinskaya, a Christian poet of rare power, is also well worth reading for her account of how her faith enabled her to survive the prison camps.[8] The former Romanian dictator Ceausescu had outlawed the private ownership of typewriters, correctly understanding the relationship between writing and freedom, but he has been swept away. In Czechoslovakia, Vaclav Havel, a playwright who was imprisoned and whose works had been banned, became the post-Communist regime's first head of state. The pen has proven to be more powerful than armored divisions.

If the social realists focused on society, sometimes at the expense of the individual, another branch of realists delved into the human mind to create a psychological realism. The rise of modern psychology encouraged the view that, as far as human beings are concerned, the mind is the locus of reality. That is, reality is mediated through a person's consciousness, which is shaped by early experiences and innate mythical patterns as well as by the environment. Writers such as Henry James explored the infinitely subtle nuances of individual personalities. James Joyce invented the stream-of-consciousness novel, reproducing the inner life of his characters and relating them to primal myths and psychological archetypes. In doing so, he pushed realism itself closer to fantasy.

The best modern realistic novelists draw on both the outer and the inner realities. William Faulkner captured the people and places of the backwoods South in vivid detail, but he also plunged into the minds of the characters, reflecting the complexity of their thoughts and emotions in the very style of his prose. Faulkner's realism anatomized the social structure of the South while at the same time affirming the complexity and the dignity of his characters. Faulkner is profoundly democratic in the respect he shows for ordinary people. His "white trash" share-croppers, black farm hands, and seedy aristocrats lack refinement, but he never belittles them. Instead, he reveals that ordinary life contains material enough for the highest art.

The same can be said for Hemingway and Steinbeck, the other great modern American realists. Hemingway's style, nearly opposite to Faulkner's, is spare, terse, and cut to the bone. Disdaining flowery descriptions and commentary by the narrator, Hemingway's mastery of dialogue and point of view create the effect of immersing the reader in the world of the characters. Steinbeck was more interested in the social problems of the country, but he never neglected the individual, whom he set against the backdrop of a natural world evocatively described. Steinbeck often turned to the Bible to amplify his themes (consider his titles *East of Eden* and *Grapes of Wrath*), and, like Faulkner, operated with a strong moral sensibility.

From a Christian point of view, realism can be a way of coming to grips with the world and the human condition. Christianity is not primarily subjective, but objective. That is, it is not simply a matter of mystical feelings experienced in the private sanctum of the self. Rather, Christianity is the revelation of a God who exists independently of the self, a God who created the external world, who became incarnate in that world, who acts in history, and who calls His people to become involved in society through concrete moral actions. Christians will therefore be drawn to literary realism, interpreting what they read the same way they interpret what they experience, in light of their faith. In this regard, it does not matter too much if the author of a realistic novel is a Christian or not. If the novel is truly realistic, if it reflects the world as it actually is, the Christian reader can notice the same patterns of creation, sin, and love evident everywhere in "real life."

CHRISTIAN REALISM

The limitation of realism, from the Christian perspective, is that many writers exclude God from their picture of reality. In much modern fiction, spiritual or moral issues have no place. The characters are motivated solely by their own desires; they struggle against sheerly impersonal forces; they remain insulated in their own psyches. In other words, as in the materialistic view of the world, they exist in a closed system. In many realistic novels, characters are grotesquely immoral, but they never feel guilty. They never wonder about God or pray or go to church. A Christian would say that such exclusion of explicit religious concerns is a lapse in the realism. With all due respect to Faulkner, his vivid portrayals of the old South almost never include the pervasive role of the church in the consciousness of backwoods southerners. This religious awareness sometimes takes strange and obsessive forms, as Flannery O'Connor shows, but it is never far from the surface.

Other authors do include spiritual issues as part of their realism. Here the Russian giants Dostoyevsky and Tolstoy come to mind. Dostoyevsky delves into the human heart and finds its need for Christ. *Crime and Punishment* deals with a cold-blooded murder, performed almost as a philosophical exercise by someone who has accepted the moral nihilism of post-Enlightenment thought. The novel shows him overtaken by guilt and self-revulsion, and holds up Christ as the only solution to human sin. Tolstoy explores the social panorama of nineteenth-century Russia and the complexities of ordinary human life, measuring them both in terms of the Sermon on the Mount.

Many modern Christian novelists are also working out of the tradition of the realistic novel. In *The Power and the Glory*, Graham Greene writes about the persecution of Christianity during the Mexican revolution. The last priest in the province is an alcoholic, conscious of his failures and his sinfulness; yet he doggedly pursues his ministry as he is being tracked down by a Marxist police official determined to eliminate Christianity via the firing squad. The novel is an unforgettable portrayal of the clash of worldviews and the unstoppable grace of God. The atmosphere of Greene's novels is typically tropical, sultry, and bleak, taking into full account the spiritual landscape of the human heart.

Contemporary Christian realists would include Frederick Buechner, Larry Woiwode, Walker Percy, and J. F. Powers. Buechner's books range from *The Books of Bebb,* a series of comic novels about an outrageous preacher, to *Godric* and *Brendan,* tales about medieval saints which manage to evoke an ancient consciousness while dealing powerfully with contemporary spiritual concerns—all rendered in delicious language. Larry Woiwode captures the poignant depths of family life. Walker Percy is a devastating social critic. J. F. Powers writes about the spiritual struggles of the priesthood in the twentieth century. A. N. Wilson writes satiric novels with an odd compassionate edge. *Gentlemen in England* is a remarkable recreation of Victorian England, featuring a conflict between a son who has fallen under the spell of the Oxford Movement (a revival of Christian orthodoxy and high church Anglicanism) and his father, a geologist who has fallen under the spell of Charles Darwin.

Other realistic Christian authors—besides the incomparable Flannery O'Connor—would include Evelyn Waugh, Muriel Spark, and John Updike (considered one of the greatest of contemporary writers, whose virtuoso literary skill and flashes of theological insight are marred, for me, by his overly explicit sexual descriptions). Others who deserve reading are Hugh Cook, Lloyd Billingsley, James Schaap, and other promising new novelists whose works are beginning to appear in Christian bookstores.

Christian realists tend to balance the social and the psychological, avoiding the double temptation of either effacing the individual in the whirl of external social forces or of being sucked into the black hole of a private ego that excludes the external world. Such writers are not necessarily trying to present lessons in piety. Rather, they are trying to write about real people in real circumstances and, in doing so, they uncover the realism of faith.

FANTASY:
Literature as a Lamp

*J*ust as there is a literature of imitation, there is a literature of creation. Fairy tales, allegorical visions, beast fables, medieval romances, Gothic tales, supernatural thrillers, epic quests in a sub-created universe, and science fiction constitute an important literary tradition. Such works have always been popular, firing the imaginations of their readers with tales of wonder and mystery that transcend everyday life.

Fantasy draws upon the inward imagination rather than external reality for its subject matter. The play of the creative imagination is an important human power. The pure, radical fictionality of fantasy—its separateness from what we already experience—is part of its value. Nevertheless, the lamp of fantasy can shed light on the world outside its pages.

Christians have always been drawn to fantasy. The great pioneers of fantasy—Spenser, Bunyan, Swift, MacDonald, Tolkien, Lewis—were all devout Christians, as are many authors and avid readers of fantasy today. On the other hand, some Christians decry unrealistic literature. Mythological tales of magic spells and demonic villains seem to them dangerously close to the occult. Yet even the critics of fantasy can hardly deny that in the hands of a John Bunyan or a C. S. Lewis, fantasy has been a way of exploring and proclaiming the Christian faith.

Fantasy, by projecting the inner life and by symbolizing the intangible, will by its very nature raise spiritual issues. The battle between good and evil, the inner struggles of the mind, the contest between God and Satan for the soul—such momentous truths are in the realm of the unseen, but fantasy can express them in symbolic form. Something spiritual may be evil or it may be good. Fantasy's spiritual orientation means that it can embody the occult and promote immorality, or it can embody Christianity and promote virtue. Most fantasy—the great fantasy—comes down on the side of Christianity.

FANTASY OF THE SPIDERS

There are good reasons for Christians to be cautious with fantasy. The external world is the creation of God. Turning one's back on what God has made in favor of figments of the imagination would seem presumptuous or at best trivial. Basing literature on dreams and private fancies would seem to diminish its scope and relevance and to waste the time of its readers.

Jonathan Swift dealt with the relationship between literature drawn from the outside world and literature spun out of the private imagination in his fable of the bee and the spider. The two insects debate which one is superior. The bee describes how it leaves its hive to range far and wide among the flowers. The nectar found in nature the bee takes into itself, processing it into honey and wax. The spider, on the other hand, disdains nature, living by itself in a dark corner which it never leaves. The spider asserts his superiority to the bee because he spins elaborate creations—his webs—without any help, wholly out of himself. This is true, rebuts the bee, but consider the end result: "By assimilating material taken from nature and creatively transforming it, I produce works of real value, which humans can use for sweetness and light" (that is, honey and beeswax candles). The spider's result is a web of complex design (the bee praises the spider's skill in mathematics and architecture), but it is flimsy and made out of filth. According to the bee, "the question comes down to this":

> Whether is the nobler being of the two, that which, by a lazy contemplation of four inches round, by an overweening pride, which feeding and engendering on itself, turns all into excrement and venom, produces nothing at last but flybane and a cobweb; or that which, by an universal range, with long search, much study, true judgment, and distinction of things, brings home honey and wax.[1]

Swift was comparing the "ancients" (who imitated nature) with the "moderns" (who created from their own self-sufficient minds). In the process, he was ridiculing the human propensity to spin out elaborate philosophical systems, which so characterized the rationalism of the Enlightenment. More deeply, he was advocating the neoclassical position that the mind is a mirror and criticizing the newly emerging romanticism that would see it as a lamp.

His analogy is unanswerable. As he frames the argument, bees are undoubtedly nobler than spiders. If we accept his fable, what does it mean for fantasy? First of all, the fable of the spider and the bee is itself an example of fantasy; insects in nature do not normally talk, much less debate their relative merits. Swift, the author of *Gulliver's Travels,* was a virtuoso of fantasy, yet he was clearly on the side of the bee. Swift must have believed that fantasy too, including this tale, could produce sweetness and light.

Notice that the bee does not simply fetch nectar—such a purely natural product is not particularly useful to human beings. Rather, the bee digests the nectar, internalizing and working upon it with his own powers ("much study, true judgment, and distinction of things"), turning it into something that would not exist apart from the bee's efforts. Just as honey and wax are made from nectar but are not identical with it, a fantasy can be made from truth without being true itself. The fantasy writer, like the bee, takes elements from the real world and, by the creative process, turns them into a work of art that can be both aesthetically delightful (as honey is sweet) and illuminating (as wax candles can light up a dark room).

There is, of course, spiderish literature. His description of the spider's "lazy contemplation of four inches round," and his "overweening pride, which feeding and engendering on itself, turns all into excrement and venom," reminds me, frankly, of much modern realistic writing. An author's self-centered perspective on the universe and prideful rejection of God's truth can poison his vision of the world. To be sure, there is also spiderish fantasy.

Christians are right to be skeptical about the products of the human mind. "For the imagination of man's heart is evil from his youth" (Genesis 8:21 KJV). The doctrine of original sin implies that evil resides in the deepest crannies of the mind and that it contaminates everything we might create or accomplish. Scripture suggests that the imagination is the source of idolatry and false religions, and the prophets continually warn God's people to base their faith upon the Word of God rather than upon the imaginations of their hearts (see Jeremiah 23:16-32).

Christians today are rightly concerned about connections between fantasy and the occult. Our pop culture's fascination with magic, ESP, astrology, and other superstitions are all evidence of neo-paganism insinuating itself throughout the mass culture. Sometimes the occult is presented in sanitized forms, as in cartoons that make witches and demons cute, while sometimes the occult is presented in all of its darkness, as in Stephen King novels and horrific movies. Role-playing fantasy games such as "Dungeons and Dragons" have led some into experimentation with black magic and satanic ritual. Just as the idol-

atrous religions decried by the prophets expressed themselves in mythological stories, pop paganism sometimes finds expression in fantasy.
L. Ron Hubbard, founder of the scientology cult, writes best-selling
science fiction. Scientology, in turn, teaches that human beings are rein-
carnated extraterrestrials, a theology that is itself science fiction. I have
heard of fantasy conventions which offer separate worship services for
Christians and for pagans, the latter consisting of outdoor rituals modeled somewhat after the ancient Druids', except without the human
sacrifices. Both idolatry and fantasy find their origin in the imagination.
When the sinful mind is unleashed and indulged without restraint, the
result will inevitably be some version of idolatry and abject slavery to
Satan.

However, the problem is not fantasy as such. Christians are
offended by fantasy that flirts with the occult because they know that
the occult is *not* fantasy. Witchcraft, necromancy, and demonism are
real spiritual dangers. Nor do those seduced by occultism think of it
as fantasy; they consider it real. Some people might begin by being fascinated with fantasy literature, dreaming about magic and superhuman
powers, but once they cross the line into occultism, they no longer see
fantasy as purely imaginary. Rather, they treat it as the pagans did their
myths, as actual descriptions of the universe. Fantasy, by definition, is
not an imitation of the external world. Once the radical fictionality of
fantasy is clearly understood, its dangers diminish. Sanity involves
being able to distinguish fantasy from reality. Such discernment is necessary for spiritual sanity as well as for psychological sanity.

We can use our minds and imaginations in either a wholesome
or a degraded way; by the same token, human beings can produce good
fantasy or bad fantasy. Both draw on the inner world of the soul, and
both can be a way of making spiritual realities tangible, presenting
goodness and evil in concrete terms. Good fantasy elevates and disciplines the imagination, awakening its readers to the beauty of goodness
as well as to the repulsiveness of evil. Tolkien eloquently speaks of how
fantasy can create a sense of recovery (helping us see existence in something of its Edenic wonder), a sense of consolation (the experience of
wholeness and reconciliation that comes from the happy ending), and
a sense of escape (helping us transcend the narrow materialism of modern life).[2] Good fantasy projects a universe of grandeur and meaning.
Good and evil are a matter of moral absolutes. The principles of virtue
are austere and all-demanding, yet full of splendor. Evil is presented
in all of its hideousness. The reader's moral sensibility is sharpened,
and spiritual truth is thrown into high relief.

Bad fantasy, on the other hand, is concerned only with the self.
The writers of much contemporary fantasy are doing nothing more
than manufacturing daydreams for the reader. In line with the demands

of mass culture, they are designed solely for self-gratification and often do little to elevate or instruct the imagination. Many Sword and Sorcery novels typically portray a big-thewed warrior clad in leather and metal, hacking apart his enemies and raping pliant maidens. Obviously, these are little more than projections of male dreams—to be so big and strong that no one could despise me, to get back at those who do by stomping them to a bloody pulp, to take what I want when it comes to sex. Such fantasizing is the mark of a frustrated and lonely mind. It is also morally evil. Rape and compliance can never go together, yet such is the twisted fantasy. Such novels have the same appeal as slasher movies and Heavy Metal concerts. In a self-obsessed culture that suppresses no desires, we should not be too surprised at their popularity.

This is not to say that the Sword and Sorcery genre is bad in itself—a classic progenitor such as *Beowulf* proves otherwise. One difference between the barbarians of contemporary pop fiction and the sword-wielding warriors of quality literature lies in their atmosphere. Beowulf's adventures are suffused with the spirit of Germanic heroism, the code of honor in which the hero's greatest deeds are accomplished when he knows that he faces certain doom. Here is the stoic pessimism of the old pagan culture which has just been supplanted by the grander moral idealism of the newly embraced Christianity. Tolkien also has his wandering warriors and evil wizards, and he is shamelessly plagiarized by many of the Sword and Sorcery authors. The difference is that Middle Earth conveys a sense of eerie beauty and a moral order which is part of that beauty. The world of many of his imitators is dark, cynical, and repugnant—an imaginative landscape that is spiritually, morally, and aesthetically barren.

Such fantasies are usually bad not only morally but aesthetically. Writers who reject objective morality can hardly portray a convincing battle between good and evil. In many contemporary horror novels there is no battle—we wallow in unrelieved and unchallenged evil. In other superficial fantasies, such as the pseudo-realistic romance and adventure novels, the heroes are indistinguishable morally from the villains. The main difference is that the "good guys" are physically attractive and the "bad guys" are physically ugly. The modeling power of literature is sometimes askew: we find evil characters attractive and good characters (if they exist at all) repulsive. We may enjoy an imaginative rush from descriptions of battle, witchcraft, or sex; but the experience has no point, and the reader is left with nothing of value once the stimulation fades.

Those who delve deeply into the self with no restraints or safeguards will encounter horrors. Innate sin dwells deep within the human soul, like goblins that lurk in subterranean caverns. The self in isolation will become a source of malevolence and corruption. This is why the untrammeled pursuit of fantasy's dark side leads some into the occult. Like Faustus, they play at being sorcerers, only to find themselves in the hands of Satan, a necromancer that, far from being a fantasy, is horribly, implacably real. Good fantasy, on the other hand, can be nourishing to the imagination and the soul.

CREATION

Not only can fantasy be in accord with the Bible; the Bible has actually made fantasy possible. The Greek concept of imitation, which has been so influential in Western aesthetics, issued from their worldview. According to Plato, the physical world is an imitation of an ideal realm. Art, in turn, is an imitation of that imitation (so that Plato minimized its importance).[3] The Biblical emphasis upon creation rather than imitation, on the other hand, helped provide the conceptual basis for fantasy.[4]

Most societies based on a mythological religion, including that of the Greeks, have no true creation story. For them, the universe is a phase in a cosmic cycle. Their myths speak of a new world being born out of a pre-existing world, which itself was made out of an earlier world. The cycle never ends and, more to the point, never begins. (Compare the emerging neopagan worldview of some contemporary scientists, who speculate that the universe continually expands, then collapses in upon itself until a new big bang starts the process all over again.)

Greek thinkers rationalized the myths by postulating that the universe came into being when the primal chaotic matter was organized and given form by an active agent (the *demiurge*) working in accordance with the divine rational plan (the *logos*). Plato and Aristotle did reject the mythic cycles in favor of a God understood as a "first cause," an insight which led the early church to respect them highly. For the philosophers, however, as well as for the Greeks who believed in the old gods, there never was a time when there was nothing. Even the demiurge was imitating a pre-existent pattern and was simply shaping what already existed.

The Hebrews, on the other hand, stressed that God started with nothing, that the universe is not an imitation but a creation. If the Greek belief about how the world came into being had implications for their view of art, so did the Hebrews'. To keep the Israelites from contaminating their faith with their neighbors' mythical worldview and its accompanying idolatry, the Bible warns against the dangers of imitative art. The commandment against graven images strikes explicitly against the very principle of imitation: "You shall not make yourself a graven image, or *any likeness of anything* that is in heaven above, or that is in the earth beneath, or that is in the water under the earth" (Exodus 20:4 RSV).[5]

Prohibiting making "any likeness of anything" obviously inhibited realistic art.[6] This did not prohibit art that was *not* a likeness of anything. Designs could be created that were beautiful in themselves, not because they imitated natural beauty. Art could be nonrepresentational. Consider the carpets, tapestries, and mosaics of Middle Eastern art even today. Their complex geometric patterns and interlocking shapes, their vibrant colors and energetic designs, are likenesses of nothing on earth, but they are art and beauty of the highest order. (This monotheistic abstractionism is very different from contemporary Western abstract art with its minimalism and disorder.) In creating something orderly and beautiful that did not previously exist, the artist is paralleling what God did in the act of creation.

The maker of a Persian carpet, of course, is still working with colors, the laws of geometry, and physical materials made by God. Only God can truly create from nothing. The Greek view of imitation—especially the model of the demiurge shaping pre-existent matter—is still a useful paradigm for human artists. The concept of creation, in turn, emphasizes the active role of the artist's mind in the shaping of the work. An element of imitation and an element of creation are involved in any work of art and literature, whether realism or fantasy. Christians can affirm the whole spectrum of the arts in terms of God's creation, which is made manifest in realism and reenacted in fantasy.

Not only did the ancient Hebrews and the early Christians have a concept of creation and a suspicion of realistic art, they also debunked the mythology of their pagan neighbors. Prometheus bringing civilization to mortals by stealing fire from the gods, Demeter causing the crops to grow through her reunion with her daughter Persephone—such things never actually happened. The early Christians conceded that they were good *stories*, however. The myths are not imitations; rather, they are creations. Thus was born the concept of fiction.

Although the early Christians denied the factuality of the Greek and Roman myths, they retained them in their educational curriculum. As long as the stories were understood to be fiction, they could be read with delight and profit. Virgil, author of the Roman epic *The Aeneid*, retained his popularity among the Christians and occupied a central place in the teaching of Latin for centuries. Christian writers even included mythological allusions in their own work, but these were "demythologized," interpreted as sheerly artistic or allegorical devices.

By rejecting the myths as true stories, Christianity redefined them as fantasies. Fiction as an imaginative realm, separate and distinct from the "real world, became conceptually clear. Christians did not see fiction as totally unrelated to the external world; rather they saw the relationship to be thematic or symbolic. Myths and fantasies offer idealized examples that can clarify actual human experience and symbolize moral or spiritual truths. The early Christian attack on mythology opened up a space in which fantasy could develop.

Romances (fantasy tales of knights, brave deeds, and marvels) flourished in the Middle Ages, as did fairy tales. Both may well have drawn on earlier legends filtered through a Christian consciousness. Folk epics such as *Beowulf* were still treasured, although revised in terms of the new faith. Writers turned to allegory—that is, symbolic fantasies—as a way of writing about psychological and spiritual realities. *The Romance of the Rose* is an allegory about the psychology of human love; the *Divine Comedy* is an allegory about the love of God. Tales such as the quest of the Holy Grail combine secular romance with religious allegory, resulting in numinous, wonder-filled religious fantasy.

The Renaissance with its rediscovery of both the Greek and the Biblical heritage was a golden age of fantasy. Modern fantasy perhaps begins with Edmund Spenser's *Faerie Queene,* an under-read literary masterpiece that was one of C. S. Lewis's favorite books. Continuing the tradition of the medieval romances, Spenser went further to create a wholly realized, self-contained imaginative world (as Tolkien would do). Spenser's Fairy Land, inhabited by a host of heroes, villains, and monsters involved in the most labyrinthine of interconnecting plots, is also a profound allegory of the Christian character.

The first book of the *Faerie Queene,* focusing on holiness, is a *tour de force* of Reformation theology and psychology. The Red-Crosse Knight becomes disillusioned, deceived, and alienated from faith. He follows his will until it leads him to sin, to despair, and to bondage. Like all sinners, he must be rescued by the grace of God. This spiritual paradigm becomes the plot of a lively tale of love and adventure. Spenser explores the inner life of faith in luminous poetry and unforgettable characters and episodes: Archimago, the shape-shifting wizard; the virtuous Una and her sinister counterpart Duessa; the succession of Saracens who symbolize how loss of faith leads first to lawlessness and then to despair. Book I of *The Faerie Queene* ends with one of the best dragon fights in English literature, which becomes an emblem of the defeat of the Serpent in the Garden.

The reach of Spenser's symbolic imagination can be illustrated with a single detail. The Red-Crosse knight, rescued from the dungeon of the Giant of pride, is taken for healing to the House of Holiness. From the outside, it appears small and insignificant. He must stoop low to enter. On the inside, however, he finds himself in a vast, spacious court.[7] (This is in contrast to the Palace of Pride, which has an impressive appearance, but is actually only a false front like a Hollywood set.)[8] Spenser's image of a structure whose "inside is bigger than its outside" has been borrowed in Dr. Who's Tardis and in *The Last Battle* by C. S. Lewis[9] and can serve as a startling description of the human soul. Looked at physically, a human being is relatively small and circumscribed within the limits of the body. From the inside, however, a human being is as vast as the reaches of the mind. Spenser employs the image to make a point about holiness and by extension about the Christian faith, which may look forbidding, narrow, and unpleasant from the perspective of those outside the church. Experienced from the inside, holiness proves to be spacious, liberating, and, in Spenser's words, "pleasant to be walked in."[10]

A simpler but related allegorical fantasy of the Christian life would be written a century later by John Bunyan. *Pilgrim's Progress* uses down-to-earth prose rather than Spenser's elaborate poetry to explore Christian's journey from the City of Destruction to the Celestial City. Along the way he has to slog through the Slough of Despond, be ridiculed in Vanity Fair, risk giving it all up in the Valley of the Shadow of Death, and be attended upon by a host of memorable companions. This book by an uneducated tinker in prison for his faith has edified the souls and fueled the imaginations of countless readers.

The tradition of Christian fantasy continued. Swift's *Gulliver's Travels* was not only a devastating Christian satire, but it was perhaps the first science fiction novel, with its alternate worlds of microscopic people, benevolent giants, and flying islands. In the nineteenth century, George MacDonald wrote Christian fairy tales that would have a profound impact a century later on the imagination of C. S. Lewis, who also employed fantasy to explore the truth and the implications of the Christian faith. His friend J. R. R. Tolkien, a medieval scholar whose testimony to Christ led to Lewis's conversion to Christianity, wrote the monumental saga *Lord of the Rings*. Today many Christian writers are turning to fantasy as an appropriate medium for writing about spiritual issues: Madeleine L'Engle, Robert Siegel, Stephen Lawhead, Frank Peretti, Walter Wangerin.

FANTASY AND SPIRITUAL REALISM

Why are Christian writers and readers so fascinated by fantasy? Nonbelievers might say that Christians turn to fantasy because their faith is a fantasy. Such a response betrays a lack of understanding about both faith and fantasy. Faith has to do with the realm of the unseen (Hebrews 11:1), with truths that are no less real for being mysterious and beyond our full comprehension. Christianity also has to do with the inner life—the state of the soul. In fantasy, a writer can project that inner life and those invisible truths by making them tangible through symbols.

Our dreams are fantasies. The eerie landscapes, the enigmatic characters, the vivid details and shifting scenes of a dream are not exactly realistic if we consider only the surface appearances of the waking world. Yet they are expressive of the real world of the mind. Psychologists are not sure about how to interpret them, but dreams do seem to embody emotional preoccupations or unconscious concerns which are given imaginative form. Although dreams should not be taken as oracles from God (Jeremiah 23: 25-29), the dreams described in the Bible do have important meanings and consist of symbols that demand interpretation.

The world of legend and myth is akin to that of dreams.[11] Apparently, such fantasies are ways of externalizing inner, as opposed to outer, conditions. The psychological patterns that underlie dreams are paralleled by even deeper patterns of human nature that underlie the ancient tales perpetuated by the folk culture. Many myths speak of a "dying god," of sacrifice, of death and rebirth. C. S. Lewis believed that these myths are "good dreams" of the human race, evidence of the innate human need and longing for Christ who came not as myth but as fact.

Lewis was a literary scholar who had always been fascinated by myth. He shared this interest with his friend and fellow-author J. R. R. Tolkien. As a young scholar, Lewis was not a Christian, but in the course of his explorations of myth and conversations with Tolkien, he encountered the gospel of Jesus Christ. Shortly after his conversion, Lewis wrote a letter to a friend announcing his new belief in Christ, describing how Tolkien and another Christian friend witnessed to him in the context of myth:

Now what [Hugo] Dyson and Tolkien showed me was this: that if I met the idea of sacrifice in a Pagan story I didn't mind it at all: again, that if I met the idea of a god sacrificing himself to himself . . . I liked it very much and was mysteriously moved by it: again, that the idea of the dying and reviving god (Balder, Adonis, Bacchus) similarly moved me provided I met it anywhere *except* in the Gospels. The reason was that in Pagan stories I was prepared to feel the myth as profound and suggestive of meanings beyond my grasp even tho' I could not say in cold prose "what it meant."

Now the story of Christ is simply a true myth: a myth working on us in the same way as the others, but with this tremendous difference that *it really happened*: and one must be content to accept it in the same way, remembering that it is God's myth where the others are men's myths: i.e. the Pagan stories are God expressing Himself through the minds of poets, using such images as He found there, while Christianity is God expressing Himself through what we call "real things."[12]

To say world mythologies can be seen as a kind of testimony to Christian truth does not mean, as Joseph Campbell suggests, that they should be used as spiritual guides. Scripture warns us in no uncertain terms to "have nothing to do with godless myths" (1 Timothy 4:7). The Biblical worldview, as we have shown, is diametrically opposed to the mythical worldview. For Lewis, the myths that had always moved him so deeply were thoroughly "demythologized"; he knew that they were untrue. Even as a young Christian, Lewis here recognizes that they were "man's myths," the projections of human poets and thus tainted with sinful distortions and confusion. Christianity, on the other hand, is "God's myth," the revelation of God in the objective realm of truth.

Lewis's account of his conversion, though, has important implications for contemporary evangelism. Before as well as after his conversion, Lewis was an intellectual among intellectuals, and he is well known for his rational defenses of Christian doctrine. And yet, Lewis was reached not so much by intellectual argument as by the Word of the gospel conveyed through imaginative literature. Clearly, the Holy Spirit can work through the imagination as well as the intellect. Literature and the other arts may well take part in the ministry of the Word and be used by God to open some people's minds to spiritual issues and to the good news of Christ.

Lewis's autobiography *Surprised by Joy* describes another pivotal moment in his spiritual life prior to his conversion yet part of the process that would lead him to Christ. Before getting on a train, Lewis stopped at a bookstall and picked up *Phantases: A Faerie Romance,* an adult fairy tale by the nineteenth-century Christian fantasist George MacDonald:

> The woodland journeyings in that story, the ghostly enemies, the ladies both good and evil, were close enough to my habitual imagery to lure me on without the perception of a change. It is as if I were carried sleeping across the frontier, or as if I had died in the old country and could never remember how I came alive in the new. . . . I did not yet know (and I was long in learning) the name of the new quality, the bright shadow, that rested on the travels of Anodos. I do now. It was Holiness. . . . That night my imagination was, in a certain sense, baptized; the rest of me, not unnaturally, took longer. I had not the faintest notion what I had let myself in for by buying *Phantases*.[13]

In today's world of materialism and cynicism, a major obstacle to belief is the difficulty of *imagining* anything that transcends what the senses can perceive. Christianity speaks of mysteries, of absolute goodness locked in a cosmic battle with Satan, of eternal ecstasies—all of which go far beyond the constricted, empty universe of physical objects that our culture assumes is all there is. The problem with many people today is not that they have intellectual objections to Christianity—our age is anti-intellectual to begin with—but that their imaginations are so impoverished that they cannot even begin to conceive of anything spiritual. They have become incapable of recognizing the awe and wonder of holiness. Their imaginations need baptizing.

Our Christian witness is often couched in purely intellectual terms—and there is definitely a need for apologetics and for asserting the conceptual content of the faith—but it sometimes leaves little impression on an increasingly brain-dead population. Many people, like Lewis, may need to have their imaginations quickened so that they can see the "wonderful things in your law" (Psalm 119:18). Christians, whether as writers or preachers or conversationalists, can address the dreams and longings that lie deep within the human soul, unveiling the compelling beauty and mystery of the Christian faith. A. N. Wilson, a contemporary English author, argues for the truth of Christianity by focusing on the peculiar imaginative appeal of the Sermon on the Mount and the Lord's Supper.[14] G. K. Chesterton persuades his readers of the truth of Christianity by first helping them to notice the marvels inherent in ordinary life. C. S. Lewis, when defending Christianity, appeals to the mind, and he also appeals to the imagination.

His *Chronicles of Narnia* are works of fantasy that have baptized the imaginations of many, both children and adults. In *The Lion, the Witch, and the Wardrobe*, Christ is symbolized by Aslan the Lion, who gives Himself to the White Witch to be sacrificed on the Stone Table in exchange for the life of the traitor Edmund. The fantasy context, in effect, defamiliarizes the gospel. In describing how he wrote the series, Lewis describes his purpose: "I thought I saw how stories of this kind could steal past a certain inhibition which had paralyzed much of my own religion in childhood." The enforced reverence of church, with its lowered voices and heavy obligations, prevented him as a child from appreciating the magnitude of the Christian claims. It occurred to him that the fairy tale might be a way of recovering the true excitement of the Christian story. "By casting all these things into an imaginary world, stripping them of their stained-glass and Sunday school associations, one could make them for the first time appear in their real potency."[15]

The very atmosphere of fantasy is charged with beauty and mystery, the sense that anything can happen, that there is more to life than we see on the surface. It is little wonder that Christian writers and readers have disciplined their imaginations through fantasy.

FAIRY TALES

Coleridge (another Christian theorist and practitioner of fantasy) has said that reading imaginative literature requires a "willing suspension of disbelief."[16] Of course a frog cannot actually change into a handsome prince, a beanstalk growing into the clouds is a biological impossibility, and magic is a hoax or an occult obsession. We know that, but fantasy by definition is not supposed to be realistic. We surrender our disbelief to enter the alternative world of the story.

At the same time, a fantasy must possess "verisimilitude." That is, it must be similar to truth. It must be believable, if not in terms of our world, in terms of its own. Contradictions, inconsistencies, unmotivated characters, and incoherent plots will make it difficult for the reader to suspend disbelief. A good fantasy will give its imaginary world the texture of reality. Cause and effect still hold. Science fiction, an enormously popular genre, creates its own scientific assumptions, but then follows them rigorously. The wildest fantasies show their characters caught up in the consequences of their actions. Human nature is generally a constant, whether in our world, in a faraway galaxy, or in Never-Never-Land.

Fairy tales are examples of fantasies that both require a suspension of disbelief and are true to their own laws and the laws of human nature. Fairy tales are a product of the folk culture, shaped by centuries of telling and retelling. As such, they are a storehouse of human experience and cultural wisdom.

G. K. Chesterton has written about "the ethics of Elfland" and how fairy tales convey a philosophy that accords with the Christian faith:

> There is the chivalrous lesson of "Jack the Giant Killer"; that giants should be killed because they are gigantic. It is a manly mutiny against pride as such. . . . There is the lesson of "Cinderella," which is the same as that of the Magnificat—*exaltavit humiles* [the humble will be exalted]. There is the great lesson of "Beauty and the Beast"; that a thing must be loved *before* it is lovable. There is the terrible allegory of the "Sleeping Beauty," which tells how the human creature was blessed with all birthday gifts, yet cursed with death; and how death also may perhaps be softened to a sleep.[17]

Yet fairy tales as literature for children are often attacked today, both by radical feminists who object to their "rigid sex roles"[18] and by traditional moralists who object to their sometimes violent imagery.

To the consternation of many well-meaning adults, children usually prefer fairy tales to modern children's books, which are "educational" in a heavy-handed way and in which nothing very interesting ever happens. Children deprived of fairy tales may risk the plight of Eustace, a boy in Lewis's *The Voyage of the Dawn Treader* who "liked books if they were books of information and had pictures of grain elevators or of fat foreign children doing exercises in model schools." When he meets a dragon—an actual moral and emotional crisis—he is unprepared. "Most of us," Lewis writes, "know what we should expect to find in a dragon's lair, but, as I said before, Eustace had read only the wrong books. They had a lot to say about exports and imports and governments and drains, but they were weak on dragons."[19]

Noted child psychologist Bruno Bettelheim has studied children's love for fairy tales and has demonstrated their value to the child's psychological, moral, and intellectual growth:

> For a story truly to hold the child's attention, it must entertain him and arouse his curiosity. But to enrich his life, it must stimulate his imagination; help him to develop his intellect and to clarify his emotions; be attuned to his anxieties and aspirations; give full recognition to his difficulties, while at the same time suggesting solutions to the problems which perturb him. In short, it must at one and the same time relate to all aspects of his personality—and this without ever belittling but, on the contrary, giving full credence to the seriousness of the child's predicaments, while simultaneously promoting confidence in himself and in his future.[20]

An expert in working with the most severely disturbed children, Bettelheim found that fairy tales can help a child develop self-esteem, resolve emotional fears and conflicts, achieve independence, and gain a sense of life's meaning. Children need to know about dragons.

Consider the story of "Hansel and Gretel." It begins with the brother and sister eavesdropping on their parents who admit that they are so poor they can no longer take care of their children. Hansel and Gretel, to save the expense for their family, set off into the deep woods. Running away from their house of starvation, they find what looks to be the answer to their dreams: a house made of gingerbread. Here they have all the food they want; the abundant provider, however, turns out to be a wicked witch. The indulgence of their appetite only means they are being "fattened up" for the witch's own feast. By their ingenuity, they thwart her evil designs when Gretel pushes her into her own oven, and they find a great treasure. The two children return home with money enough to solve all of their parent's financial problems. They live happily ever after.

Here is a tale of abandonment, cannibalism, and burning people alive. Is such horrifying material, worthy of an R-rating on the screen, appropriate for children? Bettelheim and the experience of generations of parents and children say yes. Somehow the fantasy framework and the charmed atmosphere of fairy tales prevent most children from actually being afraid. Experience shows that the "scary" elements are part of what children love most in these tales, which they enjoy far more than the socially correct, innocuous realism of much modern children's literature. Bettelheim shows that fairy tales are in fact profoundly reassuring. What could be more terrifying to children than the thought that their parents on whom they are totally dependent can no longer provide for them? And yet, Bettelheim points out, children *do* worry about such things. In fairy tales such as "Hansel and Gretel," their most secret fears are acknowledged, respected, and resolved into a happy ending.

Such stories, according to Bettelheim, encourage a child by offering reassuring models of independence, problem solving, and success. Hansel and Gretel learn to look past superficial appearances. Whereas they did not have enough food at home, a house of gingerbread and an all-you-can-eat diet is not pleasant when your caregiver is a witch. They learn to be resourceful, to think creatively, and to act with courage. Most significantly, Hansel and Gretel are victorious. Is it any wonder that children love the story of Hansel and Gretel when they see children like themselves facing overwhelming problems and overcoming them?

Bettelheim prefers the unexpurgated tales of the Brothers Grimm to the sanitized versions of Walt Disney and the "safe" domestic worlds of much contemporary children's literature. The horrible punishment of fairy tale villains is necessary for the child's sense of justice:

> Adults often think that the cruel punishment of an evil person in fairy tales upsets and scares children unnecessarily. Quite the opposite is true: such retribution reassures the child that the punishment fits the crime. The child often feels unjustly treated by adults and the world in general, and it seems that nothing is done about it. On the basis of such experiences alone, he wants those who cheat and degrade him . . . most severely punished. If they are not, the child thinks that nobody is serious about protecting him; but the more severely those bad ones are dealt with, the more secure the child feels.[21]

The fairy tale world is dangerous, as is the real world. Child-eating witches may be exaggerated, but child abusers and child molesters are real. Yet the fairy tale world, unlike our own sometimes, is rigorously and dramatically just. The decisive end of the villains gives a child a sense of moral closure. The child is almost never frightened by violence done to the "bad guys." Rather, the child achieves a sense of security from the spectacle of the good (with whom the child identifies) being lavishly rewarded and the evil (who wishes to harm the child) being utterly obliterated.

Fairy tales might begin with the death of parents, separation or abandonment, the threat of being killed or devoured, or turmoil within the family (think of the sibling rivalry in "Cinderella"). Modern parents, observes Bettelheim, wish to protect their children from thinking about such things:

> The prevalent parental belief is that a child must be diverted from what troubles him most: his formless, nameless anxieties, and his chaotic, angry, and even violent fantasies. Many parents believe that only conscious reality or pleasant and wish-fulfilling images should be presented to the child—that he should be exposed only to the sunny side of things. But such one-sided fare nourishes the mind only in a one-sided way, and real life is not all sunny.[22]

Fairy tales give voice to the child's inner turmoil—the fears, angers, and yearnings felt in secret—and give order and direction to the child's inner life.

Behind Grimm's fairy tales one can catch glimpses of the hard lives and the triumphs of the ordinary people who shaped these tales and passed them on. Starvation, wolves, abandonment, and the death of parents would not have been uncommon among Black Forest peasants. Families were broken up, not so much by divorce as by death, and the surviving parent would often remarry. Step-mothers and the ambivalent feelings they arouse in children, sibling rivalry, and child abuse are not new problems, as the story of "Cinderella" reminds us. Contemporary children who are products of broken homes and a scary environment can find these tales especially relevant and healing.

Bettelheim is primarily a psychoanalyst, but his appraisal of modern squeamishness toward evil and the true problems of the human condition as addressed by fairy tales is in striking accord with Biblical truth:

> There is a widespread refusal to let children know that the source of much that goes wrong in life is due to our very own natures—the propensity of all men for acting aggressively, asocially, selfishly, out of anger and anxiety. Instead, we want our children to believe that, inherently, all men are good. But children know that *they* are not always good; and often, even when they are, they would prefer not

to be. This contradicts what they are told by their parents and therefore makes the child a monster in his own eyes.[23]

As Bettelheim observes, "The dominant culture wishes to pretend, particularly where children are concerned, that the dark side of man does not exist."[24] Fairy tales, on the other hand, recognize this dark side, confront it forthrightly, and bring it into the light.

Fairy tales are profoundly moral. They teach morality, however, not by didactic sermonizing nor simply by showing evil punished and virtue rewarded. Bettelheim astutely describes how fairy tales—and by extension literature in general—can shape one's moral sensibility:

> It is not the fact that virtue wins out at the end which promotes morality, but that the hero is most attractive to the child, who identifies with the hero in all his struggles. Because of this identification the child imagines that he suffers with the hero his trials and tribulations, and triumphs with him as virtue is victorious. The child makes such identifications all on his own, and the inner and outer struggles of the hero imprint morality on him.[25]

Fairy tales thus speak to the particular nature of children, to the way they think. As Bettelheim explains:

> A child's choices are based, not so much on right versus wrong, as on who arouses his sympathy and who his antipathy. . . . The question for the child is not "Do I want to be good?" but "Who do I want to be like?" The child decides this on the basis of projecting himself wholeheartedly into one character. If this fairy-tale figure is a very good person, then the child decides that he wants to be good, too.[26]

Adults too, I suspect, respond in a similar way. Good literature can edify not simply by offering an intellectual "lesson" that can be extracted from the text, but by offering models of goodness that the reader admires and wants to emulate. Bad literature can teach immorality by making the reader want to be like evil characters.

The most important part of the fairy tale is the invariable ending: "And they all lived happily ever after." Fairy tales are thus profoundly comic. They may begin in suffering, but they are resolved in the most intense happiness. According to Bettelheim, the happy ending consists of the integration of the personality (the hero resolving all inner conflicts) and the establishing of a permanent relationship with someone else (with marriage or with a reunion with one's family [cf.

Shakespeare's comedies]). This relationship, the child is assured, will never be broken. Good fairy tales end with consolation.[27]

The happy ending of a Christian's life is the consolation of Heaven, which likewise involves the integration of the personality (complete sanctification) and the establishment of a loving relationship that can never be broken (the marriage of Christ and the church). Fairy tales reflect the Christian "comic sense of life," going so far as to evoke eternity—the characters live happily "ever after," a conclusion that transforms the preceding hardships into high adventure.

REALISTIC FANTASY/FANTASTIC REALISM

For all of its impossibilities, fantasy can paradoxically be very realistic psychologically and spiritually. By the same token, realism, when pursued far enough, can include the fantastic. As the realistic novel became preoccupied with the inner psychology of its characters, it started depicting the fantasies of their minds. James Joyce's stream-of-consciousness novel *Ulysses* is hyper-realistic in its characters and in its impressionistic depiction of Dublin; it is hyper-fantastic in its mythological allusions and its dreamlike images. Just as realism can lean toward fantasy, fantasy has its own canons of realism. Fairy tales may recount impossibilities, but they can still be psychologically or philosophically true. Truth lies in their meaning, not their factuality.

Some Christian writers combine fantasy and realism. The novels of Charles Williams, Lewis's close friend, describe modern characters in modern situations in a richly textured, realistic vein. Suddenly, the supernatural breaks in. An archangel, a Platonic archetype, or a demonic plot intrude into the characters' mundane, materialistic lives. The result is an enigmatic, yet profound hybrid of realism and fantasy. Robinson Davies sustains a quirky realism throughout his novels, yet the spiritual dimension is never far from the surface.

Science fiction is an especially interesting form of fantasy which makes at least some concessions to the external world. The marvels and adventures of traditional fantasy are displaced into technological terms. Whereas in fantasy every kind of wonder is possible by invoking magic, in science fiction every kind of wonder is possible by invoking science. Whereas fantasy usually takes place in the remote past ("once upon a time"), science fiction usually takes place in the remote future. Heroes are dressed in space suits rather than armor, and they fight with lasers rather than swords. The monsters, adventures, and character types are pretty much the same.

The main difference is that science fiction addresses itself to the contemporary scientific imagination. Good science fiction (as opposed to the "space operas" that simply project conventional adventure stories into a futuristic setting) will be consistent with actual or hypothetical scientific principles, which are imaginatively extrapolated and turned into the premise for a story. Science fiction writers have been the first to imagine submarines, atomic weapons, communication satellites, and space travel, demonstrating that flights of the imagination can be imminently practical. Science fiction is hugely popular today, and for good reason—it carries on the imaginative pleasures of fantasy in a more modern key to an audience that thinks it has outgrown fairy tales. Lewis directed his Narnia chronicles to children; he wrote his science fiction trilogy to achieve the same effect for adults.

The literature of the high culture has also been experimenting with fantasy. Whereas the modernism of Faulkner and Hemingway manifested itself in terms of the realistic novel, the "post-modernism" of Borges, Barth, and Calvino has turned to fantasy. Hispanic writers such as Gabriel García Márquez have been experimenting with "magical realism." The work of such contemporary novelists is sometimes brilliant and thought provoking. In lesser hands, the new experimental fantasy is merely obscure and self-absorbed. At times fiction writers seem to be emulating abstract painters, manipulating images for their private effects, experimenting for experimentation's sake, writing fiction that is about fiction rather than anything outside its pages. Behind some of the new fantasy is a profound skepticism that believes that all external order, all meaning, and all truth are nothing more than creations of the human mind, that everything, in effect, is fantasy.

The "New Journalist" Tom Wolfe has criticized these novelists for retreating into themselves and neglecting the vast and lively social panorama of our civilization. Our society has gone through the civil rights movement, countercultures, the Vietnam War, economic and technological miracles, and moral follies of staggering proportions, yet such provocative material has been ignored by most "serious" contemporary novelists. Wolfe advocates a revival of the realistic social novel—the tradition of Dickens, Tolstoy, and Steinbeck—which can help people come to grips with their culture. "At this weak, pale, tabescent moment in the history of American literature, we need a battalion, a brigade, of Zolas to head out into this wild, bizarre, unpredictable, Hog-stomping Baroque country of ours and reclaim it as literary property."[28] Wolfe's point suggests the limits of fantasy. Authors who write with their eyes shut to the realities outside of themselves, spinning private dreams and playing elaborate imaginative games, risk trivializing their work and boring their readers. It might be time, as Wolfe suggests, for writers to recover social realism. The best fantasy, though, shuts its eyes at nothing.

Good fantasy has the ring of truth. For all of their fairy godmothers, enchanted forests, and talking animals, fairy tales are dead-on realistic when it comes to the subterranean truths of human nature. Fantasy may be a way of digging out these psychological and spiritual truths, but when it does so, it is, for all of its imaginative freedom, an imitation of the created order. The creation of a good fantasy writer pays homage to the creation of God and increases our perception and our love for the mysterious reality that God has made up.

THE TRADITIONS
OF LITERATURE

Writing makes thoughts permanent. Literature enables a
reader to enter the mind of an author who died centuries
ago, but whose insights and imagination are stored on
the printed page, ideas which can be replayed in the
mind of a reader. By the miracle of writing, readers can
still access the past and draw upon the whole range of
human achievement. Literature can function as a time
machine whereby we leave our own day to enter other
ages.

Literature ushers us into the minds of its authors
and into the heartbeat of their age. Nowhere else are
worldviews, cultural changes, and spiritual assumptions
manifested more clearly. To understand our own times
requires a knowledge of the past. One can do no better
in tracing the greatness and the delusions of Western culture than to study its literature.

Like all of the arts, literature is in a constant process of change. Styles become exhausted and no longer
communicate effectively. They give way to new styles
that again seize their readers' attention and communicate
in a fresh and compelling way. But also the older styles,
insofar as they are different from what we are used to,
can communicate very powerfully to contemporary readers. For those of us stranded in the modern age, the old
styles can cut through the fog of our culture and communicate truths that will seem refreshingly new.

Although changes in style reflect changes in culture,

Christian authors have been able to express their faith in nearly every style. In doing so, they have proclaimed Christ in terms their audiences could understand despite their culture's sometimes deficient worldviews. This section will survey some of the major phases of Western literature with the purpose of helping Christians draw upon and continue the Christian literary tradition.

THE MIDDLE AGES AND THE REFORMATION:
The Literature of Belief

Christians today face the problem of living in a post-Christian culture. The moral absolutes and spiritual assumptions which have been so influential in Western civilization are now widely rejected or ignored. The institutions and artifacts of the mass society seem to undercut Christian beliefs on every level, so that Christians feel beleaguered by their own culture. One way for Christians to find the cultural support they need is to draw on the great literature of the past.

Books that have survived the most difficult test, the test of time, tend to be greater in every sense than the fleeting here-today-gone-tomorrow titles of current bestseller lists. In graduate school I helped a professor in a research project involving nineteenth-century literary periodicals. One of them featured a glowing story about a novelist I had never heard of. From the description of this acclaimed writer's work, it appeared that her novels were typical Victorian melodramas, full of noble heroines, sinister villains, and stock sentimental plotlines. In the same issue was a list of books that the editors had received for review, but which received no mention. One of them was *Moby Dick* by Herman Melville.

The reviewer who was so taken with a stock melodrama and oblivious to *Moby Dick* was unable to discern greatness amidst the swirling but soon-changing fashions that can so dominate the taste of an age. Time has a way of winnowing out inferiority. Often works that are hugely popular at one time owe their success to the fact that they were put together solely to cash in on a passing trend. When the trend passes, the former bestseller appears dated. The formulas are painfully obvious, and the once fashionable language now seems comical (on the order of the startlingly wide ties on Bob Newhart reruns or an adult using the slang of his adolescence to try to impress teenagers). Artistic excellence, on the other hand, outlasts the trends. Works that speak to the human condition are universal in that the deepest human joys and struggles never change. What survives the test of time is what can appeal to every age.

We might wonder what literature of today will still be read in fifty years. Reading the bestseller lists of the past, even the recent past, will show how books that were once hailed and imitated turn out now to be embarrassments. (Remember *The Greening of America? Power Lunching? 100 Uses for a Dead Cat?*) What on the paperback racks or bestseller lists today will survive the test of time?[1] The very question can help us to sort out literature of quality from that that is merely trendy and soon will be passé.

We are probably too close to our own time to really be good judges of our culture and its artifacts. The nineteenth-century reviewer did not see that his taste was dominated by the limitations of his age. We need to be able to step outside of our time, looking at it from a distance, in order to view our own age objectively. We can do this by reading old books.

C. S. Lewis, in an essay entitled "On the Reading of Old Books," explains the importance of maintaining a perspective on one's own time:

> Every age has its own outlook. It is specially good at seeing certain truths and specially liable to make certain mistakes. We all, there-fore, need the books that will correct the characteristic mistakes of our own period. And that means the old books. All contemporary writers share to some extent the contemporary outlook—even those, like myself, who seem most opposed to it. . . . We may be sure that the characteristic blindness of the twentieth century—the blindness about which posterity will ask, "But how *could* they have thought that?"—lies where we have never suspected it, and concerns something about which there is untroubled agreement between Hitler and President Roosevelt or between Mr. H. G. Wells and Karl Barth. None of us can fully escape this blindness, but we shall cer-tainly increase it, and weaken our guard against it, if we read only modern books. Where they are true they will give us truths which we half knew already. Where they are false they will aggravate the error with which we are already dangerously ill. The only palliative is to keep the clean sea breeze of the centuries blowing through our minds, and this can be done only by reading old books.[2]

This is not to say that the old books are infallible. The point is, their mistakes will not be the *same* mistakes of our own age, and, with our perspective, the errors of the past will be easy to see. "They will not flatter us in the errors we are already committing; and their own errors, being now open and palpable, will not endanger us."[3]

Reading the works of statesmen such as Madison and Jefferson is an instructive exercise in an age in which politics has become relatively debased. That these great theorists of equality, freedom, and democracy also tolerated slavery is a jarring discord. From our perspective two hundred years later, we can see the contradiction that they were too close to and too culture-bound to notice; we can recognize their errors without rejecting their insights. Future generations may well look upon our own times, with our tolerance for sexual license and abortion, with the same revulsion we feel for ancient barbaric tribes, with their human sacrifices and blood feuds. The theory of evolution may one day seem as scientifically primitive as the theory of the earth being the stationary center of the universe.

"To be sure," says Lewis, "the books of the future would be just as good a corrective as the books of the past, but unfortunately we cannot get at them."[4] To maintain this "corrective" perspective on our own time, Lewis goes so far as to recommend reading at least one old book to every three new ones.[5]

From the fall of Rome through the seventeenth century, Christianity dominated the art, literature, and intellectual life of the culture. Paradoxically, these were often difficult times for genuine Christianity. Cultures as such cannot be Christians—only individuals enlightened by the Holy Spirit can have faith in Christ. Sometimes a religion that becomes wholly intertwined with its culture becomes false and idolatrous, confusing cultural customs and institutions with spiritual truth. Nevertheless, despite doctrinal disagreements and confusions, the culture accepted the basic authority of a Christian worldview. The greatest minds and the greatest writers worked within its framework.

THE MIDDLE AGES: THE RISE OF BIBLICAL DRAMA

The Middle Ages were the era of Dante, Chaucer, the fairy tales, and the comic sense of life. This was the age of the romance, the tales of high adventure and courtly love, exemplified in the King Arthur sagas. Another important literary achievement was the re-invention of drama. An ancient literary form which has survived technological change, drama today flourishes in the new media of film and television. Ironically, modern drama owes its life and its form to the Bible and to the Christian church.

The Greeks, of course, had developed drama from its origins in religious ritual into an exquisite art form. The Romans carried on the Greek dramatic tradition, but they began to depart from its canons of taste and decorum. Whereas the Greeks forbade the portrayal of violence onstage, the Romans in their late decadence reveled in bloody spectacle. Roman drama degenerated to the point that condemned criminals would sometimes be made to play a part in a play. When the time came for a death scene, the actor/criminal would actually be killed. The audience no doubt was greatly amused by such a realistic touch. Today our special-effects technology is superior to that of the Romans, but our fondness for horrific violence in movies is no different morally or aesthetically.

When Rome fell, drama disappeared, and no one really missed it. Drama had to be re-invented. Just as Greek drama grew out of religious rituals, modern drama grew out of Christian worship. Medieval church worship was liturgical, consisting largely of texts of Scripture recited by the priest and the congregation. The liturgy also prescribed actions, both on the part of the congregation (kneeling, making the sign of the Cross) and on the part of the priest (reenacting the Last Supper in the Mass). Such liturgical worship had dramatic elements, but it was not drama in the sense of acting out a complete story. One Easter morning, however, a new liturgy was introduced, and Western drama came into existence.

Remarkably, we have the actual eleventh-century text that preserves for us the very beginning of modern drama. These liturgical instructions are short enough to quote in full:

> While the third lesson is being chanted, let four brethren vest themselves. Let one of these, vested in an alb, enter as though to take part in the service, and let him approach the sepulchre [the altar] without attracting attention and sit there quietly with a palm in his hand. While the third respond is chanted, let the remaining three follow, and let them all, vested in copes, bearing in their hands thuribles with incense, and stepping delicately as those who seek something, approach the sepulchre. These things are done in imitation of the angel sitting in the monument, and the women with spices coming to anoint the body of Jesus.
>
> When therefore he who sits there beholds the three approach him like folk lost and seeking something, let him begin in a dulcet voice of medium pitch to sing, "*Whom do you seek?*" And when he has sung it to the end, let the three reply in unison, "*Jesus of Nazareth.*" So he, "*He is not here. He has risen as He said. Behold, know that He has risen from the dead.*" At the word of this bidding let those three turn to the choir and say, "*Alleluia! The Lord is*

risen!" This said, let the one, still sitting there and as if recalling them, say the anthem, *"Come and see the place."* And saying this, let him rise, and lift the veil, and show them the place bare of the cross, but only the cloths laid there in which the cross was wrapped. [The crucifix on the altar would be covered with a black veil during Lent and removed on Good Friday.]

And when they have seen this, let them set down the thuribles which they bare in that same sepulchre, and take the cloth, and hold it up in the face of the clergy, and as if to demonstrate that the Lord has risen and is no longer wrapped therein, let them sing the anthem, *"The Lord Has Risen from the Tomb,"* and lay the cloth upon the altar. When the anthem is done, let the prior, sharing in their gladness at the triumph of our King, in that, having vanquished death, He rose again, begin the hymn, *"We Praise You, O Lord"* [*"Te Deum Laudamus"*]. And this begun, all the bells chime out together.[6]

This service was for Matins on Easter morning—in effect, the Easter sunrise service. The worshipers, who themselves had gotten up early on Easter morning to come to church, were witnessing what took place in history on that first Easter morning. The gestures and responses of the liturgy here crystalize into the acting out of a *story*, an episode from the Word of God. On that particular Easter morning, drama, once the province of pagan culture, was born again.

This Easter service was so moving and so popular that a similar service was devised for Christmas, with the shepherds trooping into the church searching for the Christ child. A veil would be drawn back from the altar to reveal a picture of Mary holding her child. Soon these liturgical dramatizations became more elaborate with costumes and more complicated actions. (The Christmas programs of today with their shepherds in bathrobes and angels in white robes and tinsel crowns go back all the way to the medieval church and to the very origins of modern drama.)

Soon these plays became too long and ambitious to fit within the confines of a church service. They moved outside. Eventually, someone had a brilliant idea. Why not dramatize the whole Bible? Few people could read; Bibles, which had to be copied out by hand, were hard to come by. Why not act out the major stories of the Bible as a way of teaching the common people the Scriptures? This ambitious enterprise led to the performance of "mystery plays," so called because they portrayed the "mystery" of salvation.

On the Feast of Corpus Christi, the whole population would gather along the streets of the cities. A wagon decorated to form a mobile stage known as a "pageant" would proceed down the street and at intervals would come to a halt. An actor wearing a golden mask would declaim the Creation of the Universe. The pageant would then move on to replay the Creation for the audience further down the street. The next pageant would roll into position. It would portray Adam and Eve, tempted by the Devil until they plucked the fruit (represented by an apple, which is probably why people still today associate the forbidden fruit with apples). Next would come a pageant showing Cain and Abel. Then Noah and the Flood—this was a time for a little comic relief. Noah would be portrayed as a henpecked husband who must drag his nagging wife kicking and screaming into the Ark.

And so on, in various configurations, to the coming of Christ, the Christmas story, the crucifixion, and the resurrection. The final pageant would represent the Last Judgment, as devils in red suits and pitchforks (another survival of the folk memory) would gather up sinners and drag them into Hell (an open trap door in the wagon complete with smoke and artificial flames). The saved would be ushered by angels into Heaven. (They climbed up a ladder onto a raised platform where the gold-masked figure awaited them.)

These dramatic processions are preserved today in the institution of parades. Elaborately decorated floats—the remnants of the pageants—pass by the throngs of people watching along the street. In fact, we still speak of "Easter Pageants," "Christmas Pageants," and even "Rose Bowl Pageants," reflecting the impact of the mystery plays on our folk culture. More importantly, these plays drawn from the Bible directly determined the form and the possibilities of Western drama. There is scarcely a movie or a television show today that does not owe a debt to these mystery plays and through them to the Bible.

Classical theater required drama to obey the unities of time, place, and action, and to observe careful principles of decorum. The old Biblical plays threw out such rules, giving Western literature a legacy of dramatic freedom.

For the Greeks, the unity of time meant that the time elapsing in the plot should roughly correspond to the actual time of the performance. If an audience would sit through two hours in the theater, then the play should show two hours in the life of its characters. Portraying a character's life from birth to death or his adventures over many years was forbidden (although the rules were relaxed somewhat to allow the portrayal of at most one day in the life of the character). The unity of time does give classical drama a concentrated focus that is one of its many strengths. The audience intensely identifies with the action on stage. The unity of time is still sometimes employed to great effect, as in the classic western movie *High Noon*. (Gary Cooper's wedding day is interrupted by the news that his revenge-driven enemies are arriving on the next train at high noon. We watch what he does in the hour and a half before they arrive as the suspense builds and the camera keeps cutting away to a clock ticking closer and closer to the showdown.)

The mystery plays, on the other hand, showed dramatists how to play with time. The audiences watched the whole scope of human history from the Creation to the Last Judgment in the course of an afternoon. Time could be compressed dramatically—years or centuries could be skipped between pageants or later simply by changing the scene. Today, dramatists are free to portray time in an expansive way. Playwrights can survey a character's entire life. Flashbacks in which a scene from the past alternates with scenes from the present are commonplace. Films such as 2001 can begin with the Stone Age and jump to space ships in the remote future. We are not confused by such chronological manipulation because of the imaginative precedent set by Biblical drama.

Another unity of classical drama was that of place. The setting of the play was restricted to one location—a particular house, a palace, or a single spot outside the walls of a city. One could not jump from Thebes to Delphi and back again. To do so, the Greeks felt, was disorienting to the audience. As always, the Greeks were working with a sound aesthetic principle. Clumsily constructed television programs or poorly edited movies often become confusing in the way they cut from one place to another without adequately orienting the audience to the new setting. If the audience has to ask, "Where are we, anyway?" its imaginative participation in the scene is lost. The Biblical plays which effortlessly conveyed their audience from Eden to Egypt to Palestine showed how diverse places could be imaginatively represented without confusion. Modern drama can leap from city to city, nation to nation, and planet to planet because of the way the early Biblical plays trained the imaginations of its audience.

Greek drama also required a unity of action. This meant that there could only be one plot and that it should be as clear and straight forward as possible. Greek drama is surprisingly easy to follow even for modern readers. That is because the classical playwrights valued clarity, simplicity, and directness. There are no subplots, no digressions, no narrative dead ends—only a sequence of cause and effect events that unfold at a brisk and riveting pace. Again, modern dramatists can learn from the Greeks, who would not have tolerated the labyrinthine soap opera storylines that juggle subplots for every character but lack a single unifying story. Nevertheless, soap operas would not have been conceptually possible were it not for the mystery plays, which portrayed the overarching story of God's saving work through a series of separate narrative episodes. A skillful dramatist now can work with several plots in the same story, giving each character a personal plot, all of which are orchestrated into a larger, more complex unity.

Unlike Greek drama, the mystery plays did show violence—the murder of Abel, the crucifixion of Christ. Biblical plays set a precedent that is abused today, but still is part of the legacy of dramatic freedom bequeathed to the culture. There is nothing morally wrong with the fencing scene in *Hamlet*, a battle in a war movie, or a death scene when the story calls for a character to die. The Greek perception that extreme violence can be an aesthetic distraction is still valid, although the problem is not so much the violence itself but how the violence is portrayed and what its effect is on the audience.

The principle of decorum had other applications. Characters in Greek drama had to behave in ways appropriate to their station. Kings had to be treated like kings—with dignity and respect. A Greek tragedy would never have a king slipping on a banana peel or otherwise being mocked. Shepherds, on the other hand, could be the butt of jokes, as could foot soldiers and slaves. The Greeks, because of their worldview and class consciousness, were always more interested in types than individuals, so they enforced the decorum of character by having their actors wear masks. When the Greeks attended a tragedy, they did not see the face of an individual actor, whom they might recognize as good old Parmenides from the marketplace. This would be another distraction. Rather they would see stylized kings and commoners undergoing universal human struggles.

What we moderns value in acting, on the other hand, is a sense of individuality. Movie stars—such as John Wayne, Marilyn Monroe, and Eddie Murphy—convey the same personality no matter what role they are playing. Their fans are fascinated by the actor rather than the part, and so will flock to their next film no matter what it is about. More accomplished actors and actresses—such as Dustin Hoffman and Meryl Streep—lose themselves in the roles they are playing, submerging their own personalities in the personalities of the characters. In either case, whether we are watching a popular celebrity or a virtuoso character actor, we respond to the people on stage or screen as if relating to individual, unique human beings. The effect would be spoiled if they were wearing masks.

In the mystery plays, only God wore a mask; people of the Bible were portrayed as distinct individuals in all of their humanness. The value of every person as a unique child of God is an important legacy of Christian thought. The plays based upon the Bible reflected the Biblical worldview in their individualistic characterizations.

The rigid class system of the Greeks did not carry over into the Biblical plays. Kings themselves are under the sovereignty of God and are subject to His law. Herod, the king who tried to murder the Christ child, was portrayed as a ranting lunatic whose bombastic language degenerated into a royal temper tantrum. The character of Herod became a byword for comic overacting (as in Hamlet's criticism of actors who "tear a passion to tatters" and so "out-herod Herod"),[7] and was a great crowd pleaser for the peasants who lined the streets. Despite their rank, Herod and also Pilate were castigated and ridiculed for flouting God's Word. Notice how the Biblical heritage strikes at the root of class distinctions and how very early it was providing the conceptual basis for democratic freedoms.

The other characters too were lively and realistic. Long-suffering Noah and his nagging wife; faithful but anguished Abraham about to sacrifice his precocious little boy; the shepherds at the Nativity, as rowdy and as sinful as the real shepherds in the audience, who could thus identify with the Biblical story and relate it to their own lives. (Perhaps the best of the surviving mystery plays is *The Second Shepherd's Play*, whose comic realism was discussed in chapter 6.)

In these plays, the comical and the serious were shamelessly mixed, which would have outraged the Greeks as an offense against aesthetic unity, but which reflects the texture of ordinary life. The final pageant, the Last Judgment, established for believers the happy ending. The mystery plays constituted a comedy.

These Biblical plays soon developed into other forms. They began to be performed on stationary stages in the courtyards of inns. "Miracle plays" were the next step, portraying Christian teaching by means of allegory, a symbolic narrative, as in the masterpiece *Everyman*. Saints' lives and other instructive histories also came to be dramatized, so that the subject matter of drama grew beyond the boundaries of Bible stories. With the Reformation came distinctly Protestant mystery and miracle plays.[8]

The Renaissance rediscovered Greek culture. The intellectuals of the universities restored classical drama. Playwrights such as Ben Jonson reinstated and insisted upon the classical rules. In France, classicism was solidly established, so that even today classical dramatic conventions dominate French drama (which is one reason why many French films are so hard for English-speaking people to appreciate). So it might have been for England were it not for William Shakespeare.

Shakespeare's genius is such that some have questioned whether this ordinary middle class man with little formal education could have written these masterpieces. Surely the man from Stratford must have been only a front for the true author of the plays. The actual playwright must have been a nobleman. He must have been a university-educated intellectual. Two facts, however, are certain about Shakespeare. He could not have been a nobleman. What great work has a nobleman ever produced? The best literature has always been written by ordinary middle class people who are in closer touch with life than the insulated and pampered aristocracy. Nor could he have been highly educated. The university-educated playwrights such as Ben Jonson were all writing plays modeled after Greek and Roman drama.

Jonson was too great a writer himself not to notice Shakespeare's genius, but he was maddened by Shakespeare's neglect of the rules. Shakespeare has plays that range widely over time and space. *The Winter's Tale* skips sixteen years between act 3 and act 4. *Anthony and Cleopatra* jumps back and forth alternately between Rome and Egypt. Shakespeare's plays all contain elaborate plots and tortuous subplots. His characters are not at all the types preferred by Jonson, but complex, unique, and endlessly fascinating individuals with psychological depths that critics are still exploring.

What Shakespeare did was to borrow elements from the Greeks (such as their idea of tragedy, their relatively secular subjects, their poetic language) and combine them with the realism and freedom of the native medieval tradition going back to the Biblical plays.[9] Shakespeare's synthesis of classicism and medievalism, the high and the folk culture, set the precedent for subsequent drama, which owes its scope and freedom ultimately to the Bible.

THE REFORMATION: THE RISE OF BIBLICAL POETRY

The Middle Ages in many ways were an era of wholeness. Faith, reason, and culture were not felt to be in conflict. Human beings knew their place in society, the world, and God's Kingdom. The spiritual realm and the material realm were distinct, yet integrated. Indeed the spiritual realm manifested itself in material terms. In the course of the Mass when the priest elevated the Transubstantiated Host, the worshipers actually felt themselves to be seeing God.[10] The papacy likewise manifested the spiritual authority of the church in tangible form. The Pope was seen as the Vicar of Christ on earth and as such was an earthly monarch as well as a palpable spiritual authority. This heartfelt closeness and accessibility of the spiritual realm engendered a broad moral and philosophical consensus that united Western Europe, providing a strong conceptual foundation for religious art and culture.

But the medieval synthesis was not without its problems. Attempts to fuse Christ with human culture generally result in the deification of human beings and human institutions. Original sin runs too deep. The temptation to trust in our own works for salvation rather than the free grace of God in Christ, the temptation to erect monuments to human pride rather than to submit wholly to the Word of God—such tendencies in our inmost nature subvert some of our best efforts to achieve wholeness in our lives and in our culture.

Evangelical Christians have perhaps not valued the Middle Ages enough. There were certainly devout believers in Christ throughout this era. The Gothic cathedrals, the religious art and literature, the insights of its great thinkers should impress us. We too try to integrate our faith with every other facet of our lives, and the Middle Ages suggest some of the possibilities for doing so as well as dangers to avoid.

For all of its achievements, the Middle Ages fell into decadence. The ideals of courtly love degenerated into adultery.[11] When given temporal power, the church became corrupt. Its mysticism decayed into ritualism, idolatry, and works-righteousness. The political and social order fostered by the medieval synthesis became oppressive and enslaving as the aristocracy claimed divine sanction to exploit the lower classes. As in ancient Israel, tangible and idolatrous images displaced the Word of God.

The Reformation recovered the Bible, cultivating a spirituality based on God's revelation through human language. The idea that a lowly peasant could have direct access to God by reading the Bible shattered the religious hierarchy of medieval culture. The Reformation was accompanied by the technological innovation of the printing press and the opening of schools to teach as many people as possible how to read. That the educated peasant could thus have access to every other kind of knowledge would eventually shatter the political hierarchy, making possible social mobility, economic enterprise, and political equality.

The spiritual significance of the Reformation came in its proclamation that salvation is achieved not by human actions, but by God's actions. Salvation need not be purchased by good works, much less by the literal purchase of indulgences or by other rituals. Rather, salvation is a free gift, offered by God's grace through faith in Jesus Christ. In Christ, the incarnate God Himself achieved the righteousness we need and paid the penalty for our moral failures. Medieval theology had great confidence in the power of the human will to do good and to choose to follow God. Dante describes himself ascending to God; George Herbert, on the other hand, describes God coming down to him.

The seventeenth century was a golden age for Christian poetry. Herbert has already been discussed. John Donne experienced a dramatic conversion, so that today he is famous both for his love poetry (some of it frankly immoral) and for his religious poetry. In the course of his transition from playboy to pastor (becoming one of the most spellbinding preachers of the age), he developed a style of writing known as "metaphysical poetry," filled with paradoxes, unusual figures of speech, and an honest human voice.

Consider again the sonnet "Batter My Heart," whose metrical pattern was discussed in chapter 5:

> *Batter my heart, three-personed God; for you*
> *As yet but knock, breathe, shine, and seek to mend.*
> *That I may rise, and stand, o'erthrow me, and bend*
> *Your force, to break, blow, burn, and make me new.*
> *I, like an usurped town, to another due,*
> *Labor to admit you, but oh, to no end.*
> *Reason, your viceroy in me, me should defend,*
> *but is captive, and proves weak or untrue.*
> *Yet dearly I love you, and would be loved fain,*
> *but am betrothed unto your enemy.*
> *Divorce me, untie, or break that knot again.*
> *Take me to you, imprison me, for I*
> *Except you enthrall me, never shall be free,*
> *Nor ever chaste, except you ravish me.*[12]

Here is the primal conflict between sin and grace. The speaker knows that of himself he cannot free himself from slavery to sin. Reason, although it *should* align him with God, is itself bound by sin. He is like a walled city taken over by an enemy (Satan), whose rightful ruler (God) is outside besieging the gates. Donne then takes the familiar secular device of the lovers' triangle and in the metaphysical vein twists it into a bold theological metaphor. He is like a woman engaged to one man, but in love with another. She is betrothed to Satan (just as we all belong to him under the law because of our sinfulness). God is the lover who must steal us away from our evil husband-to-be, despite his legal right to us. The paradoxes multiply: only if God enslaves us can we escape sin's slavery to find perfect freedom; only if God ravishes us can we be sexually pure.

Throughout the poem is the Reformation gospel: We cannot save ourselves. Everything depends upon God's initiative—the grace of God the Father, the action of the Holy Spirit in our hearts, the saving work of Christ who comes to be our Bridegroom (Revelation 19:7). The tri-une God must batter our hearts—He must break us to pieces and make us new; He must crash through the gates of our hearts; He must steal us away from Satan.

Such profound meditations can be found throughout seventeenth-century literature. Besides Herbert and Donne, poets such as Henry Vaughan, Thomas Traherne, and Richard Crashaw (a Roman Catholic metaphysical poet) reward close reading and demonstrate the spiritual range and aesthetic greatness of Christian poetry at its best.

DEVOTIONAL PROSE

The prose of the seventeenth century is nearly poetic in the depths of its language and its imagery. Sir Thomas Browne, a scientist and physician, wrote about his faith in *Religio Medici* ("The Faith of a Physician") and about death and immortality in *Hydriotaphia: Urn Burial.* Jeremy Taylor wrote *Holy Dying*, treating an urgent but now-neglected subject—how a Christian should prepare for death—in incandescent language.

Some of the best devotional prose is again by Donne. His *Devotions upon Emergent Occasions* were written during a serious illness which, as far as he knew at the time, might have proven fatal. At every stage, from the first faint symptoms through incapacitation, crisis, and recovery, he meditates upon the human condition in light of God's love. In its most famous and oft-quoted section, he is in his sickbed when he hears a church bell. He knows this is the "passing bell," which would be tolled when someone is dying to summon the faithful to prayer:

> Perchance he for whom this bell tolls may be so ill, as that he knows not it tolls for him. And perchance I may think myself so much better than I am, as that they who are about me and see my state, may have caused it to toll for me, and I know not that. The Church is catholic, universal; so are all her actions; all that she does belongs to all. When she baptizes a child, that action concerns me; for that child is thereby connected to that Head which is my Head too, and engrafted into that body, whereof I am a member. And when she buries a man, that action concerns me. All mankind is of one Author, and is one volume; when one man dies, one chapter is not torn out of the book, but translated into a better language, and every chapter must be so translated. God employs several translators; some pieces are translated by age, some by sickness, some by war, some by justice; but God's hand is in every translation; and his hand shall bind up all our scattered leaves again for that Library where every book shall lie open to one another. . . .
>
> No man is an island, entire of itself; every man is a piece of the continent, a part of the main. If a clod be washed away by the sea, Europe is the less, as well as if a promontory were, as well as if a manor of thy friend's or of thine own were. Any man's death diminishes me, because I am involved in mankind; and therefore never send to know for whom the bell tolls; it tolls for thee. . . .
>
> Another man may be sick too, and sick to death, and this affliction may lie in his bowels, as gold in a mine, and be of no use to him; but this bell, that tells me of his affliction, digs out and applies that gold to me, if by this consideration of another's danger, I take mine own into contemplation, and so secure myself by making my recourse to my God, who is our only security.[13]

Such a contemplation of the intimate unity that Christians have with each other as part of the Body of Christ (1 Corinthians 12:12-26) makes much contemporary devotional writing seem anemic in comparison. Those facing suffering or death can find far more comfort and sustenance in Donne or Taylor than in today's pop psychologists or positive-thinking theologians. The devotional classics of the past are treasures that deserve to be mined by contemporary Christians.

MILTON

Finally, we must consider Milton—a colossus of English literature and a paragon of Christian authors. He is an important role model for Christians because he violates so many of the stereotypes about Bible-believing Christians, both those imposed upon us by others and those we impose on ourselves. He was a staunch Puritan, yet a great lover of beauty. He was a fundamentalist in his view of Scripture, but also one of the most learned men of his day. (Some scholars think he must have read *everything* in print in his lifetime.) He was a spiritual man and also a political activist. He was a moralist who championed individual liberty. He was a conservative who took part in a revolution that overthrew a monarchy.

Far from being an "impractical poet," Milton worked tirelessly as an official in the new revolutionary government. He went blind in the midst of his career and struggled bravely to overcome his handicap. When the monarchy was restored, he was ousted in defeat, facing persecution and the collapse of everything he had worked for. At his life's lowest point, this blind exile from power wrote his greatest poetry by dictating it to his daughters. Milton in many ways was a fierce, difficult man, by no means without his faults, but he wrote some of the most sublime poetry.

Milton was not a prolific writer. Besides his epic poem *Paradise Lost,* he wrote one tragedy, *Samson Agonistes* (on the Biblical story of Samson), one brief epic, *Paradise Regained* (on the story of Christ's temptation), and an example or so of the other major genres of his day (*Comus*, an allegorical play known as a "masque"; *Lycidas*, a pastoral elegy mourning the death of a friend; a number of short lyric poems including sonnets such as "On His Blindness," in which he struggles to reconcile his desire to serve God with his physical handicap). Much of his literary energy was sacrificed to his political cause. He wrote tract after tract on the major issues of the new republic, including *Areopagitica* on the freedom of the press. The current events about which he wrote are no longer current, so their content is elusive for modern readers; but even in these political tracts Milton's prose style is so powerful in its rhythms and imagery that it can dazzle the reader.

Milton's greatest work is *Paradise Lost,* an epic poem on the pivotal event of human history—the fall of Adam and Eve. Writers are always seeking to explore the human condition; Milton does so by going to the very heart of the matter as revealed in the pages of Scripture. What the Bible succinctly states in the first three chapters of Genesis, Milton explores in thousands of lines of poetry. The fall of the human race entails also the fall of Satan, the creation of the universe, and the promise of redemption. Milton employs his imagination in a free yet Scripturally faithful way to contemplate what Scripture reveals about sin and grace.

Milton writes in an exalted style, characterized by long rhythmic sentences and an energetic intensity. He plays with the English language like Bach playing the organ. Consider these lines on Satan being cast out of Heaven:

Him the Almighty Power
Hurled headlong flaming from th' ethereal sky
With hideous ruin and combustion down
To bottomless perdition, there to dwell
In adamantine chains and penal fire,
Who durst defy th' Omnipotent to arms.[14]

Notice the audacity of starting a sentence with the direct object ("Him"). Milton's syntax owes much to Latin, but he makes it work for English and in doing so achieves some magnificent poetic effects. By positing the object of God's judgment in the first word, we can picture Satan falling, falling, through the course of the sentence—accompanied by fireworks all the way—until the end of the sentence binds him securely in Hell, concluding with a resounding statement of Satan's crime and his folly.

Milton's long narrative poem is perhaps best approached as a novel. The characters and their points of view are rendered with a Shakespearean complexity. We see Satan's perspective. When he says, "Better to reign in Hell, than serve in Heaven,"[15] we, sinners that we are, can understand and relate to his furious pride and rebelliousness. Milton imagines Satan as holding a council in Hell with all of the defeated demons (described in terms of the pagan gods of the Bible, from warlike Moloch to hedonistic Belial). Their one way to hurt an omnipotent God, they decide, is to seduce away from Him those whom He loves—the newly created human race. We next see the counsels of Heaven as the Father works all of Satan's malice into His saving plan through the work of His Son.

We then get to know Adam and Eve. The unfallen couple is innocent, yet not naive or simple-minded. They are both strong, intelligent, and in love with each other. They love too the lush world God has given them, and they love God. An angel visits them and provides flashback accounts of the war in Heaven and the Creation, rendered with Milton's sublime descriptions. Later, Satan, enraged by their happiness, assumes the form of a serpent. As Satan is deceiving Eve, the arguments seem so plausible that, putting ourselves into the scene, we can admit that we too might have succumbed. We can see our own complicity in her fall. Adam falls without being deceived, knowing exactly what he is doing, but choosing to reject God's Word. According to Milton, Adam does not want to be separated from the woman he loves. To share Eve's fate, he eats the fruit.

The result of this romantic but idolatrous gesture is hateful recrimination between the two of them, the breaking of all natural harmony, and the tragic flaw that underlies human history. Milton has Eve come to her now-hateful husband and in a memorable scene repent of the wrong she has done to him. Adam comes to his senses, and the two turn to God for mercy. God's judgment is tempered with the promise of salvation through the coming of His Son. An angel gives Adam a vision of subsequent human history, and the two must leave paradise in order to begin the human story.

Milton is giving his own interpretation of this familiar Biblical history. His poem should not be seen as authoritative in the way he imagines the details not stated in Scripture, but it can help us understand some of this event's implications and its human depths more fully. "Sublimity" refers to that aesthetic apprehension of vastness and grandeur, the mind-boggling awe we feel when we encounter something huge, approaching the infinite. Milton is the master of sublimity in verse. Whenever I see photographs taken of outer space, I think of Milton's lines about God in Creation, "brooding on the vast Abyss":[16]

> Boundless the Deep, because I am who fill
> Infinitude, nor vacuous the space.[17]

Christians need theologians to explain the Biblical text and to apply its truths, but Christians also need poets such as Milton who can help us imagine and contemplate those truths more fully.

Milton also illustrates how Christian writers can appropriate non-Christian styles and subvert them to service of Christian truth. Milton was writing an epic; therefore, he employed all of the conventions of the classical pagan epic. In doing so, he Christianized them. Epic poems had always begun with an invocation to the Muse (a goddess of artistic inspiration). Milton obeys the convention, but the Muse he invokes is the Holy Spirit. Epic poems had always dealt with warfare, descents into Hades, catalogues of warriors, and—above all—a hero who is the center of the action. Milton includes them all, but twists them into a Biblical context.

Many critics have insisted that Satan is the true hero of *Paradise Lost,* some going so far as to say that Milton, himself a rebel against a monarchy, "was of the Devil's party without knowing it."[18] Indeed, Satan does have many of the characteristics of the pagan heroes—their *hubris,* their violence, their manic over-reaching. In so portraying Satan, Milton is critiquing the pagan concept of heroism. In the poem, Milton explicitly rejects the pagan obsession with violent action as the only criterion for heroism, celebrating instead "the better fortitude of/ Patience and Heroic martyrdom."[19] To Milton, true heroism comes not in Satan's clamorous malice, but in humility and patience in the face of suffering. True "heroic martyrdom" is evident in the cross of Jesus Christ and in Adam and Eve when they accept their suffering and set out into the world in faith.

Milton thus devises a new kind of epic with Christian, as opposed to pagan, values. Milton accepts the aesthetic forms of classical poetry, drawing on their strengths and beauty, but at the same time he challenges their assumptions. Satan *is* like Achilles (the hero of Homer's *Iliad*), but in making him so, Milton shows that Achilles in his bloody self-pitying egotism must be satanic. Milton is writing a distinctly *Christian* epic, accepting the secular form in its own terms—even outdoing some of its best practitioners—but in the process he uncovers its errors and infuses it with Biblical truth.

In subsequent centuries, Christianity would lose its dominance in thought and culture. Yet in every age, Christian authors have, like Milton, been able to write in the prevailing styles while challenging their non-Biblical assumptions. The Christian writers to come, however, would continually refer back to and draw upon these earlier ages of faith to nourish their own imaginations.

THE ENLIGHTENMENT AND ROMANTICISM:
The Literature of Nature and the Self

*B*eginning with the eighteenth century and continuing into our own time, Western culture has been hurtling away from the Biblical view of life. The alternatives have come in quick succession. At first, each new worldview addressed the issues of its day and had a certain plausibility; but in time each has proven partial, unbalanced, and humanly disastrous. Each is soon answered by a new secular view of the world, which itself is soon challenged. The history of thought since the eighteenth century can well be summarized in the words of Scripture: "The first to present his case seems right, till another comes forward and questions him" (Proverbs 18:17).

Nevertheless, even the exploded worldviews of the past continue to shape people's thinking. The typical man on the street may know nothing of intellectual history and may have never heard of utilitarianism, pantheism, or existentialism. Yet he may very well live out these belief systems more consistently than the philosophers who formulated them.[1] To understand the crazy quilt of contemporary thought, one must know the alternative ways of thinking, and perhaps the best way to do so is through literature. History, philosophy, and concrete human life come together in literature. In an author's imagination, abstract ideas find expression in tangible forms, so that we can see more clearly their human implications.

Surveying the literature of these times also demonstrates the

strength and wholeness of the Christian perspective. Each new movement attacks Christianity for a different reason. Each seizes upon some
one truth (which Christians might agree with) and tries to build a
whole view of life around it to the exclusion of the more complex reality described by Scripture. They have taken Christ's seamless garment,
ripped it apart, and then tried to clothe themselves with the pieces.[2]
Conversely, Christianity provides a way to fit together the fragmented
pieces of truth. Christians can learn from a wide range of non-Christian
authors without falling into their errors. Studying literary history also
demonstrates how Christian authors in every age have responded to
their times with the truth of Scripture.

I have never been satisfied with the old nostrum that we should
study history to avoid the mistakes of the past. That is one good reason
to study history, but it is too negative. It denigrates the very real achievements of our ancestors. We should study history also to learn from the
accomplishments of the past. Besides unveiling human problems, literary
history helps us discover works of innate greatness which transcend their
times and which help us to transcend our time. The 1700s brought forth
an inhuman rationalism, but that century also saw the birth of the novel.
The 1800s brought forth a morbid concentration on the self which still
plagues us, but during this time imaginative poetry gained a new energy.
Both centuries, for all of their problems, saw revivals of Christianity and
produced Christian writings that have stood the test of time.

THE ENLIGHTENMENT

Unfortunately, the heights of the Reformation degenerated into the
catastrophic religious wars of the seventeenth century. Milton's experience has already been mentioned—the English Puritans led a revolution which overthrew and then executed King Charles I. The new
Christian republic, however, turned sour. Milton complained that "new
presbyter is but old priest writ large"; that is, the new religious leaders,
once they were in power, became as corrupt and tyrannical as the old
ones.[3] Utopian dreams always face the rude awakening of human sin.
England lived with the republic for a few years, but then, despite
Milton's pleas, reinstated the monarchy.

The result was a widespread reaction against Puritanism and religious fervor in general, which had led to such bloodshed. England's
Civil War was mild compared to the utter desolation wrought in
Europe by the Thirty Years War in which Catholics and Protestants
brutally massacred each other in the name of Christ. Although religion
was still vitally important in the culture, it was little wonder that across
Europe religious emotions began to prompt a fearful caution and in
some circles a mood of skepticism.

At the same time, the accomplishments of the human mind were accelerating. Phenomena that had baffled human beings for centuries were given rational explanations by the new science. When Newton explained the motions of the planets and gravity itself by a series of mathematical formulas, it seemed that everything could be understood by the power of human reason operating upon the data of the senses. In the words of Alexander Pope, a poet who was putting into words the sentiments of his age:

Nature and Nature's Laws lay hid in Night:
God said, Let NEWTON *be*: And all was Light![4]

God is still in the picture, but the creation of Newton seems to over-shadow the creation of the universe. The past has all been shrouded in darkness until now. With the advent of modern science, all mysteries are disclosed and "all is light." This assumption is the essence of the movement known as "the Enlightenment."

NEOCLASSICISM

The eighteenth century was more than just an "age of reason." If it was characterized by confidence in human reason, it was also characterized by skepticism toward all human knowledge (as evident in *Candide* by Voltaire, who demonstrates both an excessive trust in reason and an excessive skepticism). Some of the new thinkers, such as Leibnitz and Spinoza, spun forth elaborate rational systems; others such as Locke stressed empiricism, trusting the evidence of the senses rather than abstract reasoning. Others such as Hume subjected reason itself, as well as Christianity, to a withering skepticism. Still others such as Samuel Johnson and Jonathan Swift on behalf of Christianity subjected the skeptics to a withering skepticism. This was the age of the great conservative philosopher Edmund Burke, of the economist Adam Smith, of the authors of the American Constitution. The discovery of foundational scientific principles, the technology of the Industrial Revolution, and the establishment of American democracy were all begun in the eighteenth century. It was an age of undoubted achievement when ideas made a difference, even when they clashed.

A common thread uniting both conservatives and radicals of the time was a literary and artistic movement known as neoclassicism. This was a continuance of the reemphasis upon Greek and Roman thought that began with the Renaissance. Artistic styles often develop for their own reasons regardless of the intellectual milieu. Despite their contempt for the recent past, even radicals such as Voltaire loved the ancient past, holding up the ancient Greeks as models.

The complexities of metaphysical poetry and the sprawling scope of Shakespeare, both of which are filled with passion and ambiguity, were displaced by a new style. In accord with the Greek ideals, this new style was clear, simple, and elegantly constructed. Consider some more lines from Pope:

> A little learning is a dangerous thing;
> Drink deep, or taste not the Pierian spring:
> There shallow draughts intoxicate the brain,
> And drinking largely sobers us again.[5]

Compare these lines to those of Herbert or Donne. Pope's verse is lucid on first reading. Unlike the complex levels of meaning in a metaphysical poem, Pope's lines call for little if any interpretation. (The reference to the Pierian spring is a classical allusion to the spring of the Muses, goddesses of learning, and would have been easily recognized by the eighteenth-century reader.) There are no "hidden meanings." Everything is on the surface. There is humor and wit, but little passion. All is logical. The meaning itself is a shrewd insight based on common sense: a *little* learning can be dangerous as opposed to extensive learning. (As when a college freshman takes one introductory psychology course and then presumes to psychoanalyze all of her friends or when a man reads one book questioning Christianity and abandons his faith. In both cases, more courses and more books would reveal there is more to psychology and to Christianity than they dreamed of in their superficial acquaintance.)

Despite their apparent simplicity, the lines show the skill of a master poet. There is the paradoxical metaphor: learning is like drinking. The image first refers to water and then shifts to alcohol, whereupon it is turned upside down. When it comes to learning, drinking a *little* is intoxicating, but drinking a lot is sobering. The rhythm and rhyme scheme are characteristic of neoclassicism. Each line has the same regular rhythm (iambic pentameter), and each line rhymes with the next (a form known as "heroic couplets"). The effect is that each line seems to "clinch" its point—the poem is a logical, orderly mechanism that processes ideas into an engaging form.

One can see why neoclassicism was favored in the Enlightenment—its rationalism fit the spirit of the times, and the self-reliance of the Greeks corresponded to the emerging humanism. And yet conservatives and Christians employed a neoclassical style as well. The eminent hymn writer Isaac Watts—author of "Joy to the World," "When I Survey the Wondrous Cross," "Our God, Our Help in Ages Past," and many others—wrote in a neoclassical style that was greatly admired in his day. (Notice that in these hymns, however, Watts employs a logical style but feels free to appeal to human emotions, thus correcting the Enlightenment overemphasis on the mind alone. Like other Christian writers, Watts employs the dominant secular forms but challenges some of their assumptions. A good dose of neoclassicism might well be a good tonic for the obscurity, emotionalism, and formlessness of much contemporary writing.)

Neoclassicism meant the return of classical rules—the drama of the period follows the unities—but it also meant the clarification of prose. Up to now, most serious literature was written in poetic form, from the dramas of Shakespeare to the extended storytelling of Spenser and Milton. Prose was reserved, for the most part, for nonfiction—for history, philosophy, devotions, and record keeping, not works of art. English prose of the earlier centuries was sometimes ornate and quasi-poetic, sometimes pointed and terse. More often, in the hands of lesser writers, it was syntactically awkward and difficult to follow. The neoclassical emphasis on clarity and simplicity, exemplified in the prose of Dryden (d. 1700)—combined perhaps with the Puritan emphasis on "the plain style" of easily understood preaching and the new demands of scientific discourse—helped to turn prose into a flexible medium for communication.

THE NOVEL

As a result of the neoclassical penchant for clarity, combined with developments within the English language itself, books written during the eighteenth century are easily understood by modern readers. Even those who have problems understanding the King James Bible, published in 1611, will have little problem understanding Dryden, born a mere twenty years later. The newly invigorated medium of prose made possible two major literary inventions—the newspaper and the novel.

In 1709, Joseph Addison and Richard Steele began a publication known as *The Tatler.* Instead of being a book or a once-only pamphlet, *The Tatler* came out three times a week. Its successor, *The Spectator,* came out every single day. Addison and Steele did not invent the newspaper. It had developed in the seventeenth century as the need grew for people to keep up with the swirl of Civil War events and controversies. Addison and Steele, both superb prose stylists in the neoclassical vein, *did* establish the newspaper as a literary and cultural institution. Their early papers consisted of essays on art, ethics, and social life—not news in today's sense. But their success led to imitators and competitors and eventually to modern journalism.

Not only did Addison and Steele's clear, conversational prose become a stylistic model for subsequent writers, but their early newspapers were a way station in the development of modern fiction. Addison and Steele began a series of character sketches featuring familiar personality types such as the rake, the coquette, and the country squire. (This interest in character types was itself neoclassical, with precedents in Ben Jonson's comedies of humors.) Sometimes these characters would tell anecdotes about themselves; some of them such as the country gentleman Sir Roger DeCoverly were so amusing that they almost achieved a fictional life of their own. With the American writer Washington Irving, such journalistic sketches would in the next century develop into full-blown short stories.

The new field of journalism also begat pseudo-journalism. Daniel Defoe, a working class Puritan, was something of an early gonzo-journalist.[6] Hearing about a man who had just been rescued from a desert island, Defoe decided to make up an account that might appeal to the tabloid readers of his day. The result was *Robinson Crusoe* (1719). This tale, one of the best adventure stories in literature, was taken as fact by most of Defoe's readers. This was because, strictly speaking, realistic fiction had not been invented yet.

Some credit Defoe with inventing the novel either with *Robinson Crusoe* or with his later masterpiece *Moll Flanders* (1722), the rags to riches story of a woman's adventures in the London underworld until she makes her fortune in America. Defoe deserves credit as a literary genius, but these works are not quite novels. Technically, they are realistic prose romances.

The medieval romances had been tales of knights and magical adventures. They did not have a single plot developed throughout the narrative. Rather, they were episodic; that is, they consisted of a series of separate episodes rather than a single plot sustained through the entire book. Most of the King Arthur stories were originally in verse, although Malory's brilliant renditions gave a precedent for prose romance. The genre of the romance still involved strange adventures and supernatural events—in other words, they were fantasies. Swift's *Gulliver's Travels* (1726) was a prose romance, episodic in structure and wildly imaginative in its incidents.

Defoe's contribution to fiction was to make up realistic romances. *Robinson Crusoe* is unforgettably realistic, although the subject matter—being shipwrecked on a desert island—was a common motif in the old romances. Its plot, like that of *Moll Flanders*, is episodic with one fascinating day following the next, but without a unified action. Moll Flanders is one of the great characters of literature, but her story follows the model of the "picaresque" tales of Europe—episodic stories of lower class rogues—which were originally parodies of the upper class romances (as in the greatest of the genre, *Don Quixote* by Miguel Cervantes [1605]).

Before a novel—a long, sustained narrative about realistic people—could be written, writers had to overcome some formal obstacles. How could an interesting story be told about ordinary people? Tales of knights and dragons, supernatural adventures, doomed love, and exotic locales—these could lend themselves to exciting fiction. Defoe wrote about ordinary people who led extraordinary lives. Could there be fiction about the rest of us? If a story about ordinary folk could be managed without being too boring, how could it avoid being brief? How much is there to say about the events of an ordinary life?

The solution to these problems and the invention of the modern realistic novel came about almost through accident. Printer and journalist Samuel Richardson was asked by a publisher in 1739 to write a self-help book illustrating the proper way of writing letters. This was a time of great social mobility, and hundreds of country folk were coming to the city, acutely aware of their lack of education and their ignorance about the ways of London society. This book was to be, in Richardson's words, "a little volume of letters, in a common style, on such subjects as might be of use to country readers who are unable to indite for themselves." In addition, it would contribute to their social and moral education by showing "how to think and act justly and prudently in the common Concerns of Human Life."[7]

Richardson began by composing letters supposedly written by a young country girl named Pamela to her parents. Pamela has come to the city and is working as a maid for a wealthy aristocratic family. The reader follows her model letters and picks up tidbits of information about what it is like to be a servant in the big city. After awhile, the reader begins to notice that her master, "Mr. B____," is making improper advances to the poor girl. Pamela in her naivete at first does not seem to notice. Mr. B____ becomes more and more overt in his assault on Pamela's virtue until she finally realizes what is happening.

From this point, the stated purpose of offering model letters is forgotten. Richardson has introduced a conflict, all that is necessary for a full-blown plot. Pamela rebuffs the attempts to seduce her; Mr. B____ kidnaps her; he takes her to a sinister mansion in the country; she escapes. All the while Pamela is frantically writing letters (one wonders when she found the time).

Richardson published these letters in several volumes. As they were released serially, they captivated the nation. Nearly all of England was swept up in what was, in effect, the first soap opera. Ultimately, Mr. B____ , stealing her personal papers, manages to read Pamela's own account of her trials. In effect, the villain is reading the book in which he appears, the same book everyone else in England has been reading. (This first novel, paradoxically, thus becomes the first Postmodern novel!) The villain is moved by Pamela's goodness and appalled at his evil actions. Mr. B____ repents. He asks Pamela to marry him. She accepts. The servant girl, by preserving her virtue, becomes the wife of a nobleman, the ultimate social mobility. (Richardson then wrote a sequel—setting still another annoying precedent for popular literature—about her efforts to become accepted by high society.)

Despite the unlikely melodrama of the letters, Richardson inadvertently had invented the novel. He had solved the formal difficulties with the genre in a way that would prove a model for all other novelists. By conveying the story through a series of letters, Richardson presented a plot from the *point of view* of a character. The story was written in first person, as all letters are, giving Pamela's innermost thoughts about what she was experiencing. The focus therefore was on *character*. A story about ordinary people could be fascinating when the characters are fascinating—not so much because of the spectacular adventures they might have—but because the reader relates to them and cares about them. A long story could be written about the actions of ordinary people by delving into their minds. The letter format allowed Pamela to dwell on minute details, to turn them over in her mind and to think deeply about them. By going inside the characters through his pioneering experiments with point of view and character, Richardson broke the ground for the modern realistic novel.

Pamela (1740) was so successful that it created a booming market for more novels. Richardson wrote another collection of letters, *Clarissa* (1747), featuring letters from the villain as well as the heroine, allowing for a fascinating clash of points of view. Henry Fielding parodied Richardson in *Shamela* (1741), suggesting that his heroines were just money-grubbing manipulators. Fielding's *Tom Jones* (1749) dropped the letter format (a device to be known as an "epistolary novel"), finding that one could present a character's point of view directly, even with third person narration. Nothing more needed to be done. The novel was up and running.

The very beginnings of an art form often represent its most creative moments. Eighteenth-century novels are still delightful to read. Although works such as *Moll Flanders* and *Tom Jones* are a little bawdy at times, they assert a definite moral framework. They are almost all comic novels, filled with satire upon human foibles and an exuberant comic energy. I recommend Lawrence Sterne's *Tristram Shandy* (1760), one of the funniest and strangest books in English literature. It purposely breaks every "rational" rule (the preface does not appear until after Book III, chapter 20; the hero is not born until the middle of the book; chapters may be only one sentence long; pages may be blank or totally dark). The eighteenth-century novel perhaps culminates in the work of Jane Austen whose wit, mastery of construction, and insights into human relationships mark her as one of the greatest novelists of the English language. (*Pride and Prejudice, Sense and Sensibility,* and *Northanger Abbey* were written in the 1790s although they were not published until the first decade of the nineteenth century.)

Knowing something about the history of fiction is important for Christians because of what it implies for the historicity of the Bible. Some contemporary Bible scholars are arguing that the Bible is fiction, not history. We should read the Bible as a novel, they say, drawing out of it valuable themes without considering it to be historical. The novel, however, was not invented until 1739. Up until that time, with few exceptions, imaginary stories were written in poetry. Prose was reserved for fact. The realistic narratives of the Gospels, if they are not historical, would have anticipated the techniques of modern fiction by 1,700 years, which in itself would be miraculous.[8]

THE DARKNESS OF THE ENLIGHTENMENT

For all of the literary, scientific, and political achievements of the eighteenth century, it marked the beginnings of the eclipse of Christianity as a unifying worldview for the entire culture. Science had made such progress that it seemed everything could be understood by the scientific method. The universe began to be seen as a closed natural system of cause and effect. Every phenomenon must be understood in terms of a cause from within the system. Such a scientific methodology is useful in analyzing the processes of nature, but when it is applied to every sphere of life, it excludes any kind of transcendent reality. God is excluded; absolute moral values are negated; humanity is reduced to a cog in a machine, void of freedom, responsibility, and transcendent worth.

Seeking a rational religion, the Enlightenment devised an alternative to Christianity known as Deism. It began by offering a logical proof for the existence of God. Suppose you were walking in the woods, so their argument would go, and you found a watch lying on the ground. The watch is an intricate mechanism, full of little gears and cogs that work in a predictable and reliable order to measure the time. Would it be reasonable to think that such a complex machine sprang out of the ground from nowhere? The obvious design of the watch proves that there must be a designer, a mind behind the invention. A watch is evidence for a watch-maker. The universe itself is like a watch—indeed, it is far more intricately designed than any human invention, its tiniest parts working for the whole, operating in perfect harmony according to mathematical laws. The design of the universe is evidence for a Designer; the order that we see all around us is evidence for a Mind that is the source of the order. This designer, this mind, this cosmic watch-maker, is God.

So far, so good. Christians could agree with such an argument, and in fact it was first put forward by a Christian, William Paley. Enlightenment rationalism, with its emphasis on the meaning and order found everywhere in life, is very different from the modern view that life is empty and meaningless. And yet, the Deists went further with the metaphor. God, they implied, was like a watch-maker who made the watch, wound it up, and then put it on the shelf to run on its own.

According to the Deists, God does not intervene in His creation. To do so would be to imply some imperfection in the original design. The Deists rejected miracles because, for them, a miracle would imply that God did not do a good job in setting up the natural order. They rejected revelation, of course, on principle—the Bible was part of the irrational religious tradition that they were trying to replace through reason alone. They also rejected Jesus Christ—the idea that the Watch-maker would enter his machine was preposterous.

The first theorist of this "rational religion" was, ironically, Edward Herbert, the brother of George Herbert, the great Christian poet. Thomas Jefferson was a Deist. He went so far as to edit the New Testament, cutting out all of the miracles and other supernatural references. The religion found a church home in American Unitarianism. It continues today with the statistically large number of people who do believe in God, but who assume that God's existence does not really make any difference for their lives.

Interestingly, the Deists did believe in Heaven and Hell. Since the design of the universe is perfect, justice must be part of that perfection. We know that on earth, evil people often prosper and good people often suffer. There must therefore be a realm after death in which justice is meted out. What they rejected was the doctrine of original sin (that we are *all* by nature sinners) and the doctrine of grace (that God intervenes in Christ to grant us forgiveness and salvation despite our sin). The result of this minimizing of the gospel and consequent stress on good works as the only means of going to Heaven was a new legalism, one taught even in "progressive" Christian churches of the day.

Many of these churches did not go so far as Deism, but they were influenced by it. The Enlightenment marks the beginnings of liberal theology in Christendom. The historical-critical method of Biblical scholarship which continues to hold sway in mainline denominations and seminaries today was an Enlightenment invention. The assumption was that the Bible must be treated like any other ancient text and must be seen like everything else in terms of a closed natural system of cause and effect. The Bible must be explained by natural causes. Since we know that miracles do not take place in the closed natural system, then we must explain Biblical miracles as symbolic rather than realistic. If an Old Testament prophecy predicts the Babylonian captivity, that is seen as evidence (since predictive prophecy cannot occur) that the text must have been written *after* the Babylonian captivity.

Such a procedure begs the question of the Bible's authority. By assuming that the Bible is a purely human document, scholars ruled out any reason to consider it a sacred text. Today, Biblical scholars in the Enlightenment tradition ingeniously construct possible naturalistic explanations of the Biblical text, which are then presented with scholarly fanfare as the objective discoveries of modern research. The doctrine of the supernatural inspiration of Scripture and the possibility of the supernatural intervention of God into history are excluded with methodological rigor.[9]

This assumption of the closed universe—as opposed to the open universe of the Bible in which God interacts with and enters into a relationship with His creation—means a different way of looking at morality as well. Instead of looking to moral absolutes, as the Bible teaches, morality becomes nothing more than a mechanism for making the cogs of the cosmic machine move more smoothly. The new way of looking at ethics was termed utilitarianism. What is good is what is useful. If an action interferes with the smooth running of the social system, then it is bad. Stealing is bad, not because of God's transcendent law grounded in His own righteousness and the nature of existence, but because it disrupts the economic order. Again, a *tangible* reason for morality must be found from within the closed, observable natural order.

Utilitarian ethics could justify the inhuman treatment of child workers in the newly emergent Industrial Revolution by proving that subsistence wages, dangerous working conditions, and abysmally cruel treatment were necessary for the efficiency of the economy. Enabling children to work in factories gave them a useful social purpose. True, many of them might fall into the machinery, but safety devices would drain investment from more socially useful projects. Any apparent injustice to the individual would be subsumed in the big picture. The whole is more important than its parts. Reducing issues of right and wrong to purely utilitarian terms is commonplace today—many believe in abortion because it will reduce the welfare rolls.

Enlightenment rationalism ground up the individual in the cogs of the cosmic machine. Human emotions were held in disdain. Utilitarianism meant that the claims of the individual were overwhelmed by the requirements of the whole. Deism taught that the status quo was the perfect design of God, who remains utterly distant, inaccessible, and uncaring.

Pope wrote a poem whose purpose, similar to Milton's stated purpose in *Paradise Lost,* was to vindicate the ways of God to man, to somehow explain the purpose of human suffering. Whereas Milton had turned to Scripture for his answers, Pope employs pure reason. His conclusion is inevitable, but chilling:

> *All this dread Order break—For whom? For thee?*
> *Vile Worm!—O Madness! Pride! Impiety!*
> . . . .
> *Submit—in this, or any other Sphere,*
> *Secure to be as blest as thou canst bear.*
> . . . .
> *And spight of Pride, in erring Reason's spight,*
> *One truth is clear; "Whatever Is, is RIGHT."*[10]

The Enlightenment sought to free humanity from the ignorance of the past and to exalt human reason. In doing so, it chained humanity to an impersonal and inexorable system of Nature.

Writers tend to both reflect their age and to struggle against it. Pope himself, a Catholic and a political conservative, vented his skepticism against the more radical skeptics that were emerging. Samuel Johnson, composer of the first English dictionary and the dominant neoclassical critic of his day, was a devout, gospel-believing Christian. The sentimental melodramas of the novelists also helped to balance the one-sided rationalism of the intellectuals.

Jonathan Swift, for all his outrageous satire, was a conservative Protestant minister. In addition to reading about the big and little people of *Gulliver's Travels,* be sure to read the account of the Flying Island and the Academy of Lagado. Here, researchers try to extract sunshine from cucumbers and turn excrement back into food. Convinced that words are only names for things, linguists try to eliminate language by communicating with objects which they carry in a bag on their backs. Other scientists try to write all possible books by combining words in all possible orders with the aid of a machine that actually anticipates the modern computer. Swift's lampoon of scientism gone mad, still hilariously relevant, is a clear counterattack on the pretensions of Enlightenment rationalism.

Christians made themselves heard across the culture, addressing the blind spots of Enlightenment thinking. The utilitarianism that justified slavery was challenged by Christians such as William Wilberforce. The evangelist John Wesley led stirring revivals which brought thousands of spiritually starving children of the Enlightenment to a heartfelt faith in Christ. The mental disciplines of the Enlightenment also encouraged some orthodox theologians to systematize the truths of Scripture.[11] Eighteenth-century Christians were not of the Enlightenment, but they were in the thick of it.

ROMANTICISM

Enlightenment rationalism proved insufficient for the human spirit, which reacted against it to form yet another secular way of looking at the world. In the midst of the Enlightenment, William Blake—a mystic in an age of reason—was raving against the emotional and spiritual deadness of the age:

I wander thro' each charter'd street,
Near where the charter'd Thames does flow,
And mark in every face I meet
Marks of weakness, marks of woe.

In every cry of every Man,
In every Infant's cry of fear,
In every voice, in every ban,
The mind-forg'd manacles I hear.[12]

Blake, who goes on in the poem to attack the exploitation of children and the moral breakdown of society, wanted human beings to break the manacles forged by the overly rational mind, to experience the world in a very different way.

In another poem, which can almost be seen as an answer to Pope's lines on Newton, Blake addresses the key Enlightenment philosophers:

Mock on, Mock on, Voltaire, Rousseau:
Mock on, Mock on; 'tis all in vain!
You throw the sand against the wind,
And the wind blows it back again.

And every sand becomes a Gem
Reflected in the beams divine;
Blown back they blind the mocking Eye,
but still in Israel's paths they shine.

The Atoms of Democritus
And Newton's Particles of light
Are sands upon the Red Sea shore,
Where Israel's tents do shine so bright.[13]

The scientific reduction of the universe into particles is here transfigured. Newton and the others make the universe seem so small—Blake wants us to see its sublimity, its mystery, its place in a larger spiritual reality. Blake was a visionary, a professing Christian (although with his own idiosyncratic and not completely orthodox theology). He was a pioneer of romanticism, which—with the help of Wordsworth, Coleridge, Shelley, and a host of German philosophers—would dominate the century to come.

Briefly, romanticism turned the rationalism of the Enlightenment on its head. Nature is not a vast machine; rather, Nature is a living organism, suffused with mystery and beauty. God is not far away; rather, He is very close—indeed, immanent in Nature and in ourselves. Reason is not the most important human faculty; rather, emotion is what makes human beings most alive. Vast, impersonal systems are not the basis of morality; rather, individuals, in all of their uniqueness, determine morality in their quest for fulfillment.

The two poles of romanticism were Nature and the Self. The Enlightenment also stressed nature as the measure of rational order, but the Romantics spiritualized nature. They were captivated not by nature's order but by its wildness. They stressed, in a way no one had before, the beauty of nature—the awe-inspiring mountains, the serenity of the forests, the sublimity of a panoramic landscape. Knowing nature in a scientific way is fine, but that is not the same as "being in touch with nature" or "becoming one with nature," phrases that originated in the Romantic movement.

Nature was seen as the source of goodness. If we would only follow the harmony of nature, all would be well. A corollary of this idealization of nature is the concept of the "noble savage." Civilization was seen as corrupting the natural innocence of human beings; more primitive societies are closer to nature and are therefore morally superior to technically advanced societies. Children too were seen as noble savages. Children are born innocent and full of creative life; education squelches their creativity, and as they grow older they are increasingly corrupted by "society" (which became a bad word thanks to the Romantics). Children should not be disciplined, but should be free to express themselves and to grow as nature intends. Notice how Romantic assumptions are still evident in today's culture—from the natural food craze and the environmental movement to child-raising books and educational theory.

The Romantics also fostered a new emphasis upon the self. Passions and experiences began to be valued for their own sake. Introspection was emphasized, as was the quest for experience. Self-fulfillment was an obligation, the key to life's purpose. What is good is what fulfills the self; what is bad is what stands in the way of the self's fulfillment. Morality was seen neither as a matter of absolutes nor of what might benefit the whole; instead, it was seen in terms of "being true to oneself" and "finding fulfillment."

Shelley left his wife and children to find his personal fulfillment with Mary Godwin. His abandoned wife committed suicide. Similar scenarios have been repeated over and over in our present day. The self-fulfillment advice of pop psychology is nothing more than a remnant of Romantic egotism. Those who advocate abortion because a pregnancy might interfere with a woman's education or career or otherwise conflict with her plans for self-fulfillment are also exhibiting a Romantic ethic. Such moral solipsism is one of the worst legacies of romanticism.

The glorification of nature sometimes led to a neopagan worship of nature, sometimes manifesting itself in a pantheism similar to that of Hinduism or modern New Age mysticism, in which God, the Self, and Nature are all one. The glorification of the self sometimes led to self-worship, in which the individual assumes the qualities of God—creator, lawgiver, and redeemer.[14]

And yet romanticism did provide a necessary balance to the Enlightenment. The cultivation of the feelings as well as the intellect; the discovery of nature's grandeur and mystery as well as its scientific order—these were important correctives. Nor was the society as a whole ready to jettison traditional morality as some of the more radical Romantics were—the reigning monarch in England over most of the nineteenth century was, after all, Queen Victoria. Despite its excesses, romanticism invigorated literature and offered some distinctly Christian applications.

ROMANTICISM AND LITERATURE

Romanticism manifested itself in many different ways. Some Romantics, such as Wordsworth and the American poet Walt Whitman, expressed a joy simply in existing and celebrated the beauty inherent in ordinary life and everyday surroundings. Others, the "Dark Romantics" such as Byron, Shelley, and Poe were more questioning and cynical. When they focus on themselves, they find little reason for joy. Their work sometimes is melancholy and self-pitying, but they are often aware of the evil in the world and in human nature.

Romanticism was accompanied by an aesthetic revolt against neoclassicism. The neoclassical theorists saw artistic form as an external scheme imposed upon the material. If you want to write a play, you must follow the rules set down by Aristotle, including each of the unities. If you want to write a poem, you must choose a scheme of rhythm and rhyme (preferably heroic couplets) and squeeze your ideas to fit the form. In the landscape gardening of the eighteenth century, trees were pruned to rational geometric shapes—cubes, pyramids, and spheres.

The Romantics, on the other hand, tried to achieve an "organic form," a form that grew out of the life of a thing instead of forcing it into a predetermined artificial pattern. A tree does not need to be in the shape of a perfect sphere to be beautiful. A tree is already beautiful. That the branches go every which way, manifesting individual uniqueness rather than a symmetrical order, is part of its beauty. Whereas eighteenth-century gardens featured symmetrical walkways through sculptured trees and homogeneous plots of flowers laid out according to a grand design, nineteenth-century gardens featured winding paths through natural-seeming trees and scattered tracts of flowers. The Romantic authors tried to achieve this organic, living form in all of their writing.

In drama, this meant the rediscovery of Shakespeare. His rich language, elaborate plots, and meanings that elude simple rational analysis, as well as his energetic violation of the classical rules, made him a model of the "natural genius." His characters, explored in such depth, also appealed to the Romantic's interest in the self, in unique personalities and all of their inner depths.

In fiction, this meant the rediscovery of fantasy. In fact, romanticism gets its name from the medieval romance, the old sagas of knights and magical adventures that nineteenth-century writers found strangely moving. Whereas the Enlightenment scorned the Middle Ages, the Romantics were captivated by them. The Romantics were fascinated by the past. Sir Walter Scott invented the historical novel in medieval recreations such as *Ivanhoe* and strongly influenced early romanticism. Gothic novels—tales of haunted castles and eerie mysteries—became popular, appealing to the nonrational side of the mind. The canons of imitation and strict realism of the neoclassical authors gave way to the imaginative creations of fantasy. Edgar Allen Poe and Charlotte Brontë exemplify Romantic fiction at its best.

In poetry, the Romantics rejected the artificiality of neoclassical verse in favor of a more "natural" language. Wordsworth tried to bring the language of the common people into his verse. Writers conveyed their own personalities in their verse, writing about their own feelings and inner lives. Nature poetry was a distinctive of the Romantic poets, as was deeply reflective and personal verse. Keats excelled in both.

Perhaps ironically, it was the Bible that enabled the Romantics to unburden themselves of the neoclassical literary tradition and to forge a new aesthetic. The poetry of the Bible obeyed none of the classical rules. The psalms and the prophets seemed unorganized, overly passionate, and formless to neoclassical critics. The Romantics saw in Biblical poetry a model of "natural" verse—spontaneous, heartfelt, and sublime. Biblical poetry is based not on meter or other external patterns; rather, its poetic form is based on parallelism and internal devices. The Bible offered the Romantics a prime example of organic form.[15]

The Romantics also found in the Bible the concept of creation, as opposed to imitation (which, as we have shown, dominates classical aesthetics).[16] Coleridge stressed the role of the creative imagination in literature and developed the concept with Biblical analogies.[17] Since the prophets were poets, it followed for many Romantics that poets should play the role of prophets, speaking out boldly against social evils and claiming authority for their poetic insights.[18]

To be sure, this Biblical influence was often secularized and distorted. Some Romantics may have put their own "inspirations" on a par with the prophets inspired by the Holy Spirit; some may have put their creative power on a par with God's, exaggerating the role of the human mind in shaping the external world. Yet the Bible provided an authority great enough to outweigh that of the Greeks and Romans. After being minimized for a while by the Enlightenment, the Bible regained some influence on the culture.

ROMANTIC CHRISTIANITY AND CHRISTIAN ROMANTICISM

Christianity was challenged during the age of romanticism, but it also had its victories. Just as Deism led to one brand of theological liberalism in the church, romanticism led to a different brand, one just as harmful in its own way. The theology of Schleiermacher, a German theologian who became a major influence in modern theology, drained Christianity of its objective doctrinal content, reducing it to nothing more than subjective feelings.

On the positive side, romanticism promoted a new respect for the past, including the ages of faith. Many Romantics discovered the gospel. The novelist George MacDonald, whose fantasies "baptized the imagination" of C. S. Lewis, was a Christian whose emphasis on feeling and the creative mind reflect the age of romanticism. Francis Thompson can also be seen as a late Romantic, whose quest for experience led him to degradation until his conversion to Christianity. His autobiographical poem "The Hound of Heaven" portrays a soul running away from God, who relentlessly pursues the sinner to bring him to salvation. This dramatization of God's grace is one of the greatest Christian poems.

The story of Coleridge, the most important thinker of English romanticism, likewise shows the power of the gospel. Author of "The Rhyme of the Ancient Mariner" and "Kubla Khan," and collaborator with Wordsworth in the trend-setting *Lyrical Ballads* (1798), Coleridge was a poetic and philosophical genius. Whether because of the bungling medical practices of the time or because of the Romantics' ill-conceived quest for experience, Coleridge became an opium addict.

This addiction wrecked his personal life and inhibited his writing. He struggled vainly to break the habit. Coleridge then began reading seventeenth-century theologians. These early Anglicans, saturated with the spirituality of Luther and Calvin, stressed that salvation is by grace through faith and not by works. Coleridge came to realize the impotence of his will. He could not simply choose to stop taking opium—he had tried that, but he was still enslaved.

When his addiction brought him to his lowest point, he saw from bitter experience that the self glorified by the Romantics is radically incapacitated by sin:

> O I have seen, I have felt that the worst offences are those against our own souls! That our souls are infinite in depth, and therefore our sins are infinite, and redeemable only by an infinitely higher infinity; that of the Love of God in Christ Jesus. I have called my soul infinite, but O infinite in the depth of darkness, an infinite craving, an infinite capacity of pain and weakness, and excellent only as being passively capacious of the light from above.[19]

He cried out, "O! only for the merits, for the agonies, for the cross of my blessed Redeemer! For I am nothing, but evil—I can do nothing, but evil! Help, Help!—I believe! help thou my unbelief!"[20] The good news of God's unconditional grace in Christ broke through his guilt-ridden heart, and he found, as he put it, a "practical FAITH" as opposed to a mere intellectualized "speculative BELIEF."[21] Coleridge secured the care of a Christian doctor, who took him into his home and brought his addiction under control. He lived under the care of this family for sixteen years, the rest of his life, not trusting himself to leave their supervision. Coleridge, reinvigorated, became a sophisticated defender of Christianity.[22]

Wordsworth too became a conservative Christian toward the end of his life. In Europe, the Pietist movement, which emphasized personal religious experience, dovetailed in many ways with the Romantic emphasis upon individual experience and the cultivation of the emotions. Pietism was also related to the resurgence of evangelicalism in England and America. Even genuine Christians could be adversely affected by the spirit of their times. The Enlightenment mentality could result in a sterile, overly intellectual religion, while the Romantic mentality could result in over-reliance upon subjective emotions rather than upon the objective Word of God. Nevertheless, true balance of objective doctrine and subjective response could and did occur in both periods.

Another strain of romanticism led to a "high church" revival. The Romantics' fascination with the past, especially the Middle Ages, led some to a new appreciation of the ancient creeds and liturgies of the historic church. In England, the "Oxford Movement" led by John Henry Newman reemphasized liturgical worship and dogmatic theology against the religious emptiness of "broad church" liberalism with its hybrid of Enlightenment-era rationalism and Romantic subjectivism. Many influenced by this movement, including eventually Newman, became Roman Catholics. Their decisions often signaled a commitment to a supernatural Christianity which they did not find in their own Protestant church.

One such convert was Gerard Manley Hopkins. Although he wrote at the very end of the nineteenth century and is classified as a "Victorian" or even as a "Modern" poet because of his radically new style of writing, Hopkins seems to have developed a true Christian romanticism. A Jesuit priest, Hopkins wrote out of a deep personal devotion to Jesus Christ. His celebrations of nature and his explorations of himself (those Romantic concerns) were carried out in accord with a thoroughly Biblical worldview. Moreover, he outdid the early Romantics by crafting a genuinely original poetic style and a truly organic form.

In the poem "God's Grandeur," Hopkins writes about nature in a distinctly Christian way and in a form both strict and free, growing perfectly out of its content:

> *The world is charged with the grandeur of God.*
> *It will flame out, like shining from shook foil;*
> *It gathers to a greatness, like the ooze of oil*
> *Crushed. Why do men then now not reck his rod?*[23]

Hopkins employs distinctly modern and scientific metaphors to describe timeless truth. He begins with the metaphor of electricity. God's grandeur permeates the world like electricity charging an object. Electricity is invisible and does not change the appearance of the object, yet the power is real and palpable, as when it "flames out" in an arc that can knock us down. Hopkins switches to the related but more traditional image of light. He describes what a sheet of foil does to light, how the reflection, especially when the foil is shaken, scatters the light in free profusion. In the same way God's grandeur sometimes "jumps out at us" as we suddenly glimpse His presence in the world He has made. His presence is in the world like oil in an olive which is crushed to manifest its pure essence.

Thus far, Hopkins is writing about nature in a way that the Romantics would understand. Nature *is* glorious, as the Romantics perceived. God *is* very near, unlike the distant deity of the Enlightenment. And yet God is described as being distinct from nature as well as being intimately involved with it. God is both transcendent and immanent, as Christian orthodoxy has always proclaimed (see Acts 17:24-28).

The question with which Hopkins ends the stanza points to an issue that the Romantics, for all of their appreciation of nature, often forgot—human sin. "Why do men then now not reck his rod?" If nature is so glorious, so permeated with God's grandeur, why are people oblivious to it? Why do they not submit to God's loving discipline?

> *Generations have trod, have trod, have trod;*
>   *And all is seared with trade; bleared, smeared with toil;*
>   *And wears man's smudge and shares man's smell: the soil*
> *Is bare now, nor can foot feel, being shod.*

Human beings have become absorbed in their own narrow interests—the drudgery of their work, their exploitation of and their detachment from nature (acutely evident in the fact that we wear shoes, which keep us from feeling the soil we walk on). The underlying problem, Hopkins insists, is original sin, in which the fall of Adam has dragged down creation itself (Romans 8:19-22). The creation "wears man's smudge and shares man's smell." Our dirtiness has smudged nature; our smell pollutes the world. Hopkins's language with its unpleasant and embarrassing connotations is both theologically and metaphorically precise.

This stanza illustrates too Hopkins's organic form. He uses rhythm, rhyme, sound, and other devices of language to forcefully express and reinforce his meaning. The repetition in "Generations have trod, have trod, have trod," conveys the drudgery, the treadmill of everyday life, the same routine repeated over and over, which can obscure the beauty of existence. The rhyming within a single line of "seared," "bleared" and "smeared," words in which the sounds themselves run together in a rather ugly way, reinforce the dirtying effect of human activity on nature, like a child smearing mud on whatever he touches. Hopkins's alliteration, rhythm, and twists of language allow him to tie words together and to make them leap off the page.

Despite the unusual style and the free energy of the poetic form, "God's Grandeur" turns out to be a sonnet. Organic form does not mean being formless, at least for Hopkins. The first stanza describes the grandeur of God in nature; the second stanza describes the dull sinfulness of the human race which refuses to acknowledge that grandeur. In accord with the traditional sonnet form, these first eight lines set up a conflict. The last six lines convey the conflict's resolution:

And, for all this, nature is never spent;
There lives the dearest freshness deep down things;
And though the last lights off the black West went
Oh, morning, at the brown brink eastwards, springs—
Because the Holy Ghost over the bent
World broods with warm breast and with ah! bright wings.

Nature retains the God-given vitality and freshness that resides in its very core. Although the darkness increases (he describes the stars—"the last lights"—disappearing right before dawn), the sun joyfully leaps into the sky for a new day. (Compare the Bible's personification of the sun as "a champion rejoicing to run his course" [Psalm 19:5-6].) The metallic metaphor for sin (the "bent" world) is in contrast to the organic metaphor for the Holy Spirit (a warm and living Dove) whose love encompasses all of the creation.

Hopkins revels in the physical world not because of the nature-mysticism of the Romantics, but because he believes in the doctrines of the Creation and the Incarnation. His verse reflects the exhilaration of mere existence. He praises God for the uniqueness of each creature, for the variegated texture of the created order, "for all things counter, original, spare, strange."[24] Hopkins can write with an infectious joy, and his poetic range is such that he can also write about suffering—"The Wreck of the Deutschland," about nuns perishing in a shipwreck, and the "sonnets of desolation," about his own depression and spiritual struggles. Throughout his poetry, insights will flame out. On the resurrection of the redeemed at Christ's return: "In a flash, at a trumpet crash, /I am all at once what Christ is, since he was what I am."[25] On the presence of Christ in others:

. . . . *For Christ plays in ten thousand places,*
Lovely in limbs, and lovely in eyes not his
To the Father through the features of men's faces.[26]

Hopkins also illustrates that a Christian writer can be innovative and original. He was not afraid to experiment with the music of language and the metrical techniques of poetry writing. Nor did he hesitate to express his Christian faith in fresh language and contemporary metaphors. Hopkins shows how a Christian writer can address the imagination and the concerns of the age without sacrificing Christian doctrine to the partial, unbalanced worldviews of the time.

The Enlightenment grasped an important truth: God created and transcends the world. Romanticism also grasped an important truth: God manifests Himself in and is intimately involved in the world and in the inner life of the self. The Enlightenment and romanticism contradict each other, but Christianity provides a framework for upholding the insights of each while avoiding their errors. This is why Christian readers can profit from reading authors from both periods, allowing them to balance and complement each other, challenging them and integrating them in terms of Biblical truth.

MODERNISM
AND POSTMODERNISM:
The Literature of Consciousness
and Self-Consciousness

Worldviews do not go away. Belief systems that emerged from a specific historical context tend to stay in a culture, even when the forces that brought them into existence have faded. Today, there are many Deists, although they may not recognize the term. Multitudes believe in "a God," but they do not allow that belief to make a difference in their lives. Theirs is a distant deity who leaves them alone. Many more are Romantics. The environmental movement and the natural food craze, for all of their scientific analysis, are fueled by the Romantic view of nature. The self-absorption and emotionalism that characterizes our culture today are direct legacies of romanticism. Contemporary pop psychology—with its ethic of self-fulfillment, its emphasis on "getting in touch with your feelings," and its "you-create-your-own-reality" ideology—reads like a parody of romanticism at its most naive.

Ours is an age of pluralism when many worldviews exist side by side. Sometimes they compete with each other. Other times people slide back and forth from one to the other without awareness or consistency. Christians too can easily slip out of a Biblical framework to pick and choose from the philosophical smorgasbord of twentieth-century culture. I have heard people I know are committed Christians articulate utilitarian ethics when it comes to politics and Romantic ethics when it comes to themselves. Reading literature can sharpen our awareness of other people's thinking and of our own.

Contemporary pluralism has led many to question whether there is absolute truth. So many worldviews exist—can any of them be true? Is there objective truth? The conventional wisdom now is that truth is relative. Every generation, every culture, even every individual has different beliefs. What is true for one person may not be true for anyone else. Tolerance is the only virtue. Different lifestyles and beliefs should all be accepted in a pluralistic society. The only exception would be "narrow-minded" and "intolerant" people who "seek to impose their ideas on everyone else." Philosophies that do still cling to the idea that truth exists, such as orthodox Christianity, are thus excluded from the canons of tolerance.

More thoughtful pluralists push their conclusion to its logical end, to complete skepticism that ends in despair. If there is no truth, or if truth is inaccessible or irrelevant, then there is no meaning. Life is futile, a cruel joke, a pointless interlude between nonexistence. Good writers tend to be honest, and in the twentieth century we see authors pursue the assumptions of the culture to their bitter end.

Human beings, as Francis Schaeffer has shown, cannot live consistently with their non-Christian presuppositions.[1] God is the author of humanness and reality, and efforts to evade Him can only result in tension and contradictions between one's life and one's beliefs. The twentieth century has been characterized by change as people try one way of looking at the world and then another, discarding one philosophy only to take up another. They are searching, not necessarily for God—their desire to cling to their sinning impels them rather to run away from God—but they are desperately seeking some kind of meaning for their lives and some kind of happiness. They do not know that it is God they really seek and that in the maze of their futile quests, God is searching for them.

We may have passed into a "post-Christian" culture, but Christianity has never been more relevant. There is a profusion of facile alternatives to faith, from the ego-building pop psychologies to the full-blown neopaganism of the New Age movement. These new religions are growing in influence and appeal. And yet our age in its honest moments admits its lostness. Jesus Christ, "the same yesterday and today and forever" (Hebrews 13:8), speaks to every one of its needs. Christians must avoid the temptation to become just another self-contained interest group, one of many "pluralistic" alternatives, and learn how to address this post-Christian culture in its own terms with the gospel of Jesus Christ. Modern and contemporary literature makes clear the terms of our culture, and Christian authors are already demonstrating the modernity of the Biblical faith.

NATURAL SELECTION

The Romantic trust in Nature and the Self was shaken to the core in the latter half of the nineteenth century. The first blow was dealt by Charles Darwin, whose *On the Origin of Species by Natural Selection* (1859) shattered the Romantic view of nature. We often think of Darwin's theory of evolution as challenging Christianity, which it did, but its impact upon romanticism was even more devastating. Theories of evolution existed before Darwin; in fact, the idea of "progress," that nature, the individual, and societies are getting better and better was part of Romantic idealism. In that sense, Darwin's theory of evolution was simply a manifestation in the field of science of the Romantic belief in progress.

What undercut romanticism was the mechanism by which this progress occurred. Evolution takes place, Darwin argued, by natural selection. Animals compete with each other for survival. The animals that cannot adapt die out in the competition for survival while the most successful pass on their traits to the next generations. The fundamental law of nature to which species including the human race owe their existence is the survival of the fittest. Contrary to the assumptions of the Romantic nature lovers, nature is not a realm of perfect harmony. Rather, it is a realm of violent competition. Nature is not peaceful and serene. It is merciless and cruel. Tennyson refers to "Nature, red in tooth and claw."[2]

Darwin's theory is also a manifestation of the culture, in this case the burgeoning capitalism of the day with its ideals of free-market economic policies and untrammeled competition. What may be perfectly valid in the realm of economics may not be valid biologically or morally. People were right to appreciate the marvels of a free economy; the heady economic expansion caused many, though, to see in the laws of economic competition the meaning of life itself. The law of the jungle became the law of the marketplace; the origin of wealth was extrapolated to explain the origin of species. Natural selection became the keystone of a new materialistic worldview.

Social Darwinism, the application of Darwin's theories to social policy, manifested itself in many forms. Nineteenth-century industrialists used it to justify ruthless business behavior. Today, many political conservatives are followers of Social Darwinism even in its attacks on Christianity. The "libertarians" who stress that no restraints should be put upon the individual are, for the most part, followers of Ayn Rand. Her philosophy is summed up in the title of one of her books, *The Virtue of Selfishness*. Ayn Rand's militant atheism manifested itself in brutal attacks on Christianity. Her main argument is that by teaching love, Christianity weakens society, in which the strong should prevail and the weak should die out.

Social Darwinism also can take an anti-capitalist form. According to Karl Marx, conflict between social classes—not individuals—is the essence of human history. The middle class threw off the feudal class in the revolutions of the eighteenth century, and soon the middle class must be overthrown by the workers. These class conflicts constitute an evolutionary struggle that will someday culminate in a classless society, the utopian paradise of the progressive's dream.

Another manifestation of Darwinism in the late nineteenth and early twentieth centuries was the attempt to relate politics and biology by means of racial theories and eugenics programs. If human beings are only animals, and if progress can only come from the survival of the fittest, then correct social policy will weed out the inferior gene pools which inhibit the evolution of the human species. The respectable social scientists who held to this view went on to classify various races as superior or inferior. They recommended birth control, sterilization, and even euthanasia for the "unfit," those of less intelligence or of a less desirable race. Margaret Sanger, founder of Planned Parenthood, was a prominent advocate of this philosophy, as was Adolph Hitler.[3]

Fascism's economic theory was based on the competition of nations rather than individuals or social classes.[4] Its theories of social progress were blended with an especially virulent form of romanticism—the unleashing of the Self and its darkest impulses. Fascism, as we shall see, was also a manifestation of existentialism, which is still endemic to modern thought. The Holocaust may be the central event of the twentieth century, giving the lie to claims of modern progress and humanistic optimism. The ideas that spawned the Holocaust still lurk in the shadows of our culture.

MATERIALISM

What Darwin did to nature, Sigmund Freud did to the self. Freud's theories revealed the self to be, like nature, filled with conflict and violence. Underneath one's civilized exterior, according to Freud, rage incestuous perversity, aggressive sexual fantasies, cravings to murder and destroy. These abhorrent desires of the "id" (the unconsciousness) must be suppressed by the "super-ego" (the socially imposed conscience). The "ego" (the conscious personality) is a battleground for these psychological impulses. The self is not a benign, innocent flower that simply needs to bloom; rather, it is more like a monster which must be tamed. Freud's theories are completely distorted by advocates of sexual freedom who speak as if psychological problems are caused by "suppression" of natural impulses. These impulses *must* be suppressed in the right way, according to Freud, or the result will be psychological chaos and the unleashing of horrific evil.

One need not agree with Darwin or Freud in their exclusion of God or their reductionism of human nature to appreciate their iconoclastic demystification of nature and the self. A Christian could say that Darwin and Freud (although they themselves did not recognize it) had rediscovered original sin. Both the Enlightenment and romanticism had left sin out of their equations. Darwin's observations demonstrated that nature cannot be the source of moral values. Rather, as Scripture teaches, the physical world itself is part of the network of suffering due to the fall (Romans 8:19-22). Freud's excavations into human nature demonstrated that the self is not the source of moral values. Rather, the inmost self is appallingly sinful in its very nature—not just in its overt acts but innately—just as Scripture teaches.

The effect of such scientific theories in the nineteenth century, however, was a new worldview—materialism. Only the observable physical universe is real. Everything can be explained in terms of the closed natural order. This was the Enlightenment without a deity, without even the eighteenth-century confidence in humanity. There is no God. Human beings are nothing more than brute animals.

In philosophy, this worldview has manifested itself in "positivism," which holds that any statement that cannot be reduced to empirical observation is meaningless. (One would think that, by their own criterion, the preceding sentence stating their position must also be meaningless.) Swift was both anticipating and ridiculing positivism and its offspring "linguistic analysis" in his Academy of Lagado. His scholars, convinced that only objects are real, try to communicate by holding up objects which they carry with them in a bag. Still dominating much twentieth-century academic philosophy, positivism rejects not only theology, but metaphysics itself. By an odd circular logic, a materialistic worldview is assumed, and then turned into a method to dissolve all nonmaterialistic arguments without having to deal with them in their own terms. Philosophy is made to reject its own subject matter.

In literature, this new materialism manifested itself in naturalism, the brand of realistic fiction discussed in chapter 7. Good authors, again, tend to be honest. The scientists and the philosophers may have enjoyed banishing the spiritual dimension from human life, but many of the novelists and poets such as Stephen Crane and Thomas Hardy saw the bleakness and the pointlessness of such a world. Here is a love poem by Hardy, who believed the materialists to be correct, but realized the human implications of this claustrophobic worldview:

We stood by a pond that winter day,
And the sun was white, as though chidden of God,
And a few leaves lay on the starving sod;
  They had fallen from an ash, and were gray.

Your eyes on me were as eyes that rove
Over tedious riddles of years ago;
And some words played between us to and fro
     On which lost the more by our love.

The smile on your mouth was the deadest thing
Alive enough to have strength to die;
And a grin of bitterness swept thereby
     Like an ominous bird a-wing.

Since then, keen lessons that love deceives,
And wrings with wrong, have shaped to me
Your face, and the God-curst sun, and a tree,
     And a pond edged with grayish leaves.[5]

Here is no sentimental paean to nature's beauty—the leaves are gray and rotting, the grass is dead, the colors are all "neutral tones" (the title of the poem). God is mentioned to emphasize His absence. The bleakness of the sun makes the poet think it must have been cursed by God, so devoid it is of any life or significance. (Atheists such as Hardy are often bitter at God for not existing.)

The stark, hard-edged plainness of the materialistic universe is not only devoid of God, it voids humanity as well. Personality, relationships, and human values have no real basis. The lovers look on each other with boredom, seeing the past as a series of "tedious riddles." They talk, but language itself is only a futile game—"some words played between us to and fro." The lovers are enervated, their smiles are dead or predatory, their thoughts are bitter. The poem ends with sweeping disillusionment—"love deceives"—and a catalog of material objects, the only realities: her face, the sun, a tree, and a pond ringed with grayish leaves.

EXISTENTIALISM

Sensitive people began to feel the tension, in Schaeffer's terms, between their humanness and the materialistic worldview. As Hardy's poem shows, love has little place in a purely materialistic world, and yet human beings cannot help loving. Christianity provides a basis for love and everything else that is truly human by seeing their origins in the love and personality of God, who underlies all of reality. Instead of turning to Biblical wholeness, many people responded to this crisis by splitting off the physical world and the human world into two rigidly separated categories. The material world may run its monotonous course according to unalterable scientific laws, but what does that have to do with me? As a human being with thoughts and feelings and dreams, adrift in an indifferent universe, I can at least forge meaning for myself.

Matthew Arnold, a late Victorian author, expressed the dilemma of the modern world and especially the century to come with acuteness and foresight. He does so in another love poem, "Dover Beach," written on his honeymoon. He and his bride were staying at Dover on the English channel. The poem opens with a vivid description of the sea at night:

> *The sea is calm to-night,*
> *The tide is full, the moon lies fair*
> *Upon the straits;—on the French coast the light*
> *Gleams and is gone; the cliffs of England stand,*
> *Glimmering and vast, out in the tranquil bay.*
> *Come to the window, sweet is the night-air!*
>
> *Only, from the long line of spray*
> *Where the sea meets the moon-blanch'd land,*
> *Listen! you hear the grating roar*
> *Of pebbles which the waves draw back, and fling,*
> *At their return, up the high strand,*
> *Begin, and cease, and then again begin,*
> *With tremulous cadence slow, and bring*
> *The eternal note of sadness in.*

Listening to the waves come in and go out, come in and go out, in a never-altering rhythm, the speaker's mood changes. The sound of the waves strikes him as somehow depressing. Sophocles, over two thousand years ago, heard the same never-changing waves. As the tide goes out, the poet contemplates the loss of religious faith:

> *Sophocles long ago*
> *Heard it on the Aegean, and it brought*
> *Into his mind the turbid ebb and flow*
> *Of human misery; we*
> *Find also in the sound a thought,*
> *Hearing it by this distant northern sea.*
>
> *The Sea of Faith*
> *Was once, too, at the full, and round earth's shore*
> *Lay like the folds of a bright girdle furl'd.*
> *But now I only hear*
> *Its melancholy, long, withdrawing roar,*

Retreating, to the breath
Of the night-wind, down the vast edges drear
And naked shingles of the world.

Faith was once like a sea, full and at high tide, encompassing and adorning the world. But now faith is retreating, and the noises it makes are like the roar of the ebbing tide. When the sea of faith has retreated, what is left are bare rocks, the "naked shingles of the world," mere physical reality in all of its starkness and harshness.

Arnold sees how the loss of faith has led to a barren materialism, but he does not leave it at that. His concluding stanza anticipates the quandaries of the twentieth century as well as the characteristic response to them:

Ah, love, let us be true
To one another! For the world, which seems
To lie before us like a land of dreams,
So various, so beautiful, so new,
Hath really neither joy, nor love, nor light,
Nor certitude, nor peace, nor help for pain;
And we are here as on a darkling plain
Swept with confused alarms of struggle and flight,
Where ignorant armies clash by night.[6]

Many Victorians were idealistic believers in progress, seeing their own time and the coming century as "a land of dreams," a time when the old ideas were being cast away in favor of a new way of life that would be various, beautiful, and new. Arnold here sees such optimism as illusory.

Once the sea of faith has receded, there can be "neither joy, nor love, nor light, /Nor certitude, nor peace, nor help for pain." The relentless succession of *nor*'s, each negating a major human need, drives the point home. "We are here as on a darkling plain"—that is, the landscape is getting darker and darker. In the darkness, confused armies are alternately fighting and running away from each other. Both sides are ignorant, oblivious to what they are fighting for, but they are clashing in the darkness. This is sometimes taken to refer to the bloody ideological wars, but it seems to apply just as well to the modern clash of ideas, all of which are in darkness apart from faith.

Arnold was not a Christian, but he boldly faced the consequences of the erosion of faith. His poem, however, posits an alternative to the hopelessness he sees in the world: "Ah, love, let us be true/To one another!" Why should they be true to one another? "For the world, which seems/To lie before us like a land of dreams . . . /Hath really neither joy, nor love, nor light, /Nor certitude, nor peace, nor help for pain." In other words, the world will offer them no consolation; therefore, they must cling to each other. Their love, their commitment to each other, will enable them to carve out their own private order in an otherwise meaningless world.

Arnold, remarkably, is anticipating the philosophy of existentialism, which would loom as a major influence in twentieth-century culture. There is no meaning in life, say the existentialists. You can, however, create a meaning for yourself. There is no order, no absolute, no essence that is given to you; rather, by your own free choice and deliberate action, you must create your own order. Those who blindly follow the roles set forth for them by other people, never taking responsibility for their own lives, are "inauthentic." Those who face the truth about their existence may become "authentic" by living according to their own codes or committing themselves to some cause even though it may seem absurd. The content of that commitment is not important—a person may choose a life of crime or a life of selfless virtue; a person may choose communism or even Christianity. What validates that commitment is the choice.

Existentialism is a complex and problematic philosophy, but it nevertheless has come to permeate modern culture. Again, consider the debates over abortion. Those who favor legalized abortion call themselves "Pro-*choice*." They are advocating in the purest form an existentialist ethic. To pro-choice advocates, the content of the woman's decision (whether to have an abortion or to keep the child) is not important. Nor are objective scientific or moral questions (whether the fetus is a human being, whether killing the fetus is morally wrong). The *only* relevant issue, the *only* consideration permissible in the moral debate, is whether or not the woman has made a choice.

Pro-choice advocates often say that "I am personally opposed to abortion, but I can't impose my beliefs anyone else." This statement lays bare the whole existential metaphysics and its implications. There is no transcendent moral law binding on everyone. There are no objective truths that exist independently of the individual. Or, as in another slogan of pop existentialism, "That may be true for you, but it is not true for me." Belief is sheerly a matter of one's own private inner commitments and has no bearing upon the external world, which lacks any innate meaning of its own. Belief is subjective, nonrational, and isolated, something to comfort one's personal life, but unrelated to external reality and to other people, each of whom dwells "in his own world."

If every person has "his or her own reality," then each person is isolated and alone. Communication which assumes some common ground becomes problematic. Existentialism minimizes reason as having to do only with the purposeless repetitions of the external world, having nothing to do with the subjectivity of human meaning. Objective moral laws have no bearing. ("Values Clarification," in which children are asked what they "value" instead of being taught what is right and wrong, is another example of existential ethics.) Since "beliefs" are not bound by correspondence to the objective world, they need not be rational. Indeed, the rational can be a barrier to their sense of meaning. An educated and sophisticated person can accept uncritically the most outlandish statements of the New Age charlatans if these can in some way "give meaning" to his life. The channelers, gurus, and cultists give a jolt of subjective meaning without requiring their devotees to abandon their self-directed lives and in fact encourage them to live only for themselves. "Truth is relative," according to another pop existentialist slogan, justifying the profound anti-intellectualism that exists today even among intellectuals.

There is thus a cleavage between the personal realm (capable of meaning) and the objective realm outside the self (which operates according to scientific laws but is meaningless as far as the individual person is concerned). People can learn to function well in the objective realm as scientists, managers, or laborers, but when it comes to questions of meaning, they retreat into their private, subjective worlds.[7]

Just as the Enlightenment and romanticism infected Christianity, so "Christian existentialism" has become a major strain of modern theology. The historic truth of the Bible and what one believes about God make no difference—they are part of the objective realm which, according to existentialism, is irrelevant to the inner life.

Some theologians do stress the significance of a personal inner response and commitment to the "Christ-event." This refers not to the historical Christ (whom we can never know, since objective history is problematic and existentially irrelevant), certainly not the Incarnate God-Man (which is an existentially irrelevant objective dogma). Rather, Christ is defined almost gnostically as a mystical encounter, a spiritual model or paradigm, resulting in a commitment to a life of faith defined not in terms of any object but as a life of authenticity and "openness."

Existential theologians often attack the historicity of Scripture and the historic doctrines of the faith, imagining themselves as "casting down idols" which "limit faith." They minimize the moral teachings of the Bible in favor of "situation ethics," which rejects any absolute ethic based upon God's transcendent law. Instead, the morality of an action depends upon an individual's "responsible" decision based upon a particular situation. Christian existentialism allows people who no longer believe any traditional Christian doctrines to still consider themselves Christians.

If Christian existentialism is a major brand of theological liberalism, those of us who are more orthodox should also be on our guard. Evangelicals sometimes are unaware that they are using the existentialist language and categories of the age. Sometimes we speak of "decisions," "commitments," and "choices" for Christ as if conversion were a purely autonomous act of will power. The old theologians such as Augustine, Luther, and Calvin saw the human will as very problematic, enslaved by sin and powerless of itself to choose God. They stressed the role of the Holy Spirit in conversion. Even those such as Arminius and Wesley who did assert that conversion involves a free choice still stressed the need to cooperate with the Holy Spirit, who is ultimately responsible for bringing someone to faith. Evangelicals who use existentialist terminology are still proclaiming the gospel, in which the Holy Spirit is at work *enabling* the sinner to choose Christ. Still, evangelicals need to be careful, lest this philosophy which dominates the age subtly undermine the Biblical worldview. This may have already happened in some of the "positive thinking" theologies. In stressing the power of the mind over reality and in preaching self-fulfillment rather than self-denial, such theologies are clearly part of the spirit of the age, going farther than most existentialists in their exaltation of the human will.

In criticizing existentialism, I have oversimplified and perhaps misrepresented its positions and the variety of its forms. I should acknowledge my admiration for the existentialists who take their dilemma seriously: Kierkegaard, a devout and passionate Christian in his own way, fiercely rebelling against the dead orthodoxy of his day which reduced faith to an intellectual formula; Camus, who insisted on moral behavior in an immoral world; Sartre, who lamented the "burden of freedom" in a world characterized by "nausea," a man who accepted the consequences of a world without God (although on his deathbed he seems to have converted to Catholicism). Such thinkers would scorn what I have termed the "pop existentialism" of contemporary culture, which minimizes the anguish of the existential dilemma and uses the lack of objective order as an excuse for hedonism and self-aggrandizement.

And yet, these thinkers bear some responsibility for what the culture has made of their thought. They also bear a certain responsibility for another ideology which likewise stressed the "triumph of the will" and which rejected transcendent ethics as a "Jewish invention."[8] Fascism had its intellectual origins in the thought of proto-existentialist Friedrich Nietzsche. Heidegger, the greatest existential philosopher of them all, still cited as an authority by critics and theologians, we now know was a dedicated, ruthless, fully committed Nazi.[9] Once more, a modern philosophy must be indicted for its complicity in Fascism, in which many strains of modern thought make clear their horrific consequences.

MODERNISM

Existentialism seems to me to be the informing philosophy of the twentieth century, manifesting itself in various ways throughout the culture. Art began to be seen as "imposing order on the chaos of experience." As a sort of neoromanticism, without the optimism and without the love of nature, existentialism saw the artist as a creator of meaning. Visual artists turned away from the external world, which was seen to be irrelevant and meaningless. Realistic paintings were purposefully ugly and unsettling, trying to awake their viewers to an existential despair. The device of the collage, taking unconnected scraps from the actual world and putting them together according to the artist's own design, illustrates well the existentialist aesthetic. Other artists turned to abstract art, pure projections of their creative imaginations, owing nothing to the meaningless world outside of themselves.

In literature, we see motifs such as the alienated hero. Aloof and isolated, misunderstood by society, possessed of a sensibility that ordinary people do not share, the hero is on a quest to give his life meaning. Hemingway's heroes typically cling stubbornly to a "code," principles of honor, whether of a bull fighter, a soldier, or a sportsman, which give purpose to their lives and enable them to live with courage. Hemingway's existentialism is evident too in a story such as "A Clean, Well-Lighted Place." The owner of an all-night café maintains an orderly, human haven in the midst of the all-pervading darkness. At its best, existentialism in literature portrays people doing what they can against chaos. In "The Waste Land," while civilization is collapsing and "London Bridge is falling down falling down falling down," the speaker asks, "Shall I at least set my lands in order?"[10] Existentialism is also evident in the carefully crafted poetry of Wallace Stevens, which sometimes explores how human beings create order and sometimes playfully becomes the poetic equivalent of abstract art.

Modern literature is also characterized by the quest for new forms. The old ways of writing fiction and poetry seemed exhausted and inauthentic. Poets wondered why they should write orderly poetry with its neat patterns of rhythm and rhyme when life itself lacks order. Fiction writers questioned the validity of conventional narrative techniques. If there is no omniscient God, how can we employ an omniscient narrator? If history is not logical, how can a plot be logical?

This is not to say that the writers of the early twentieth century were abandoning order. They were seeking it. In poetry, free verse became the norm. At its best, free verse is not formless; rather, it establishes its own form by its orchestration of images and language. Fiction writers plunged into the points of view of their characters, sometimes dissolving all narrative conventions by reproducing the stream-of-consciousness of the character's mind.

Both poets and fiction writers, faced with the chaos of modern life, sometimes turned to myth as a way of giving order to their writing. James Joyce organized his stream-of-consciousness novel *Ulysses* according to Homer's *Odyssey*, employing Greek mythology to comment upon the action and to hold it together. Yeats, one of the most talented of Modern poets, turned first to the myths and legends of his native Ireland to give his poetry a conceptual foundation. Later, he invented his own mythology, which went along with an elaborate historical and metaphysical system of his own construction. Yeats would then write poems that allude to and are structured by this private, solitary worldview. Poems such as "The Second Coming" and "Byzantium" manage to be provocatively effective despite their private frame of reference. Some writers found order in Marxism, some in Freud's psychological system. Perhaps the most important theorist of Modern literature was the poet and critic Ezra Pound. Like many Modernist thinkers, he found order by becoming a Fascist.[11]

Modernist poet T. S. Eliot (whose verse is discussed in chapter 5) set the course for subsequent poetry with his experimentations. He too turned to myth, such as the Grail legend in "The Waste Land," as well as to seventeenth-century literature. Eliot came to see in modern culture what he described as a "disassociation of sensibility"; that is to say, thought and feeling now go in different directions.[12] Those who think, valuing logic and objectivity (as in the Enlightenment), seem cold, passionless, and machinelike. Those who feel, valuing passion and subjectivity (as in romanticism), seem sentimental, subjective, and self-absorbed. He found in the ages of faith, the poetry of Dante and of Donne, a wholeness, the working together of thought and feeling essential to him as a poet. He realized that this integration of the mind is made possible ultimately by a Biblical view of the world. Eliot became a Christian.

C. S. Lewis was approaching the same realization from a different angle. His first book after his conversion was *Pilgrim's Regress,* subtitled, *An Allegorical Apology for Christianity, Reason, and Romanticism.* In the twentieth century *both* reason and romanticism were under attack (reason by existential irrationalism and romanticism by scientific materialism). Furthermore, both reason and romanticism were attacking Christianity from different sides (one because Christianity was too irrational and the other because Christianity was too dogmatic). Lewis, like Eliot, found that Christianity could affirm both thinking and feeling, the best of the Enlightenment and the best of romanticism, thereby offering a view of the world that could give wholeness and meaning to modern life.

Eliot continued to be a Modernist even after his conversion. Indeed, Christianity was a Modernist alternative. Modernist writers such as T. E. Hulme, Allen Tate, Robert Penn Warren, W. H. Auden, Evelyn Waugh, and Flannery O'Connor embraced Christianity (often of a Roman Catholic or high church Anglican variety). These writers still depicted the external world as bleak and empty—according to Christianity, the modern world without Christ *is* bleak and empty. They still experimented with bold, original, idiosyncratic styles—Christianity by no means hindered their literary creativity. These writers were inspired all the more to devise unique and distinctive styles to express their convictions to a world oblivious to the meaning that they themselves found in Christ.

POSTMODERNISM

Literature is always in a state of change, so that what once seemed daring and experimental seems quaint and old fashioned only a few years later. Modernism in its various modes dominated the first half of the twentieth century and was practiced by writers who have made their mark but are no longer living. Ironically, modernism, once the quintessence of radicalism, now does not seem so modern. Contemporary writers, artists, and thinkers are presently turning against modernism. A new cultural movement is in the air.

"Postmodernism" promises to be as varied and difficult to define as modernism. Like all secular movements, postmodernism holds both peril and promise for Christians. Already it has enlivened architecture and moved literary criticism, of all things, to a central place in the intellectual establishment. Disdaining elitism, the Postmodern movement reaches out to the popular culture. Postmodernism refuses to take itself too seriously, which is healthy in any literary movement; the problem is that it sometimes fails to take anything seriously.

Acutely aware of the decline of religion, Matthew Arnold offered literature as a substitute. "Most of what now passes with us for religion and philosophy will be replaced by poetry." As a result, "More and more, mankind will discover that we have to turn to poetry to interpret life for us, to console us, to sustain us."[13] Many people today do turn to literature or other works of art for a sense of meaning, an experience of transcendence, and guidance for their lives.

In literary criticism, religious language has been displaced into the realm of literature. Critics speak of the author's "inspiration." They argue over principles of correctly interpreting the text, speaking of "hermeneutics," a term originally used for the techniques of interpreting Scripture. They debate over what works should be included in the "canon," a term referring to the list of inspired books that constitute the Bible. In effect, this has meant that all literature is treated as Scripture. Authors are treated as authoritative prophets, their words reverently scrutinized and found to reveal depths of complex meanings. This devotion to secular scriptures has led to whole theologies of literature, systems of interpretation which often inspire the zeal, the fanaticism, and the inquisitorial spirit of real theologies.

Contemporary art and criticism are still guilty of this pseudo-religious posturing, but the Postmodern aesthetic makes it more difficult. Matthew Arnold's criterion for the new literature, which must take the place of religion, was "high seriousness."[14] When literature presumes to take upon itself the functions of religion, it is not being true to its nature. It becomes stuffy, pretentious, and esoteric, adjectives which do characterize much of the work that came out of the Modernist movement. Postmodernism proclaims that art and literature are only art and literature, reclaiming the playfulness, decorativeness, and entertainment value that were squelched by the "high seriousness" of modernism.

In architecture, for example, modernism has given us the glass and steel monoliths that dominate city skylines. The skyscrapers of the Modernist period are austere, intimidating, and impersonal. Form follows function for the Modernist architects who scorned any "decorative" touches or any concessions to the human scale. Postmodern architects, on the other hand, are building skyscrapers that might include an elaborately sculpted roof, bright colors, and ornate decorations. Inside, the building may feature a vast atrium filled with trees and shops, a space designed for people to gather and interact. Such decorativeness and wasted space would be anathema to Modernist purists, but the Postmodernists want to restore the human scale, to make buildings that give pleasure to human beings rather than overwhelming them with the impersonality of modern life.[15]

Whereas the Modernists were obsessed with being different from everything that had gone before, Postmodernists are not afraid to draw on the past. A Postmodernist building might well throw in a touch of art nouveau, a salute to Victorian design, an allusion to classicism or some other style recently scorned as outmoded. This openness to history sometimes results in an incoherent pastiche of styles or to unfocused nostalgia. On the other hand, it has resulted in architectural preservation, the revival of the historical novel, and other attempts to capture the flavor and the significance of the past.

Postmodern design calls attention to its forms, flaunting its constructedness. Buildings which lay bare their structural supports and do not even try to hide their heating ducts are part of this new aesthetic.

A good example of a Postmodern television program is the Gary Shandling Show (or, to use its correct Postmodern title, "It's Gary Shandling's Show"). As is the convention with all television shows, a theme song is played while the credits roll. The lyrics to this particular theme song make us self-consciously aware of the convention: "This is the theme to Gary's show. . . . This is the music that they play while they roll the credits. . . . Gary called me up and asked if I would write his theme song. . . . How do you like it so far?. . . . Now it's almost finished. . . . This is the theme to Gary Shandling's show." Gary comes out, talks to the TV audience, and then steps back into the set for a typical sit-com story. Every now and then, he breaks the dramatic illusion and addresses us directly, reminding us that he is an actor playing a part on a TV show and that none of this is real.

If the plot requires that he leave his apartment and drive his car, he is likely to walk out of the apartment set, get in a little toy pedal car, drive it around the cameras, past the studio audience, and over to another set. He flaunts the "realistic" conventions of TV and then makes fun of them. In one episode, the subject of shaving came up. He offered to shave the TV audience. The camera pulled in for a close-up, whereupon Gary put shaving cream over the lens (darkening our living room screens), and then scraped it off with a razor. By blurring the distinction between the real world and the TV world, Shandling makes us highly conscious of television's artificial conventions and makes us laugh at them.

Postmodern literature similarly plays with the conventions of literature, blurring the distinctions between fiction and life and thereby calling both into question. Michael Ende's fascinating children's fantasy *The Never-Ending Story* is about a child reading a book, who becomes drawn into the story so much that he becomes a character in the book. We discover that this magical book is none other than the book that we are holding in our hands, *The Never-Ending Story,* which we are reading ourselves and into which we are drawn. Postmodern fiction often sets up levels within levels, story-lines packed within each other like Chinese boxes or reflecting each other like two mirrors placed together. The author may address the reader or describe the process of making up the story and putting words onto paper. The reader becomes highly conscious of being in the act of reading a story, of being manipulated by the workings of the author's and his own imagination.

This formal self-consciousness makes us realize that realism too is a set of literary conventions, a set of techniques that create an illusion of reality rather than reality itself. Postmodernist fiction is often realistic, but it is likely to undermine its own realism by intrusions of fantasy (as in the work of many contemporary Latin American novelists such as Gabriel García Márquez) or by drawing attention to the artificial conventions of realistic fiction (such as the intrusive narrator from nineteenth-century fiction, familiar character types, or clichés from historical melodramas or murder mysteries).

Enamored of conventions and tired of modernism's "high seriousness," postmodernism has drawn on popular culture for its subjects and forms. On the one hand, this has meant Andy Warhol's Campbell soup cans and the general trivialization of the high culture, as Kenneth Myers has shown.[16] In literature, it has had the salutary effect of rehabilitating genres that were once scorned as being subliterary: mysteries, science fiction, adventure stories, and thrillers. Larry McMurtry, one of the most respected contemporary novelists, won a Pulitzer Prize for *Lonesome Dove*, a hugely entertaining western. Umberto Eco, a structuralist academician, wrote a philosophically complex exploration of language and thought in the guise of a historical novel, *The Name of the Rose*, using the plot and all of the conventions of a murder mystery.

His second novel, *Foucault's Pendulum*, is a conspiracy-thriller, filled with accurate historical lore about Templars, Masons, and European occultism. His main characters, in digging up such arcane information, dream up a possible "plan" whereby a secret society has been manipulating history in a plot to take over the world. The characters at first intend their research and their elaborate interpretations to be nothing more than a game, an intellectual exercise, showing how interpretations of facts can be made to demonstrate anything one pleases. Then there is a murder and evidence that what they have invented has become real.

Now, following the conventions of Christian books about culture, I must show the theological errors of postmodernism. I will do so by deferring to a critic, Mark Edmundson, who is in agreement with postmodernism and who articulates its anti-religious assumptions:

> One might think of postmodernism—in its negative or demystifying phase—as trying to get done what its practitioners sensed modernism had failed to do; that is, to purge the world of superstition in every form. Major modern thinkers such as Marx and Freud strove to come up with ways of conceiving of life as lived in the West that would be genuinely post-religious. Both of them practiced and promoted what Paul Ricoeur has called, "the hermeneutics of suspicion." Nothing, their work taught, could be taken at face value. . . . But the problem with this Modern tendency to disenchant the world was that it turned the old religious drive upside down. The traditional man of faith seeks transcendence. He wants contact with God, the One, the Truth. The Modern thinker, inspired by Marx and Freud, found truth in repressed or hidden

impulses, but he *found truth* nonetheless. . . . The postmodern man sees religious residues in *any* way of thinking that affirms the Truth.[17]

Edmundson argues that modernism rejected God, but erected other absolutes in His place.

Postmodernism, in turn, is attacking these substitutes for God. "If you want to be genuinely secular, then give up on transcendence in every form. . . . Don't replace the deity with some other idol, like scientific truth, the self, the destiny of America, or what have you."[18] Citing the work of Postmodernists such as Samuel Beckett and William Burroughs, Edmundson concludes that "the objective of much of this work is to trash whatever existing God replacements the culture has latched on to, whether it be Reason, the Self, the Artist, the Magnum Opus, or whatever."[19]

Some Postmodernist fiction implies that reality itself is fictional, a set of arbitrary conventions imposed by the human mind and culture upon a meaningless world. These structures, some say, are determined by those in power. Marxists disclose the oppressive economic structures that determine "reality." Feminists see the power structures of the "patriarchal, male-dominated" society. And yet, the Marxist and feminist Postmodernists must see that their programs too must be as arbitrary and "privileged" as the systems they oppose.

An important corollary of Postmodernist criticism is that the old "high culture" with its humanistic values and civilizing authority is an artificial construction. Marxists and feminists claim that the traditional "canon" of great literature simply perpetuates the power and the values of the rich white men who produced it. Who is to say that the literature of the anthologies is superior to other kinds of literature? What were women writing during the Renaissance? If they were restricted by the male-dominated society from writing plays, they did write diaries and letters which also deserve inclusion in the literary tradition. What about people of color? We teach the great books of the West, but this is cultural imperialism. Instead, we should read Third World authors.

Debates over what should constitute "the canon" of great literature are now raging among literary scholars. What is emerging is an affirmative action plan for anthologies and educational curricula no less than for the workplace. Works are chosen out of fairness to ethnic groups rather than upon intrinsic merit, a concept thoroughly discredited by Postmodern criticism. Christian critics have often been maligned for valuing authors on the basis of their theological position, rather than their literary significance, and for reducing works of aesthetic complexity to a theological formula. Today, some of the most progressive critics are valuing authors on the basis of their gender or race and reducing work of aesthetic complexity to a political formula.

Postmodern philosophers and literary critics often go much farther. Deconstructionists such as Jacques Derrida stress the arbitrariness of language, the lack of a "transcendental signifier" that can ground language in objective reality. They delve into a literary text to find not so much its meaning as its essential contradiction. The deconstructionists emphasize that if there is no God, there can be no transcendent meaning. We Christians are quick to agree, but if there *is* a God, as we believe, then meaning *is* grounded in Him and only in Him. Moreover, we assert that God became flesh in Jesus Christ, who is the Word, the *logos* underlying all of existence, accessible to us in the form of a written text, the Holy Bible, the unique Word of God. The Postmodernists may be right that language constitutes reality, but Christians must insist that it is God's language which constitutes reality.[20]

Christians agree with the Postmodernists that substitutes for God are futile, and we heirs of idol-smashing prophets can appreciate the "trashing" of false gods. We can appreciate too the way many contemporary thinkers and artists are finally facing the implications of atheism and seeing through the false promises of humanistic ideals. And yet, because we believe God *does* exist—moreover, that He has made the universe—and because we have no wish "to be genuinely secular," then we can never completely accept the Postmodernist program. The playfulness and the literary games are facades for nihilism and despair.

Mark Edmundson, however, suggests that postmodernism may be moving beyond despair to some sort of renewal. Once the wreckage of human ideals has been removed, he suggests, something positive may arise out of the rubble. He sees this particularly in certain Third World authors who live between cultures, writers such as Salman Rushdie, at home neither in his native country nor in the West. Edmundson cites the Czech writer Milan Kundera, author of the novel *The Unbearable Lightness of Being,* who writes, "If God is gone and man is no longer master, then who is master? The planet is moving through the void without any master. There it is, the unbearable lightness of being."[21]

Kundera's novel depicts characters who want their lives to be "substantially weighted," to have stability, permanence, and a sense of order. One character, though, Sabina, embraces the "lightness of being." She is open to change. She allows herself to be tied down to nothing. She changes cultures and lifestyles. She is sexually promiscuous. She commits herself to nothing, blithely floating through existence. Edmundson sees her as a paradigm of Postmodern freedom from meaning.

The new way of thinking, reflected also in Rushdie's *Satanic Verses,* affirms pluralism, cultural diversity, and continual change and self-revision. Whether this renewal manifests itself in a Zenlike acceptance of existence, a New Age mysticism, or sheer secular hedonism, it promises to be competition and a temptation for contemporary Christianity.

And yet, hard-edged reality has a way of interrupting human complacency even of the Postmodern variety. Kundera himself describes the "lightness of being" as ultimately "unbearable."[22] Sabina's independence is interrupted when Soviet tanks smash into Czechoslovakia. Salman Rushdie's fun and games with the Islamic religion has resulted in bloody riots throughout the Islamic world and a death sentence upon the author, who may have to spend the rest of his life in hiding. Postmodernists did not create these realities.

Those trying to be not only Modern, but Postmodern, not only contemporary, but post-contemporary,[23] may find to their shock that the old ideas they think have been surpassed may have only gone out of fashion. An ancient religion such as Islam is still a formidable power. The "lightness of being" could not stop Soviet tanks, although the "weightiness" of Christianity and the people's zeal for national freedom did drive out the tanks in Czechoslovakia and throughout once-Communist Europe. Ideologies of "transcendence" were rejected once before in the twentieth century, resulting not in a euphoric relativism nor in "an unbearable lightness of being" but, such is the evil within human nature, in the Holocaust. The deconstructionist Paul de Man, it has recently been discovered, was also a Nazi.[24] Ernst Nolte, one of the foremost analysts of the movement, has gone so far as to define fascism as "resistance to transcendence."[25] The resistance to transcendent meaning, transcendent values, and transcendent language has characterized Modern and Postmodern culture. The litany of still influential Modern and Postmodern thinkers—Heidegger, Pound, de Man—whose bold new ideas led them to embrace Adolf Hitler should encourage us to question their questioning.

CONTEMPORARY CHRISTIAN WRITERS

Are there Postmodern writers who are Christians? Certainly the metaphysical assumptions of the more radical Postmodernists are incompatible with a Christian view of the world. The same could be said of modernism, and yet some of its leading figures, such as T. S. Eliot, became Christians. Postmodernism with its skepticism towards human creations of every kind may well force some people to confront the Word of God and the all-consuming claims of Christ. If they did so, they would have to modify their philosophical assumptions, as Eliot did, but a Christian postmodernism may well be a formidable combination.

Styles change of themselves. When everything has been done with a style that can be done and it no longer communicates freshly, new styles always emerge. Christians can certainly react against the rigidities and clichés of modernism, and the varieties of postmodernism show them ways of doing so. Postmodern reactions against modernism are evident in the rehabilitation of fantasy, the new interest in historical fiction, and the treatment of nonfiction as an art form, all of which Christian writers are exploiting. A number of contemporary Christian writers are on the cutting edge of their craft and exhibit some of the most intriguing traits of postmodernism.

I am not sure whether Walker Percy is exemplifying postmodernism or attacking it; probably both. In *The Thanatos Syndrome*, Percy carries out a sustained guerrilla warfare against Modern thought—its pleasure-centeredness coupled with a bizarre embrace of death (as in its advocacy of abortion and euthanasia). His novel is charged with ideas, yet in a Postmodern touch he casts it in the form of a science fiction thriller. *Lost in the Cosmos: The Last Self Help Book* defies classification, which is certainly a Postmodern trait. This parody of self-help books contains quizzes, fiction, a serious discussion of how the mind seeks meaning, and a mock TV script ("The Last Donahue Show," in which Donahue's program on contemporary sexual practices is rudely interrupted by John Calvin, a Confederate colonel, and an alien determined to blow up the earth).

Modernist writing has tended to stress clarity in language. Good writing is transparent, calling attention to its subject matter instead of to itself. Postmodernism has tended to question the assumption that language is nothing more than a blank pane of glass which conveys a truth distinct from its words. One need not question the referentiality of language to appreciate that words do have power of their own, a point supported by Scripture (Proverbs 16:21, 24; Hebrews 4:12).

A number of contemporary Christian writers are distinctive for bringing their language to the surface, for making not only their meaning but their words burn in the reader's mind. Walter Wangerin and Annie Dillard are striking examples (see the quotations from chapter 3). Frederick Buechner also devises a rich, heavily textured language in *Brendan*, a novel about a saint in ancient Ireland. In this passage in which Brendan is explaining the Gospel to a Celtic bard, notice the cadence and the music, the archaic yet revelatory frames of reference, the poetry of the prose:

> Christ was the king of all kings, Brendan said from MacLennin's knee. He was the wizard of all wizards. He turned water to beer

easy as breathing. When he commanded the foaming waves to lay flat, they laid flat. He straightened the bent legs of cripples out and peeled the blue milky scales off the eyes of the blind. When he called out of darkness the first light as ever was, the morning stars sang together at the sweet ring of it and all the sons of heaven shouted for joy.

"Ah well, he was a bard then," MacLennin said. It was the part about Christ's voice that struck him hardest.

"MacLennin, he was so mighty a bard his songs have ravished the hearts of men from that day on," Brendan said. "He was a song himself you might say. King Christ is a song on the lips of the true God."[26]

These new prose stylists are sometimes nearly baroque in the passion, ornateness, and swirling beauty of their language. Sometimes criticized for over-writing, for quirky inversions and excessive descriptions, these writers are unintimidated by Modernist austerity as they revel in God's gift of language.

Other contemporary writers I do not know how to classify, whether they are Modern or Postmodern. I would say that they are just good, often striking the classic, universal chords that transcend passing styles and trends—novelists such as Larry Woiwode, and Madeleine L'Engle; poets such as Luci Shaw, Eugene Warren, and John Leax.

Newer writers of great promise are also emerging, such as Harold Fickett and Shirley Nelson. I must also recommend Robert Siegel, a master of both fiction and poetry, and Hugh Cook, author of memorable short stories. Other contemporary Christian novelists who write with honesty and spiritual insight are James Schaap, Lloyd Billingsley, William Griffin, Peggy Payne, Michael Malone, Calvin Miller, and Stephen Lawhead. Frank Perretti's best-selling spiritual thrillers, although not high art, have convinced a mass popular audience of the reality of spiritual warfare and the power of prayer. Nor should readers neglect nonfiction writers such as Philip Yancy and Virginia Stem Owens who are artists in their own right.

Christian authors today can address their age, as the best Christian writers have always addressed their age, with intelligence, sophistication, artistry, and a faithfulness to the Word of God which never becomes outdated.

THE MAKERS
OF LITERATURE:
Writers, Publishers, and Readers

*L*iterature is a relationship between the writer and the reader as mediated by the words on paper. Many writers express themselves privately, writing their reflections in a journal or pouring out their inmost thoughts in secret poems no one is allowed to read. This sort of writing is extremely valuable. It is more than therapy; it is a way of thinking, of articulating one's life into language, and thus understanding and appreciating it more fully. And yet, writing only for oneself is not quite literature. Someone needs to read it, and then it becomes literature.

All it takes is one person—a friend, perhaps—to read those secret poems. When the author's words are played back in the mind of someone else so that what was happening in the author's mind is vicariously shared by a reader, the circle of communication is complete. (Some Christians turn their private journals into prayer journals. God is their reader. The journal becomes not just a forum for introspection and complaints, but a means of intimate and honest communication with God.)

Since language by its very nature is a means of communication, writers sometimes have the impulse to publish their work. To go public with their ideas, research, stories, or verse is fraught with perils. Writers are generally a reclusive breed; they might feel uneasy revealing to their closest friends what they are now exposing in print to thousands of total strangers. Writers make themselves vulnerable at every stage of the publication process. They pour out themselves in their writing; then they submit their best efforts to the scrutiny of editors armed with rejection slips, to reviewers with their snide put-downs or devastatingly accurate criticisms, to the reading public which may be completely apathetic. Yet when a writer connects with a publisher, when the language that has been been composed and sweated over in private emerges on the printed page, and when someone actually reads one's work, the result is a humble satisfaction that is difficult even for a good writer to describe, a sense of having communicated.

The key role in the literary process is played, not by authors nor by publishers, but by readers. To a large extent, readers determine what gets published. They determine what books are stocked in bookstores. What readers are willing to buy, publishers and bookstores are happy to provide. The power of the marketplace is enormous, in literature as well as in the economy as a whole. Although certain ideological factors do enter into publishing, distorting the process, by and large the public gets what it wants. If sex and violence dominate the paperback racks, it is largely because readers are willing to pay for sex and violence. Conversely, if readers demand excellence, then they will find themselves swaying the literary world and thus the entire culture.

WRITERS

Writers today face a dilemma. Should they write to express the truth as they see it, or should they write to please their readers? Should their main concern be art or the marketplace? Some writers choose to do one or the other, either expressing themselves in a grand integrity (even if no one reads or understands what they are writing) or selling out to whatever the market demands (even though what they write is worthless). Probably the best writers try to do both, writing works of excellence that people will read.

Some writers devote their lives to creating a literary work with uncompromising integrity, only to be unable to find a publisher. There is no market for this kind of book, they are told. It is too difficult or too depressing. Such writers may still find a niche somewhere in the literary world. Small presses do publish "serious" or "experimental" literature, usually for a small coterie of like-minded readers. A great deal of writing, though, never finds readers.

Other authors sacrifice their artistic integrity to write works that they know will sell. They determine what the reading public wants, and they rush in to supply the demand. Today, our mass culture wants mainly to be titillated and entertained.[1] Complexity, thought, and spiritual realism are too demanding. Writers trying to make a living from their craft often keep one eye on the marketplace. If slanderous biographies are selling well, these writers will churn out a slanderous biography. If pornographic horror stories are hitting the bestseller lists, they will cash in on the trend. Many professional writers are hard at work on their "serious" novel while writing serial romances "to put meat on the table."

If you would like to write a Harlequin romance or a title for a similar series, you would first write the publisher for a set of "author's guidelines." (Try it. Anyone can ask for them.) These give the precise formulas by which each story must be written. They specify the kinds of characters allowed, what the settings should be, how the plot must be developed, and even how much sex should be included and how explicitly it should be described. The writer's own creativity and originality are excluded on principle.

This is why such products of the mass market, designed to be consumed rather than read, are by their very nature inferior as literature. This is not to say that they might not be a pleasant indulgence. One can "like" what is not objectively "good." Potato chips and candy bars may satisfy our craving for junk food, but no one would call them "good" either nutritionally or in the sense that a home-cooked meal or a dinner in a fine restaurant would be "good." Good writing, like good food, needs to be savored; it is nutritious and will prove far more satisfying than the short-lived sugar-high of junk food and its literary equivalent.

And yet authors who strive to be literary sometimes fall prey to an opposite temptation. I had a student who called himself a writer. He hung around with artists and affected the Bohemian manner—the scorn for "middle class values," the assumption that because he is an artist he is superior to ordinary people, the Byronic combination of flamboyance and self-pity. I got to know him and asked to see some of his writing. Although he always introduced himself as a writer, it turned out that he never actually wrote anything. He could not tell a story. He was too impatient to write a poem. He did have some notebooks which he let me see. They were nearly indecipherable; the entries were nothing more than ravings. Occasionally I could tell that he did have an audience in mind; he would try to be shocking. He was posing as a writer, but he could not write. Writing for him was a means of self-indulgence rather than creativity or communication. To create, by definition, means to make something outside of oneself. Creativity involves an objective craft and mastery of technique. Writing is by its very nature communication. No author dares write without a reader in mind. If an author through egotism or neglect fails to respect the reader as an equal human being with legitimate needs and interests, the work will inevitably be an artistic failure.

Writers must walk a fine line between art and the marketplace, elitism and commercialism. Paradoxically, writers who insist on their own artistic integrity while neglecting their readers will produce bad work. Without the discipline of writing for a reader, the writer will accept the first phrases that come to mind, resulting in a sloppy and inartistic style. Similarly, writers who pander to the supposed desires of readers end up cheating the very readers they try to please. Because the work tells readers what they already know and addresses how they already feel, they will get nothing from the work. After a while, formulas grow old and predictable; then they cease even to entertain. Practiced readers tend to develop a taste for quality.

Milton did not want a mass audience, asking the muse to "drive far off the barbarous dissonance of Bacchus and his revellers" (the god of wine and his frenzied followers who tore into pieces the poet Orpheus). Rather, Milton asked for a "fit audience . . . though few."[2] Milton *was* writing for an audience, but one that was "fit" for his poem, that could understand and respond to what he was saying.

Today, writers can aim their work to the right audience. There are so many readers that one can find subgroups interested in just about anything, with publishers ready to cater to their tastes. One of the most lamentable facts of the contemporary literary scene is that while many people write poetry, few read it anymore. Practically the only publishers of poetry today are small presses. Writers need not sell out to the mass taste for mediocrity, nor need they become overly elitist. They can write for a fit audience, though few.

It is possible, however, to write with artistic excellence while still appealing to a broad, popular audience. Shakespeare, Charles Dickens, Mark Twain, and Ernest Hemingway proved that. The very best writing may well demand a hearing because of its aesthetic excellence. If it is good enough, it can win over its audience. Flannery O'Connor's undiluted Christianity would not seem to win her much sympathy with secularist academic scholars, but her stories are so brilliant, her style so penetrating and so original, that no short story anthology and no survey of modern American literature can exclude her. There is much in her work that would alienate her from a mass audience. Her stories are unsettling rather than merely entertaining; she shocks more often than she soothes. And yet discriminating readers, of whom there are many, find her work far more satisfying and even more entertaining than the time-killing fare of the paperback stands.

Contemporary Christian writers face another dilemma. Often their work is considered "too religious" for secular publishers and "too secular" for religious publishers. The large publishing houses and the markets they serve are mainstays of the current intellectual establishment with its animosity toward overt, conservative Christianity. Orthodox Christian writers may therefore be at a disadvantage with the secular literary establishment.

When they turn to Christian publishers, they face another problem. If they have expressed their faith in an honest, artistically complex way, the Christian market might not be receptive. Christian readers are often not interested in reading about honest and complicated treatments of faith. Christians today typically prefer to be reassured and uplifted, not challenged. If the novel mentions sex, describes a moral failure, or portrays a theological lapse, Christians can become outraged. Christian publishers are therefore wary of publishing books that might offend their customers.

This dilemma, which I have heard many Christian writers express, does not always hold true. Again, excellent writing by Christians can win acceptance with even the major secular publishers, as Walker Percy, Frederick Buechner, Walter Wangerin, Madeleine L'Engle, and many others have proven. Christian publishers such as Crossway and Harold Shaw are publishing novels of complexity and literary merit. Nevertheless, the obstacles can be real. The publishing establishment, serving both the mass culture and the high culture, often works against the interests of Christian writers and readers. Christian readers sometimes fail to read with understanding and fail to give Christian authors the support they need.

PUBLISHERS

The freedom of the press means that governments may not decide what is printed; publishers who control the presses do. This gives the publishing industry, for better or worse, enormous power throughout the culture.

For an author's manuscript, composed in the solitude of a study, to make its way into the hands of a reader is a complicated process. The manuscript must be accepted by a publisher. It must be put into print and manufactured as a book. It must be marketed and reviewed so that readers know it exists. It must be ordered by bookstores. It must be purchased to recoup the publisher's investment. At every stage, something can go wrong. The delicate work of art becomes a business commodity, and the otherworldly author is swept up into the pragmatic world of high finance, manufacturing deadlines, and marketing strategies.

Imagine that you have written what you think is the great Christian novel for our times. You have spent years writing and rewriting, pouring everything in you into this masterpiece. You send it off to a major publisher. Editors at publishing houses receive hundreds of manuscripts and must cold-bloodedly decide which to read and which to leave unread. Of those they read, they can publish only a few, and the rest must be rejected. After months and months of checking your mailbox every day, you receive a form rejection slip.

You are crushed, but you persevere. This time you send a letter of inquiry first with a sample chapter. You also do some research to find publishers who might be interested in the sort of thing you have written. You get courteous replies, saying that they are swamped with manuscripts right now and would rather not read yours. That is disappointing, but not as bad as a rejection slip. Eventually, one expresses interest. Then you send your complete manuscript. Perhaps you are rejected again. You think about getting an agent, but unless you are a hot property, capable of provoking bidding wars among publishers, an agent can be as difficult to secure as a publisher if you are just getting started.[3] Just as you are about to give up, you write one more letter of inquiry, perhaps to a Christian publisher. They are interested. You send off the manuscript, and months later to your astonishment, you find in your mail a publishing contract.

You want to pursue your art, but you must attend to more mundane matters. The editor wants changes. Your artistic integrity rebels. Yet the first book is the hardest to publish. Wait until you are famous to become a prima donna. Do the revisions. Go over the edited manuscript and consider the suggestions. Correct the galleys. Resist the temptation to improve your prose style or to change a character, which would mean costly resetting of type. Correct the page proofs. By this time, you will be sick of every word. Later, the box of books will appear, and it will all be worth it.

But will anyone read it? Will anyone even know it exists? Your publisher's marketing department will send out review copies to periodicals and key people (usually ones you recommend). They might book you on a radio talk show or set up an autograph appearance (both of which appall you, a shy person). Maybe the novel does get reviewed. A good review in a national publication such as *The New York Review of Books* can mean enormous sales. Getting panned in even the tiniest periodical can leave you depressed for days. Reviewers exert a powerful influence on the literary scene. Perhaps your book falls into the hands of someone who scathingly attacks its Christian themes. Perhaps a Christian periodical is kinder.

At any rate, your book is out and you are reasonably happy. Your friends and family members ask where they can buy a copy. Having given away your free author's copies, you realize that you do not know what to tell them. You go into Walden Books at your local shopping mall. Your book is not under fiction. You check the religion section and find books on astral projection and the *I Ching*, but yours is nowhere to be found. This is because the large bookstore chains stock only the books they think will appeal to large markets. Even smaller bookstores depend upon wholesale warehouses to supply their shelves. The decisions of bookstore chains or wholesale middlemen can determine the life or death of a book.

Imagine that you go into a Christian bookstore and, lo and behold, there it is in a display right by the cash register. Christian bookstores and wholesale firms operate in much the same way that their secular counterparts do. Bookstores can, of course, order any book they please, but big sales generally come from the decisions of large distributors. But to give our story a happy ending, assume that Christian bookstores are stocking your novel and that it is selling like greeting cards. You outsell even the religious knickknacks. Thousands upon thousands of books are selling. You get letters from people who have been moved and helped by your work. The royalty checks are enabling you to write full time. Your editor tells you that your book is the biggest seller in the country.

You glance at the *New York Times Bestseller List* and think your editor must have been joking because your book is nowhere mentioned. It will not appear on that bestseller list no matter how many copies it sells because that list is based on reported sales from a select group of secular bookstores which do not usually stock titles from Christian publishers. Making the bestseller list, of course, would mean that chains, wholesalers, and book clubs will stock the book like mad. People will buy bestsellers just to see what everyone else is reading and to be up to date at cocktail parties. Sales will soar exponentially; trends will be set; the impact of the book on the culture will be magnified. Christian books may thus be artificially excluded from having a wider circulation and a greater impact throughout the culture.

The literary establishment, of course, makes up an important segment of the intellectual establishment, which has been hostile to orthodox Christianity in varying degrees since the eighteenth century. The editors who choose the manuscripts, the reviewers who publicize them, the booksellers who stock them, the librarians who purchase them, and a large part of the book-buying public are not usually sympathetic to conservative Christianity. They operate oblivious to Christianity, never even glancing at a book from a religious press and feeling that they need make no concessions to the tastes or the concerns of Christians.

In the past few decades, Christians have responded to this exclusion by creating their own literary establishment. Christian publishers, which at one time printed only Sunday school material and denominational tracts, have blossomed into large-scale publishing firms every bit as diverse and sophisticated as their secular counterparts. A contemporary Christian publisher, while staying true to its original mission, may publish everything from Biblical scholarship and popular theology to children's books and fitness videos. Some have even ventured into fiction and poetry as well as provocative nonfiction.

Christian bookstores have emerged everywhere. These enterprises are responsible for the explosion in Christian publishing. They have opened up the market for Christian writers and have turned thousands upon thousands of Christians into readers. A few decades ago, Bible-believing Christians simply did not read much. Today, that is no longer the case, thanks largely to Christian bookstores. Christians eagerly pore over new books, discussing them in small groups, passing them on to their friends, and growing intellectually and spiritually in the process.

Christian bookstores are stimulating personal reflection and Biblical thinking in an almost unprecedented way. People are avidly reading books which relate the Bible to current issues and apply theology in a way comprehensible to the laity. Books on evangelism and spiritual growth, warnings against cults and other spiritual dangers, counseling for specific personal problems, and the classic offerings such as Bible studies, testimonies, and devotional materials—all of these can build up the church immeasurably. Christian bookstores have been catalysts of evangelical renewal. They have become crucial institutions of the contemporary church.

That Christians have successfully constructed an alternative literary establishment (complete with a network of Christian reviewers and a Christian Bestseller List) is a great achievement, although not without its problems. As it stands, the Christian literary establishment is oriented to a mass market. This popularizing tendency is part of its strength—rescuing theology from the elite domain of academic specialists and restoring it to laypeople has been a great service to the church. The hazard of appealing only to a mass popular audience is that the marketplace tends to be ruled by pleasure and self-gratification rather than truth and objective value. The mass market wishes only to be entertained, stimulated, and affirmed, values which can run counter to authentic Christianity.

Kenneth Myers has shown how popular culture tends to be oriented toward sentimentality, celebrity worship, sensationalism, simplistic answers, and self-centered desires.[4] Such values are evident in Christian bookstores, no less than in their secular counterparts. Books by newly converted celebrities outsell those by seasoned pastors. Books promising worldly success have more appeal than those proclaiming the disciplines of the cross. Sentimentality, moralism, and bad theology often prove more marketable than the gospel. In general, today's popular culture prefers television, rock music, and any sort of graven image to words and books. In some Christian bookstores, the few shelves of books are almost lost amidst the records, video tapes, greeting cards, jewelry, and knickknacks.

Books which demand thinking on the part of the reader, works of intrinsic excellence which prove challenging or troubling, may receive a chilly reception in the Christian marketplace. This proves frustrating for Christian writers, as well as for many editors and bookstore owners. It is a problem for the secular literary establishment no less than for the Christian. Myers argues that Christians must be especially careful about succumbing to the popular culture because its sensibility of self-gratification is diametrically opposed to a Christian worldview. Despite the temptations of the mass market, Christians are at least reading. There is reason to think that the more they read, the more they will develop a taste for excellence.

Another potential problem for the Christian literary establishment is that by being separate from the secular publishing world, it can promote a Christian ghetto. The pattern of Christian bookstores selling books from Christian publishers by Christian authors to Christian readers is appropriate to a point—the various facets of the church must serve each other and build each other up (1 Corinthians 12). Unbelievers, though, stand most in need of Christ and His message. Somehow Christian writers and publishers must reach those outside the church. Otherwise, Christians preach only to the converted and have no way of either evangelizing or influencing the culture as a whole. By creating a self-contained subculture, Christians risk becoming nothing more than another competing interest group, one isolated segment of a "pluralistic society," talking only to themselves.

Christians are told to be in the world, but not of the world (John 17:14–18). This means that Christians should be present and active in the secular world, although operating from a completely different spirit. Too often, as Myers has said, we have managed to do the opposite:

> It has not been uncommon for evangelical Christians to give up trying to come to terms with "secular" popular culture, and to boycott it altogether. But often they have simultaneously endorsed the creation of an extensive parallel popular culture complete with Christian rock bands and night clubs, Christian soap operas and talk shows, Christian spy and romance novels, and Christian exercise videos. They have thus succeeded in being of the world, but not in the world.[5]

In creating a parallel culture, Christians sometimes segregate themselves from the world while ironically retaining its spirit. Instead, Christians should encounter the world in the power of the Spirit of God.

Christian writers and publishers should strive to be "in" the literary world as a whole, writing and publishing for nonbelievers as well as believers. Dorothy Sayers was not writing "Christian mysteries" for a Christian audience. She was just writing good mysteries which all mystery fans avidly enjoy. She was a Christian writer, "in" but not "of" the world. So was Flannery O'Connor, T. S. Eliot, Gerard Manley

Hopkins, and the other great writers mentioned in this book, whose Christianity and literary art mutually nourished one another. Excellence is a great ideological equalizer.

Christian writers of originality and exceptional merit can find secular publishers. Such writers need the support of the "Christian market." Christian bookstores should stock the works of Flannery O'Connor and other distinguished Christian authors who are now, ironically, known mainly to secular readers. Classic writers such as George Herbert and John Milton, as well as contemporary authors such as Frederick Buechner, Madeleine L'Engle, and Larry Woiwode should be available in Christian bookstores and should be eagerly bought up by their patrons. Conversely, concerted efforts should be made by Christian publishers to break through into the secular marketplace. I came across Stephen Lawhead's retelling of the King Arthur legend published by Crossway in a B. Dalton bookstore. This series of novels is permeated with Christianity, but it is capable of attracting non-Christian readers as well. Other evangelical presses are also making inroads in the big retail chains. This puts their books in the hands of non-Christians as well as Christians and enables them to infect the culture as a whole with their Biblical perspective.

The secular publishing industry is by its nature driven by the need to make money. The free market is oblivious to ideology and is thus relentlessly fair to Christians. When Christian books become big sellers, the large chains and wholesalers are only too pleased to accommodate the buyers. If enough Christians ask for Christian titles in secular bookstores, the individual orders may give way to large orders on the part of the warehouses and to large-scale distribution. The booming "Christian market" has encouraged some major secular publishers (most notably, Harper & Row) to start printing books of interest to orthodox Christians. Whether Christians develop more of an impact on the contemporary literary world depends upon how active they are as readers.

READERS

That Christians should patronize worthy writers does not mean that they should only read works by other Christians. Milton refers to "the benefit which may be had of books promiscuously read."[6] Milton was advocating wide, random, voracious reading. Even works of error and accounts of sin, he felt, should be read:

> That which purifies us is trial, and trial is by what is contrary. That virtue therefore which is but a youngling in the contemplation of evil, and knows not the utmost that vice promises to her followers,

and rejects it, is but a blank virtue, not a pure. . . . Since therefore the knowledge and survey of vice in this world is so necessary to the constituting of human virtue, and the scanning of error to the confirmation of truth, how can we more safely, and with less danger, scout into the regions of sin and falsity, than by reading all manner of tractates, and hearing all manner of reason?[7]

"The true warfaring Christian,"[8] to use Milton's words again, must understand error and vice in order to do battle against it. Reading enables the Christian warrior to "scout" the territory of the enemy.

"Promiscuous reading" involves reading a wide range of material. Ours is an age of tunnel vision, and it is especially healthy today to break out of our narrow specialties. I sometimes will go to the library just to browse. In the periodical section, I will see what the scientific journals are printing these days. Then I will see what is new in the arts magazines. I will scan the liberal political periodicals, then their conservative counterparts. Sometimes I will wander through the stacks, taking down a history book, sampling some systematic theology, reading the introduction to a new book on film. As a literature professor, reading is my job. So that I can keep alive the love of reading that drew me into this line of work, I force myself to read for pure pleasure, a discipline that means I will probably leave the library with a mystery or a spy-thriller or a P. G. Wodehouse farce under my arm. (I know some of this is "popular culture," but I justify my reading it on Milton's authority.)

Christians cannot read everything, of course. Stewardship of time, money, and the imagination should be taken seriously. Some books are so bad, so stereotyped and clumsily written that I cannot get through them. Even when I read popular fiction, I insist on at least some literary merit—an interesting character, vivid descriptions, an intriguing plot, an accomplished style. Some books, often the same ones that are inept stylistically, are abhorrent morally and spiritually. I am not overscrupulous, but I am selective. I want to gain something of value even when I read for pleasure—a techno-thriller can enlighten me about the latest electronic wizardry; a historical novel can help me imagine a medieval court; a science fiction novel can send my imagination reeling through outer space. Some books give me nothing of value, and I refuse to spend my time with them. Extremely well-written books usually have a value of their own even though I might disagree with their ideology. These books gain me entrance to worldviews and human feelings that I need to understand. I can appreciate the aesthetic excellence of a novel and appropriate what it has to offer without surrendering my own Christian worldview. Even when I am lost in a good novel, wholly absorbed in the imaginative experience, I notice its implicit values and worldviews, and I relish its skillful techniques and manipulations of language. I read promiscuously, but always critically.

Christians to one extent or another *have* to read. They are "people of the Book," whose spirituality and conceptual framework is centered upon the linguistic revelation of the Word of God. As the culture moves farther and farther away from the printed word, Christians will still read. As their neighbors plug themselves in to their video images, Christians may find themselves making up a greater proportion of the reading public. Their tastes and values may matter again. Because readers exert the most influence in a society, however the masses amuse themselves, Christians may find themselves once again the thinkers and the leaders of society.

Something similar happened 1500 years ago in the first Dark Age when the Vandals trashed a civilization based on law and learning.[9] Amidst the moral anarchy, staggering ignorance, and image-centered paganism that prevailed for centuries, the tradition of literacy was preserved in the church. Behind the protective walls of the monasteries, books were cherished. They were copied out by hand, carefully stored, and eagerly read. The church was concerned for all kinds of books—Bibles, of course, but also books of medicine and science, works of pagan philosophers such as Aristotle, the poetry of Virgil and the comedies of Plautus. The Vandal aesthetic may be coming back in the anti-intellectualism of the mass culture and in the Postmodern nihilism of the high culture. Christians may be the last readers. If so, they need to be in training.

A READING LIST

What follows are a few suggestions for Christian readers. This list is by no means complete. Other suggestions are given throughout the book and can be tracked down through the index. This list focuses on Christian writers working more or less with explicit religious themes.

Other writers, such as Chaucer, Shakespeare, and Dickens, are also in the Christian camp, but they are not included here. They are certainly worth reading. I also recommend the satires of Jonathan Swift, the fantasies of J. R. R. Tolkien, the mysteries of Dorothy L. Sayers, and the work of other Christian writers who freely range over "secular" subject matter.

This list does not pretend to be exhaustive. Many works by non-Christians certainly deserve to be read, as do many Christian writers not included here (many of whom I simply have not read yet). These are nothing more than some of my personal favorites, works of literature which have shaped my imagination and my faith:

CLASSICS

DANTE
The Divine Comedy is one of the greatest poems ever written, and it is one of the richest examples of Christian literature. Protestants should not let Dante's medieval Catholicism be a stumbling block. Victimized by the Pope, Dante was a voice of reform. The key in understanding this classic is to see it as allegorical, not literal. Dante's Hell symbolizes the state of human beings who reject God; Purgatory symbolizes the spiritual dimension of suffering; Heaven symbolizes the love of God. Just as Dante needed Virgil to explain what he was seeing, modern

readers need a guide. The best are Dorothy L. Sayers, *Introductory Papers on Dante* and Charles Williams, *The Figure of Beatrice*.

SPENSER, EDMUND

The Faerie Queene. Another spiritual allegory, this one cast in the form of a medieval romance which comprises a fantasy world of its own. Sprawling, long, and somewhat difficult, this masterpiece, which was one of C. S. Lewis's favorite books, is worth the effort.

HERBERT, GEORGE

The Temple. The Reformation Dante. Here the poetry is centered in a personal relationship with Christ. Herbert's poetry is clear on the surface, but contains incredible depths. He is a supreme master of poetic form. A guide to his verse is my book *Reformation Spirituality: The Religion of George Herbert*.

DONNE, JOHN

Collected Poetry. Donne's verse, following his life, ranges from the erotic to the deeply spiritual, with poems of struggle in between. *Devotions Upon Divergent Occasions* is his prose masterpiece. Also read his *Sermons*, which are so electrifying you can understand why the church he pastored was always packed.

MILTON, JOHN

Paradise Lost. Paradise Regained. Samson Agonistes. "Areopagitica." The most sublime of poets, thoroughly Biblical in his subjects and astonishing in his poetic power.

BUNYAN, JOHN

Pilgrim's Progress. Another profound—and entertaining—spiritual allegory. Bunyan explains his own symbolism as he writes. He is also saturated in Scripture and possesses a keen, sympathetic understanding of the soul and its struggles.

DOSTOYEVSKY, FYODOR

Crime and Punishment. The Brothers Karamazov. The Idiot. Deep, sometimes disturbing explorations of the human soul by the preeminent Russian novelist. Dostoyevsky's faith, tempered by suffering and struggle, shines through the darkness he portrays.

THOMPSON, FRANCIS

"The Hound of Heaven." This is one of the most moving Christian poems, the semiautobiographical account of a person running away from God. God, though, keeps pursuing.

HOPKINS, GERARD MANLEY
Collected Poems. Bold, original verse that stretches the language in a celebration of Christ and an affirmation of existence.

MODERN WRITERS

CHESTERTON, G. K.
Orthodoxy. Heretics. The Everlasting Man. One of the wittiest and most incisive defenders of the Christian view of life. His nonfiction often deals with topical names and issues, so that contemporary readers sometimes miss the references. Nevertheless, Chesterton's shrewd and funny refutations of modern thought and his exuberant joy in ordinary things make him indispensable.

ELIOT, T. S.
"The Waste Land." "Ash Wednesday." "The Four Quartets." Other poems and essays. Eliot's verse is sometimes difficult, but few poets see more deeply into the failures of modern culture, and few have expressed the orthodox faith in poems of such sophistication.

LEWIS, C. S.
Screwtape Letters. The Great Divorce. The Chronicles of Narnia. Out of the Silent Planet. Perelandra. Mere Christianity. Lewis has become the essential writer for contemporary Christians. A lucid and imaginative apologist for the Christian faith.

WILLIAMS, CHARLES
Descent into Hell. All Hallows Eve. Williams was one of Lewis's best friends. Of the "Inklings," the circle of Christian writers around Lewis, Williams may have been the most original. His novels are unusual and somewhat eerie, setting forth realistic, psychologically realized characters confronted by tangible spiritual forces. Throughout his writings, Williams is developing an original, yet orthodox theology centered around the "co-inherence" of the Trinity (in which the three persons of the godhead are distinct, yet united), a model of love which he applies to individuals, relationships, and societies. Williams also explores "the way of affirmation" and "the way of negation" as two legitimate styles of spirituality. For a guide to Williams, see Mary McDermott Shideler, *The Theology of Romantic Love: A Study in the Writings of Charles Williams.*

O'CONNOR, FLANNERY
The Violent Bear It Away. Wise Blood. Short Stories. A writer of uncompromising theological orthodoxy, O'Connor is unorthodox in

her fictional style. Her characters and plots are both funny and shocking. Throughout her stories of the American South, one finds human sin countered by the grace of God.

CONTEMPORARY WRITERS

BUECHNER, FREDERICK

Brendan. Godric. A presbyterian pastor turned outstanding novelist, Buechner's lives of medieval saints are filled with wonder and wisdom. His series of novels about a fraudulent, yet sympathetic evangelist, collected in *The Book of Bebb,* is not as funny as it used to be. Buechner has also written some fine nonfiction: *Telling the Truth: The Gospel as Tragedy, Comedy, and Fairy Tale; The Alphabet of Grace;* and others.

DILLARD, ANNIE

Pilgrim at Tinker Creek. Holy the Firm. Teaching a Stone to Talk. Her nonfiction combines scientific subject matter with spiritual contemplation, all rendered in a prose style of remarkable power. She does speak of evolution, but evangelicals should not let that be a stumbling block to learning new things for which to praise God.

GREENE, GRAHAM

The Power and the Glory. A Burnt-Out Case. Brighton Rock. The Heart of the Matter. Sometimes I find myself in a melancholy mood in which nothing will satisfy me except a novel by Graham Greene. "Greeneland" is tropical, seedy, and bleak, yet open to the grace of God. Greene distinguishes between his more serious novels and "entertainments," lighter fare about spies and crime. These thrillers, which also have theological depth, include *Orient Express, This Gun for Hire, The Confidential Agent,* and *Our Man in Havana.*

L'ENGLE, MADELEINE

A Wrinkle in Time. A Wind in the Door. A Swiftly Tilting Planet. These Christian fantasies are good enough to please children as well as adults. Her realistic novels such as the Austin series affirm the value of family life and show understanding for adolescents without condescending to them.

PERCY, WALKER

Love in the Ruins. The Second Coming. Lancelot. Thanatos Syndrome. Lost in the Cosmos. Percy, a southern physician, takes on the decline of Western civilization in these novels. Percy's writing is satirical, polemical, and philosophical. He deals fairly frankly with sex (excoriating the scientific research that has brought us "sex clinics," for example), which may be distasteful to some readers. He is, however, for the most part on their side.

SHAW, LUCI

Listen to the Green. Other poetry and anthologies. Her verse is clear, well-crafted, and evangelical to the bone. A good place to begin for appreciating contemporary Christian poetry. From Luci Shaw one might go on to John Leax, Eugene Warren, and others.

WANGERIN, WALTER

The Book of the Dun Cow. The Book of Sorrows. A Lutheran pastor turned novelist and prose-poet, Wangerin plunges us deeply into the faith and into its implications. His novels take the beast fable to some of its greatest heights since Chaucer. See too his children's stories such as *Thistle.* I especially recommend his nonfiction about his experiences ministering in an inner-city parish and about his own life and family: *The Ragman and Other Cries of Faith, Miz Lil and the Chronicles of Faith, The Manger is Empty.*

N O T E S

1. See for example Leland Ryken's excellent treatments of the subject, *Triumphs of the Imagination: Literature in Christian Perspective* (Downers Grove, IL: InterVarsity Press, 1979) and *Windows to the World: Literature in Christian Perspective* (Grand Rapids, MI: Zondervan, 1985). See also Susan V. Gallagher and Roger Lundin, *Literature Through the Eyes of Faith* (San Francisco: Harper & Row, 1989).

2. My theological perspective is that of an evangelical, Bible-believing Christian of the Lutheran tradition. This book might be seen as something of an experiment in Augustinian aesthetics. Augustine believed that aesthetic forms—because of their orderliness, their participation in created existence, and their beauty—are a manifestation of the divine *logos*, the Word which underlies all of creation (Hebrews 1:3; 11:3). Thus, the formal aspects of art or literature, those properties that give them their beauty, are good in themselves. Sinful human beings, both as authors and as readers, tend to misuse these forms, but the forms themselves are inherently valuable. Literary forms in general can express created truth. The literary mode of comedy, for example—our universal urge to laugh and to craft funny stories—points to some spiritual truth, some aspect of the divine *logos*.

   To be fully Augustinian involves examining also how sin distorts the aesthetic experience. Literature can be used for evil as well as for good. Nevertheless, aesthetic forms have an objective value and must be in accord with God's law whether or not the writer knows God. Christian writers must still employ good craftsmanship even if their theology is correct in order to make a good book. Both Christian and non-Christian writers are bound to the same standards of craftsmanship, and if they achieve them, both may lead their readers into valuable pleasures and insights. Thus, this book examines both form and meaning, aesthetics and theology, the value and the limits of literature.

CHAPTER ONE: *The Word and the Image: The Importance of Reading*

1. For the centrality of language to Christianity and its implications, see Jacques Ellul, *The Humiliation of the Word*, trans. Joyce Main Hanks (Grand Rapids, MI: Eerdmans, 1985).

2. See Francis A. Schaeffer's discussion of the centrality of language to personality and relationships in *He Is There and He Is Not Silent*, in *The Complete Works of Francis A. Schaeffer* (Westchester, IL: Crossway, 1982), 1:323, 344.

3. Except where otherwise indicated, quotations from the Bible are taken from the *New International Version* (Grand Rapids, MI: Zondervan, 1973). See chapter 5, n5.

4. Neil Postman, *Amusing Ourselves to Death: Public Discourse in the Age of Show Business* (New York: Viking, 1985), p. 9.

5. Neil Postman, *Teaching as a Conserving Activity* (New York: Delacorte Press, 1979), pp. 47-70. Postman was also the author of *Teaching as a Subversive Activity*, which promoted radical leftist educational theories. In this later book, Postman recants much of what he had earlier advocated. Postman's first book is still on the reading lists of many teacher education programs while his new defense of conservatism in education is strangely missing.

6. *Ibid.*, p. 57.

7. *Ibid.*, p. 77.

8. *Ibid.*, p. 79.

9. *Ibid.*, p. 72.

10. See Postman's chapter "Reach Out and Elect Someone" in *Amusing Ourselves to Death*, pp. 125-141.

11. See Postman's chapter "Typographic America" in *Amusing Ourselves to Death*, pp. 30-43.

12. See Postman, *Teaching as a Conserving Activity*, pp. 76, 78.

13. Postman, *Amusing Ourselves to Death*, pp. 116, 117.

14. *Ibid.*, p.121.

15. For a sophisticated exploration of idolatry as it relates to the contemporary domination of images, see Ellul, *The Humiliation of the Word*, especially his chapters "Idols and the Word," pp. 48-111, and "The Religious Conflict Between Image and Word," pp. 183-203.

16. Postman, *Teaching as a Conserving Activity*, pp. 15-25, 129ff. Postman is also somewhat hopeful about computers which require "languages" and modes of thinking analagous to human language. On the other hand, the cutting-edge of computer research is "computer visualization." The advances in computer animation have caused some experts to predict the further eclipse of language as a means of thinking. Computers will operate "in a vocabulary of images, not words. In effect, the sort of literacy that computers will demand will be visual. . . . Computers are now moving us into a post-visual, post-literate culture where the interactive story board is going to be the media metaphor of choice." Michael Schrage, "Computers Shift Culture to Images," *The Milwaukee Journal*, 7 January 1990, p. 5J.

17. See my book, *The Gift of Art: The Place of the Arts in Scripture* (Downers Grove, IL: InterVarsity Press, 1983) and my upcoming book on art for the Turning Point Christian Worldview Series.

18. John Milton, "Areopagitica," in *The Student's Milton*, ed. Frank Allen Patterson (New York: Appleton-Century-Crofts, 1957), p. 738.

19. Postman, *Teaching as a Conserving Activity*, p. 78.

CHAPTER TWO: *Vicarious Experience and Vicarious Sin:*
The Importance of Criticism

1. See Kenneth Myers's chart comparing "popular culture" and "high culture" values in *All God's Children and Blue Suede Shoes* (Westchester, IL: Crossway Books, 1989), p. 120.
2. Matthew Arnold, "The Study of Poetry," in *Poetry and Criticism of Matthew Arnold,* ed. A. Dwight Culler (Boston: Houghton Mifflin, 1961), p. 306.
3. C. S. Lewis, *An Experiment in Criticism* (Cambridge: Cambridge University Press, 1961), p. 137.
4. Walter Wangerin, Jr., Keynote Address, Midwest Conference on Christianity and Literature, Concordia University-Wisconsin, 29 September 1989.
5. Gallagher and Lundin, *Literature Through the Eyes of Faith,* p. 139.
6. *Ibid.,* p. 141.
7. I am not saying this is necessarily the etymology of the word, which the *Oxford English Dictionary* considers uncertain. The word is taken from the Latin, with pretty much the same meaning that it has in English. *Scene* does derive from the Latin *scena,* the word for stage, which is a transliteration of the Greek word for tent or booth, the backdrop in front of which the actors would perform. "Ob" is a Latin preposition meaning, among other things, in opposition, "implying the injurious or objectionable character of an action" (*OED*).
8. Other forms of obscenity—realities that ought not to be shown publicly—would include references to "bodily functions" and other intensely private human activities. In my city, a musician performing at a punk rock club was recently arrested for defecating onstage. This was too much for even the avant garde patrons of this club, who called the police. The charge with exquisite accuracy was obscenity—he did onstage what he should have done in private.
9. William Kirk Kilpatrick, *Psychological Seduction* (Nashville, TN: Thomas Nelson, 1983), p. 223.
10. See the entry in the *Oxford English Dictionary.*
11. Studies have shown that 77 percent of child molesters of boys and 87 percent of child molesters of girls admitted that they were imitating what they had seen in pornography. Among rapists, 57 percent confess to "trying out" what they had seen in pornography. See David Jeremiah, "The Porno Plague," in *The Rebirth of America* (Philadelphia: Arthur S. De Moss Foundation, 1986), pp. 99-103.
12. See the entry in the *Oxford English Dictionary.*
13. Robert Hughes, "A Loony Parody of Cultural Democracy," *Time,* 14 August 1989, p. 82.
14. *Inferno,* cantos XIV-XVII.
15. See E. K. Chambers, *William Shakespeare* (Oxford: The Clarendon Press, 1930), 1:98-117; 238-242.
16. This is a figure of speech known as "metonymny."
17. From *William Shakespeare, The Complete Works,* ed. Peter Alexander (London: Collins, 1951).
18. Christopher Marlowe, *Dr. Faustus,* 1.3.47. The devil Mephistopheles is explaining that Faustus's occult incantations raised him not by their intrinsic power, but because devils see that anyone who would so "abjure the Scriptures and his savior Christ" will be easy prey. Quoted from The New Mermaid Edition, ed. Roma Gill (New York: Hill and Wang, 1966).

19. Flannery O'Connor, *Wise Blood* in *Three by Flannery O'Connor* (New York: New American Library, 1962), pp. 41, 43.
20. John Milton, "Areopagitica," *The Student's Milton*, p. 752.
21. Mortimer J. Adler, *Six Great Ideas* (New York: Collier, 1984), p. 114. See also pp. 111-119.

CHAPTER THREE: *Nonfiction: The Art of Truth-Telling*

1. See Aristotle's "Rhetoric" and Cicero's "Of Oratory" for systematized presentations of classical rhetorical theory. See also St. Augustine's Christian applications of classical rhetoric in *On Christian Doctrine*, Book IV.
2. See Marvin Olasky, *The Prodigal Press* (Westchester, IL: Crossway, 1988).
3. For the classic exploration of the role of language in manipulating ideas, see George Orwell's "Politics and the English Language," as well as his novels *1984* and *Animal Farm*.
4. Jacques Barzun and Henry F. Graf, *The Modern Researcher*, 4th ed. (New York: Harcourt, Brace, Jovanovich, 1985), pp. 32, 33.
5. Cited by Edwin A. Newman, "Language on the Skids," *Reader's Digest*, November 1979, p. 43.
6. C. S. Lewis, "What Are We to Make of Jesus Christ?" in *God in the Dock*, ed. Walter Hooper (Grand Rapids, MI: Eerdmans, 1970), p. 160.
7. C. S. Lewis, *Mere Christianity* (New York: Macmillan, 1952), p. 41.
8. William Zinsser, *On Writing Well*, 3rd ed. (New York: Harper & Row, 1985), pp. 54, 55. Zinsser's book is a good introduction for writers to the techniques and artistry of nonfiction.
9. *Ibid.*, p. 54.
10. Annie Dillard, *Holy the Firm* (New York: Harper & Row, 1977), pp. 58, 59. See also *Pilgrim at Tinker Creek* (New York: Harper & Row, 1974).
11. See Wangerin's *Miz Lil and the Chronicles of Grace* (San Francisco: Harper & Row, 1988).
12. Walter Wangerin, Jr., "Modern Hexameron—De Aranea," in *The Ragman and Other Cries of Faith* (New York: Harper & Row, 1984), p. 26.
13. *Ibid.*, pp. 26, 27.

CHAPTER FOUR: *Fiction: The Art of Story-Telling*

1. See the entry in William F. Arndt and F. Wilburg Gingrich, *A Greek-English Lexicon of the New Testament and Other Early Christian Literature* (Chicago: University Chicago Press, 1957), pp. 617-618.
2. See Leland Ryken's discussion in *Triumphs of the Imagination*, pp. 12-17, and the way he answers these problems throughout his book.
3. Sir Philip Sidney, "An Apology for Poetry," in *Criticism: The Major Statements*, ed. Charles Kaplan (New York: St. Martin's, 1985), p. 132.
4. *Ibid.*, p. 133.
5. *Ibid.*, p. 115. Sidney here is drawing on Horace, *The Art of Poetry*.
6. *Ibid.*, p. 124.
7. Kilpatrick, *Psychological Seduction*, pp. 105-107.
8. See *Ibid.*, pp. 107-121.
9. *Ibid.*, pp. 119-120.
10. All of this is in Malory's *Le Morte D'Arthur*. The best modern retelling is T. H. White's *The Once and Future King* (New York: G. P. Putnam's Sons, 1958).

11. Aristotle, "The Poetics," in *Criticism: The Major Statements*, p. 29.
12. *Ibid.*, p. 34. For "tragic wonder," see p. 31.
13. J. R. R. Tolkien, "On Fairy Stories," in *The Monsters and the Critics and Other Essays,* ed. Christopher Tolkien (Boston: Houghton Mifflin, 1984), p. 148.
14. See Lewis, *An Experiment in Criticism.*
15. Certainly, non-Christians "suppress the truth by their wickedness" (Romans 1:18). For this they have no excuse, as Paul continues, because "what may be known about God is plain to them, because God has made it plain to them" in the general revelation implicit in the created order (Romans 1:19). Many talented writers are so addicted to sin in their personal lives that they distort the truth and so refuse to accept God's revelation. However, when they write from their inmost hearts and frankly describe the human condition, this suppressed knowledge emerges, and they are often forced to acknowledge the reality of God's moral order. In their personal and spiritual lives, writers and other artists are no different from any other sinners. Their work should never be set up as having moral or theological authority apart from Scripture. When they write works of excellence—employing the aesthetic laws that are part of God's creation—they sometimes unwittingly find themselves acknowledging God's truth. Christopher Marlowe was indicted for blasphemy, yet he wrote the great Christian tragedy *Dr. Faustus.* William Faulkner was a humanist and an alcoholic, yet his novels unfold the human condition in a way that often agrees with Christian orthodoxy. Steinbeck was an agnostic, yet his use of the Bible in his writings gives them a far greater meaning than he may have realized.
16. For a searching discussion of St. Augustine's aesthetics, see William H. Pahlka, *St. Augustine's Meter and George Herbert's Will* (Kent, OH: Kent State University Press, 1987).
17. Flannery O'Connor, "The Fiction Writer and His Country," in *Collected Works* (New York: The Library of America, 1988), pp. 804-805.
18. *Ibid.*, p. 804.
19. *Ibid.*, pp. 805-806.
20. Robert Drake, "Flannery O'Connor," in *Religion and Modern Literature: Essays in Theory and Criticism,* ed. G. B. Tennyson and Edward E. Ericson, Jr. (Grand Rapids, MI: Eerdmans, 1975), p. 374. Drake's essay is an excellent introduction to O'Connor's work.
21. Flannery O'Connor, "The Displaced Person," in *Three by Flannery O'Connor* (New York: New American Library, 1962), pp. 290-291.

CHAPTER FIVE: *Poetry: The Art of Singing*

1. Holy Sonnet X, ll. 1-2. Quoted from John Donne, *Poetry and Prose,* ed. Frank J. Warnke (New York: Modern Library, 1967), p. 270. I have modernized the spelling.
2. Henry Wadsworth Longfellow, "A Psalm of Life," l. 5. From *Favorite Poems of Henry Wadsworth Longfellow* (New York: Doubleday, 1947).
3. Ralph Waldo Emerson, "The Poet," in *The Selected Writings of Ralph Waldo Emerson,* ed. Brooks Atkinson (New York: Modern Library, 1950), p. 327.
4. *Ibid.*, p. 329.
5. This is one reason why I have problems with many modern Bible translations which often interpret and translate away the vivid metaphors of the

original text. In Genesis 4:1, the Hebrew speaks of Adam "knowing" Eve, a beautiful metaphor that transfigures human sexuality. To translate this figure of speech as Adam "lay with" Eve or Adam "had sexual intercourse" with Eve is to miss the depths of the Scriptural language. "Lay" is just as euphemistic, and "intercourse" is just as metaphorical, a metaphor based on conversation rather than knowledge. Most of my Bible quotations are from the *New International Version,* but I sometimes quote from an older translation, the *King James Version* (KJV) or the *Revised Standard Version* (RSV), in order to preserve the metaphor. See chapter 8, n5.

6. See Stephen Prickett, *Words and the Word: Language, Poetics, and Biblical Interpretation* (New York: Cambridge University Press, 1986) for a sophisticated discussion of this confusion.

7. Ruth apRoberts, "Old Testament Poetry: The Translatable Structure," *PMLA,* 92 (1977): 987-1004. The discussion that follows, including the analysis of Psalm 24, is greatly indebted to her excellent article.

8. See Ruth apRoberts's in-depth analysis of this psalm's structure (*Ibid.,* pp. 991-992). She finds parallelism in even larger units, such as the pattern of questions and responses. She also works out something of a rhyme scheme in the psalm, a "rhyming" based on the repetition of ideas rather than sounds.

9. I discuss this passage in similar terms and in more detail in my book *The Gift of Art,* pp. 64-65. In both cases I am indebted to Thorlief Boman, *Hebrew Thought Compared to Greek,* trans. Jules C. Moreau (Philadelphia: Westminster Press, 1960), pp. 77-81.

10. See my book *Reformation Spirituality: The Religion of George Herbert* (Lewisburg, PA: Bucknell University Press, 1985) for a detailed discussion of Herbert, his verse, and the way he explores the Christian faith.

11. Herbert's poems are quoted from *The Works of George Herbert,* ed. F. E. Hutchinson (Oxford: Clarendon Press, 1941). I have modernized the original spelling.

12. See my discussion of this poem in *Reformation Spirituality,* pp. 68-69.

13. See *Ibid.,* pp. 52-53 and the other critics whom I cite in that discussion.

14. See Mary Ellen Rickey, *Utmost Art: Complexity in the Verse of George Herbert* (Lexington, KY: University of Kentucky Press, 1966) for a fascinating study of Herbert's word play.

15. *Ibid.,* pp. 108-109.

16. See J. Max Patrick, "Critical Problems in Editing George Herbert's *The Temple,*" in *The Editor as Critic and the Critic as Editor* (Los Angeles: William Andrews Clark Memorial Library, 1973), pp. 14-22, who also lists many other more subtle examples of Herbert's shaped verse.

17. See my discussion of the poem in *Reformation Spirituality,* pp. 171-173.

18. Simone Weil, "Spiritual Autobiography," in *Waiting for God,* trans. Emma Craufurd (New York: Harper & Row, 1973), pp. 68-69.

19. Quotations from Eliot's poetry are taken from *T. S. Eliot, Collected Poems 1909-1962* (New York: Harcourt, Brace & World, 1963).

20. In the last sentence of "A Defence of Poetry" in *Criticism: The Major Statement.*

CHAPTER SIX: *Tragedy and Comedy:*
The Literature of Damnation and Salvation

1. See Dante's "Letter to Can Grande." For the implications of Dante's view of comedy see Dorothy L. Sayers, *Introductory Papers on Dante* (New

York: Harper & Row, 1954) and Charles Williams, *The Figure of Beatrice* (London: Faber & Faber, 1943).

2. Ironically, the real-life marriage of Lucille Ball and Desi Arnaz ended in divorce. They were unable to manage a comic reconciliation in their own lives.

3. A young critic has pointed out to me that *Old Yeller* does not begin with an idyllic relationship, but that it develops in the course of the novel. Greek tragedy, which is the basis of Aristotle's analysis, follows the unity of time, so that the playwright must begin in the midst of the action. A novelist has greater leisure to develop the story. Tragic novels, therefore, may not begin with joy; rather, they may work up to it. Then the tragic catastrophe brings the happy edifice, so carefully constructed, crashing down.

4. Julian of Norwich, *Showings*, trans. Edmund Colledge and James Walsh (New York: Paulist Press, 1978), p. 225. Dame Julian was an anchoress of the fourteenth century, whose contemplations of the love of God are well worth reading.

5. Dante, "Paradiso," canto 28.

6. *Ibid.*, canto 22.

7. See the entry and its discussion in Arndt and Gingrich, *A Greek-English Lexicon*, p. 16. Although the souls of all the dead went to Hades, certain regions were reserved for the punishment of the notoriously evil.

8. Aristotle's theories about tragedy are presented in his *Poetics*. At a few points, I am interpreting Aristotle rather than reproducing his thought exactly. For example, he suggests that catharsis involves eliminating undesirable emotions, specifically, pity and fear. As a Christian, I cannot agree that pity is undesirable, yet I acknowledge Aristotle's insight in describing the audience's sensation at the catastrophe and so account for it in a different way.

9. See the entry and the discussion in Arndt and Gingrich, *A Greek-English Lexicon*, p. 42.

10. The last line of Milton's *Samson Agonistes*, a tragedy about the life of Samson. Milton follows Aristotle's rules with Biblical subjects, making it an especially valuable example of a Christian tragedy.

11. That Oedipus is fulfilling the fate predicted for him by the gods does not minimize his own responsibility for what unfolds. If he did not have the *hubris* that led him to slaughter a whole company rather than stepping aside to let them pass, he never would have killed his father, and the prophecy would never have been fulfilled. Greek tragedies may play with the paradoxes of fate and free will, but they insist on the heroes' complicity in their fate.

12. I am thinking of Milton's portrayal of Samson in *Samson Agonistes* and of Graham Greene's alcoholic priest in *The Power and the Glory*.

13. Aristotle is said to have written a treatise on comedy to go along with his analysis of tragedy, but this work was lost. He does treat the subject briefly in the *Poetics*. The classical comic tradition is set forth in the anonymous Greek treatise known as the *Tractatus Coislinianus*, in the writings of the Roman poet Horace, and in neoclassical theorists such as Ben Jonson and John Dryden.

14. Sidney, "An Apology for Poetry," in *Criticism: The Major Statements*, p. 127.

15. In Walker Percy, *Lost in the Cosmos: The Last Self-Help Book* (New York:

Washington Square Press, 1983), pp. 48-59. This entire book and Percy's work in general exemplify contemporary Christian satire.

16. For the connection between Shakespeare's comedy and that of Dante, see the following articles by Neville Coghill (a close friend of C. S. Lewis): "The Basis of Shakespearean Comedy," *Essays and Studies by Members of the English Association,* 3 (1950): 1-28 and "Comic Form in *Measure for Measure,*" *Shakespeare Survey,* 8 (1955): 14-27. See also Roy W. Battenhouse, "*Measure for Measure* and Christian Doctrine of the Atonement," *PMLA,* 61 (1946): 1029-59.

17. For another approach to these issues, see Frederick Buechner, *Telling the Truth: The Gospel as Tragedy, Comedy, and Fairy Tale* (San Francisco: Harper & Row, 1977).

18. Robinson Davies, *World of Wonders* in *The Deptford Trilogy* (New York: Penguin, 1985), p. 689.

CHAPTER SEVEN: *Realism: Literature as a Mirror*

1. M. H. Abrams, *The Mirror and the Lamp: Romantic Theory and the Critical Tradition* (New York: Oxford, 1953).

2. A Christian metaphor for the human mind and imagination might be the electric light. Unlike the old self-contained oil lamps and unlike purely passive mirrors, an electric light remains totally dark unless plugged in to an external source of power. Only because of its total dependence on an outside power can it shed light of its own.

3. The Word of God describes itself both as a mirror and as a lamp. "Anyone who listens to the word but does not do what it says is like a man who looks at his face in a mirror and, after looking at himself, goes away and immediately forgets what he looks like" (James 1:23, 24). James could be describing any sort of superficial reading in which the reader glances at the reflection of reality captured in the text but remains unaffected. Listening to or reading the Bible without seeing oneself reflected in its pages and without being changed is to miss its whole point. James goes on to describe the way one should read the Bible: "But the man who looks intently into the perfect law that gives freedom, and continues to do this, not forgetting what he has heard, but doing it—he will be blessed in what he does" (James 1:25). Looking intently and continually into the mirror of the text, at the same time carrying out what has been read into action in the external world, will bring self-knowledge and blessing.

   Moreover, God's Word can flood the darkness of the soul with Jesus Christ, the light of the world (John 8:12; 2 Corinthians 4:6) and illumine every facet of life: "Your word is a lamp to my feet and a light for my path" (Psalm 119:105). In turn, the light of God's Word can also ignite the human mind: "You, O LORD, keep my lamp burning" (Psalm 18:28).

4. See Tolkien's "On Fairy Stories," p. 139.

5. The term is from the Russian critic Victor Shklovsky. See my article, "Defamiliarizing the Gospel: Shklovsky and a Theory of Religious Art," *Christianity and Literature,* 28 (1979): 40-47.

6. David Ruenzel, "Drabness, Emptiness Make a Dreary Novel," *The Milwaukee Journal,* 14 January 1990, p. 9E. The review is of *Picturing Will* by Ann Beattie.

7. According to Irina Ratushinskaya in an interview by Ellen Santilli Vaughn, "In Solitary Cells on Winter Nights," *Christianity Today,* 15 December 1989, p. 26.

8. See *Ibid.*, for a good introduction to her personality, her faith, and her poetry.

1. Jonathan Swift, "The Battle of the Books," in *Jonathan Swift,* ed. Angus Ross and David Woolley, The Oxford Authors Series (New York: Oxford University Press, 1984), p. 9. The fable is a recurrent one and can be traced from Francis Bacon to Walt Whitman.
2. See J. R. R. Tolkien, "On Fairy Stories," pp. 145-154.
3. See Plato's *Republic*, Book X.
4. See my article, "Fantasy and the Tradition of Christian Art," *Mythlore*, 53 (Spring 1988): 34-37. Some of the material in this section is adapted from that article.
5. The *New International Version*, as it often does, interprets the metaphors of Scripture rather than reproducing them. Instead of referring to "graven images," the NIV speaks of "idols," rendering Exodus 20:4 as follows: "You shall not make for yourself an idol in the form of anything in heaven above or on the earth beneath or in the waters below." See chapter 5, n5.
6. The prohibition of realistic art was not complete. The designs for the Tabernacle and the Temple included certain representational art. See the discussion in my book *The Gift of Art*, pp. 32-33, 47-52.
7. Edmund Spenser, *The Faerie Queene,* Book I, canto 10, stanzas 5-6. Quoted from *The Poetical Works of Edmund Spenser,* ed. J. C. Smith and E. deSelincourt (New York: Oxford University Press, 1959), p. 51.
8. *Ibid.*, canto 4, stanzas 4-5.
9. See C. S. Lewis, *The Last Battle* (New York: Collier Books, 1956), pp.140-141. The quotation in this sentence is taken from this passage. Lewis uses the image to describe the Incarnation, alluding to the stable in Bethlehem which contained the Infinite God.
10. Spenser, *The Faerie Queene,* canto 10, stanza 6, line 3.
11. The word *myth* is one of those terms that has different meanings in different fields and thus is open to great misunderstanding. In ordinary usage, *myth* can refer to something that may be accepted in some circles but turns out to be untrue, as in "the story of George Washington chopping down the cherry tree is probably only a myth." In anthropology, *myth* may refer to any religious narrative. In theology, *myth* may refer to a false, idolatrous religion. In psychology, *myth* may refer to significant recurring patterns manifested in expressions of the unconsciousness such as dreams. In literary criticism, *myth* may refer to any narratives that carry so much significance that they are repeated over and over again in subsequent literature, usually having their origins in folklore or another ancient source. I have had an essay published in a book entitled *The David Myth in Western Literature.* None of the editors or contributors, as far as I know, questioned the historicity of David. They were simply studying the Bible's account of David as a powerful and recurrent influence in Western literature.
12. Letter to Arthur Greeves, 18 October 1931, in *They Stand Together: The Letters of C. S. Lewis to Arthur Greeves (1914-1963),* ed. Walter Hooper (New York: Macmillan, 1979), p. 427. For further discussions on the relationship between myth and Christianity, see "Myth Became Fact" in *God in the Dock.*
13. C. S. Lewis, *Surprised by Joy* (New York: Harcourt, Brace, & World, 1955), pp. 179, 181.

14. A. N. Wilson, *How Can We Know?* (New York: Atheneum, 1985).

15. C. S. Lewis, "Sometimes Fairy Stories May Say Best What's To Be Said," in *Of Other Worlds: Essays and Stories,* ed. Walter Hooper (New York: Harcourt, Brace, & World, 1966), p. 37. See also Kathryn Lindskoog, *The Lion of Judah in Never-Never Land* (Grand Rapids, MI: Eerdmans, 1973).

16. Samuel Taylor Coleridge, *Biographia Literaria,* XIV.

17. G. K. Chesterton, *Orthodoxy* (London: The Bodley Head, 1908), p. 73.

18. See Bruce Frohnen, "Mother Knows Best," *Chronicles,* November 1989, p. 50. The charge is absurd even in its own terms. The main character in the most beloved fairy tales is usually a girl—Cinderella, Snow White, Sleeping Beauty, Beauty and the Beast, Red Riding Hood, Gretel, Goldilocks. Moreover, she nearly always shows independence, resourcefulness, and integrity.

19. C. S. Lewis, *The Voyage of the Dawn Treader* (New York: Collier, 1952), pp. 1-2, 71.

20. Bruno Bettelheim, *The Uses of Enchantment: The Meaning and Importance of Fairy Tales* (New York: Knopf, 1976), p. 5. Bettelheim's discussions of individual fairy tales such as "Cinderella," "Snow White," "The Three Little Pigs," and "Little Red Riding Hood" are perhaps overly Freudian, but they are well worth reading and constitute an important defense of traditional folk literature and the values it embodies.

21. *Ibid.,* p. 141.

22. *Ibid.,* p. 7.

23. *Ibid.,* p. 7. Compare the approach of fairy tales to that of contemporary "problem books," the genre of children's literature that shows a child facing a realistic problem (the divorce of one's parents, the death of a friend, etc.). These books generally solve the problem with a dose of pop psychology and humanistic philosophy (the divorce is not your fault; your parents must grow in their own ways; feel good about yourself no matter what you are doing, and so on). Such books are didactic in the worst way, and from a Christian point of view, what they are teaching is nearly always wrong. In a penetrating critique of such books, John R. Dunlap criticizes their brooding, self-absorbed tone and summarizes their approach to the problems they deal with: "If, for example, divorce is really something of a crippling disaster and not a 'problem' which enlightened kids can easily adjust to; if homosexuality is a pathetic disorder and not a 'life style' impugned by craven moralists; if teen promiscuity is not a sensible 'option' for healthy youngsters; if America is not really just a congeries of bigots and victims; if sentimental naturalism is not a very natural human pose; if militant feminism is not a serious response to life's deepest yearnings; if moral choice is not exclusively a 'private matter'; if ethical relativism is not coherently admissible as life's only absolute—well, then, a lot of contemporary books for children are telling a lot of big fibs to our kids." (John R. Dunlap, "Kiddie Litter," *American Spectator,* December 1989, p. 21.)

24. *Ibid.*

25. *Ibid.,* p. 9.

26. *Ibid.,* pp. 9-10.

27. *Ibid.,* pp. 143-146.

28. Tom Wolfe, "Stalking the Billion-footed Beast: A Literary Manifesto for the New Social Novel," *Harpers,* November 1989, p. 55.

CHAPTER NINE: *The Middle Ages and the Reformation:*
The Literature of Belief

1. The best line in a recent *Star Trek* movie came when Dr. Spock and Captain Kirk were discussing the customs of twentieth-century earth. The source of Kirk's information was "The Collected Works of Harold Robbins and Jacqueline Suzanne." "Oh yes," said Spock, "The greats." What worries me is that no one else in the theater laughed.
2. C. S. Lewis, "On the Reading of Old Books," *God in the Dock,* p. 202.
3. *Ibid.*
4. *Ibid.*
5. *Ibid.*
6. Translated by E. K. Chambers, *The Medieval Stage* (London: Oxford University Press, 1903), II: 14-15. The italicized responses were retained in Latin by Chambers, and their translations here are mine, as is the paragraphing. See Chamber's chapter, "Liturgical Plays," pp. 2-67, for discussion of this text, known as *"Quem Queritas"* ("Whom do you seek?").
7. *Hamlet*, act 3, scene 2, line 9.
8. See Chambers, II: 216-226.
9. See Madeleine Doran, *Endeavors of Art: A Study of Form in Elizabethan Drama* (Madison, WI: University of Wisconsin Press, 1954). Shakespeare was not the only popular dramatist of his time to do this. His literary stature, however, has been so great that he has set the precedents for English drama.
10. The contemporary Roman Catholic practice of frequent Communion was not the norm in medieval Catholicism for laypeople, who usually only received the Sacrament once a year. The high point of the worship service for the laity was the Adoration of the Host when the priest would elevate the consecrated bread and display it to the congregation for their worship. See Theodore Klauser, *A Short History of the Western Liturgy* (London: Oxford University Press, 1969), pp. 136-140.
11. See Denis de Rougemont, *Love in the Western World,* trans. Montgomery Belgion (New York: Pantheon, 1956).
12. "Holy Sonnet X," quoted from Warnke's edition, p. 270. I have regularized the punctuation and modernized the spelling.
13. John Donne, "Meditation XVII," *Devotions upon Emergent Occasions.* Quoted from Warnke, pp. 338-339. I have regularized the punctuation and modernized the spelling.
14. Patterson, *The Student's Milton,* Book I, ll. 44-49. I am modernizing the spelling.
15. *Ibid.,* Book I, l. 263.
16. *Ibid.,* Book I, l. 21.
17. *Ibid.,* Book VII, ll. 168-169.
18. The line is from William Blake, *The Marriage of Heaven and Hell.* The idea was taken up by Shelley in *A Defence of Poetry* and by some modern critics such as William Empson in *Milton's God* (London, 1965). This view is well-answered by C. S. Lewis in *A Preface to Paradise Lost* (London: Oxford University Press, 1942).
19. Book IX, ll. 31-32. See John Steadman, *Milton and the Renaissance Hero* (Oxford: Clarendon Press, 1967).

CHAPTER TEN: *The Enlightenment and Romanticism:*
The Literature of Nature and the Self

1. These points are demonstrated most thoroughly by Francis Schaeffer. See especially *The God Who Is There, Escape from Reason,* and *How Should We Then Live?* printed in *The Complete Works of Francis Schaeffer: A Christian View of Philosophy and Culture* (Westchester, IL: Crossway Books, 1982). I also am indebted in the discussions that follow to James Sire, *The Universe Next Door* (Downers Grove, IL: InterVarsity Press, 1976).

2. The metaphorical allusion to John 19:23-24 is from G. K. Chesterton, *Orthodoxy,* p. 65.

3. Patterson, *The Student's Milton,* "On the New Forcers of Conscience Under the Long Parliament," line 20.

4. "Couplet on Newton," in *Eighteenth-Century English Literature,* ed. Geoffrey Tillotson, et al. (New York: Harcourt, Brace & World, 1969), p. 609.

5. *Ibid.,* "An Essay on Criticism," lines 215-218. I have regularized Pope's capitalization, spelling, and use of italics.

6. The term is used for eccentric, renegade "new journalists" such as Hunter Thompson who sometimes get in trouble by their personal involvement in their stories. Defoe, a Protestant Dissenter in an age that did not tolerate Puritanism, was regularly censored, imprisoned, and pilloried for his journalistic ventures and for his controversial, but outspoken political opinions.

7. Quoted in *The Oxford Companion to English Literature,* ed. Sir Paul Harvey, 4th ed. (New York: Oxford University Press, 1967), p. 694.

8. C. S. Lewis makes the same point in greater detail in "Modern Theology and Biblical Criticism," in *Christian Reflections* (Grand Rapids, MI: Eerdmans, 1967), p. 155.

9. Such a procedure is understandable for secularist scholars. And yet this method has been uncritically adopted by the theologians and seminaries of most mainline churches. The result is that the Bible is treated as a merely human document and is no longer considered a supernatural authority. Some theologians still grant it some authority, but indirectly, stressing the need to interpret the quasi-fictional texts according to the experience and needs of the church. The result is sometimes a neo-Catholic view of Scripture without the constraints of Catholic dogma: Since the church wrote the Bible, then we, the institutional leaders of the church, can interpret it as we please and proclaim our "progressive" ideas in the name of Christianity. In practice this triumph of the institutional church over the substance of Scripture can mean "holding the form of religion, but denying the power of it" (2 Timothy 3:5).

10. Tillotson, *Eighteenth-Century English Literature,* "An Essay on Man," lines 257-258, 285-286, 293-294. "Whatever is, is right" derives from the German philosopher Leibnitz. The idea is interestingly satirized in *Candide* by Voltaire, who ironically was a principle architect of the Enlightenment.

11. Some Modernist theologians argue that the evangelical doctrine of the inerrancy of Scripture originated in eighteenth-century systematic theology. As such, they say it is not an authentic doctrine of the historic church. First of all, this line of argument is extremely misleading. Statements about the veracity of Scripture abound throughout church history. Luther's *Large Catechism* (1529) states, "My neighbor and I—in short, all men—may err

and deceive, but God's Word cannot err" (*The Book of Concord,* ed. Theodore G. Tappert [Philadelphia: Fortress Press, 1959], p. 444). Even if the precise term "inerrancy of Scripture" was not defined until the eighteenth century, that can hardly argue against its truth. The Enlightenment was a time when many concepts, such as gravity and law, were scrutinized and closely defined for the first time. Evangelicals need not be ashamed of their heritage in eighteenth-century thought; rather, they should draw on its intellectual rigor to defend their positions.

12. "London," ll. 1-8, from *The Portable Blake,* ed. Alfred Kazin (New York: Viking, 1946).

13. "Mock on, Mock on, Voltaire, Rousseau" from *The Portable Blake.*

14. See M. H. Abrams, *Natural Supernaturalism* (New York: Norton, 1973), for the way romanticism secularized Christian doctrines by displacing them into the realms of Nature and the Self.

15. See Prickett, *Words and the Word,* pp. 105-123, who makes these points by tracing the influence of Bishop Robert Lowth's scholarship in analyzing Biblical poetry on Blake, Coleridge, and other seminal Romantic theorists.

16. See the quotation from Herder, a German Romantic theorist, in Prickett, p. 54.

17. *Ibid.,* p. 142.

18. *Ibid.,* p. 117.

19. Quoted from a letter in Molly Lefebure, *Samuel Taylor Coleridge: A Bondage of Opium* (New York: Stein and Day, 1974), p. 479.

20. *Ibid.,* p. 480.

21. *Ibid.,* p. 481.

22. The significance of Coleridge's faith in the gospel is insufficiently known or appreciated by readers or by scholars. For the significance of his spiritual awakening in the context of his addiction, see Lefebure's excellent study, pp. 480-481. To trace Coleridge's response to the Reformation gospel, see his *Notes on English Divines,* which consists of notes he made in the margins of the books he was reading. These are sometimes collected as "Marginalia." See my quotations and discussions of Coleridge's view of Calvinism in *Reformation Spirituality,* pp. 23, 34, 117, 131-132.

23. Gerard Manley Hopkins, *Gerard Manley Hopkins,* ed. Catherine Phillips, The Oxford Authors (New York: Oxford University Press, 1986).

24. *Ibid.,* "Pied Beauty," l. 7.

25. *Ibid.,* "That Nature Is a Heraclitian Fire" and "Of the Comfort of the Resurrection," ll. 21-22.

26. *Ibid.,* "As Kingfishers Catch Fire," ll. 12-14.

CHAPTER ELEVEN: *Modernism and Postmodernism:*
The Literature of Consciousness and Self-Consciousness

1. See *The God Who Is There,* particularly the section "Speaking Historic Christianity into the Twentieth-Century Climate," *Complete Works of Francis Schaeffer,* I: 129-148.

2. Alfred, Lord Tennyson, "In Memoriam," LVI, l. 15. *The Poetic and Dramatic Works of Alfred Lord Tennyson,* ed. W. J. Rolfe, The Cambridge Poets (Boston: Houghton Mifflin, 1898), p. 176. This poem, an elegy on the death of Tennyson's friend Arthur Hallam, shows eloquently the impact of Darwin's theory on romanticism as well as other spiritual struggles of the time.

3. For Sanger's relationship to the eugenics movement and for her connections to figures in Hitler's "race hygiene" program, see Elasah Drogin, *Margaret Sanger: Father of Modern Society* (New Hope, KY: Cal Publications, 1986), pp. 11-17, 28-33.

4. See Zeev Sternhall, "Fascist Ideology," in *Fascism: A Reader's Guide,* ed. Walter Laqueur (Berkeley: University of California Press, 1976), pp. 328-335. For the relationship between fascism and Social Darwinism, see p. 322.

5. "Neutral Tones." Quoted from *The Complete Poems of Thomas Hardy,* ed. James Gibson (New York: Macmillan, 1976), p. 76. I have altered the punctuation slightly.

6. "Dover Beach" (1867). Quoted from *Matthew Arnold,* ed. Miriam Allott and Robert H. Super, The Oxford Authors (New York: Oxford University Press, 1976), pp. 135-136.

7. Cf. Francis Schaeffer's distinction between the "upper story" and the "lower story" developed in *Escape from Reason,* in *Complete Works,* vol. I.

8. Nietzsche attacked the Jews for introducing transcendent absolute values. Nietzsche correctly saw the "Jewishness" of Christianity as well. Charles Maurras, the French theorist of fascism, developed this idea in its clearest form. He is echoed by Adolph Hitler in *Mein Kampf* and *Hitler's Table Talk.* See Ernst Nolte, *Three Faces of Fascism: Action Française, Italian Fascism, National Socialism,* trans. Leila Vennewitz (New York: Holt, Rinehart & Winston, 1965), pp. 124, 406-407, 430, 442-444, *et passim.* The Nazis were trying to recover a pure communal consciousness. Any moral absolutes which transcend the community and by which it can be judged were anathema, leading, they said, to the alienation of the individual from the community. The point is, Nazi anti-semitism was not solely racial. Rather, Nazi philosophy was aimed at dismantling the Hebraic intellectual influence upon Western culture. In other words, they were attacking the Bible and the entire Judeo-Christian tradition. Christianity itself was to be turned into a purely cultural religion, purged of its "Jewish [i.e., Scriptural] elements." This was the stated purpose of certain influential Bible scholars and theologians who attacked the veracity of the Bible. See Raymon F. Surburg, "The Influence of the Two Delitzsches on Biblical and Near Eastern Studies," *Concordia Theological Quarterly,* 47 (1983): 234-236.

9. See Victor Farias, *Heidegger and Nazism,* trans. Gabriel R. Ricci (Philadelphia: Temple University Press, 1989).

10. T. S. Eliot, "The Waste Land," ll. 426-427.

11. Pound's fascism, unlike that of Heidegger and others, is well-known. During the war, he made propaganda broadcasts for Mussolini. After the war, Pound, an American, was indicted for treason. Due to the intercession of his literary friends, he was not tried, but instead was committed to a mental hospital. After his release, he returned to Italy (giving the Fascist salute as soon as he disembarked) where he lived unrepentant, still lionized by the literary community. He died in 1972. See Humphrey Carpenter, *A Serious Character: The Life of Ezra Pound* (New York: Houghton Mifflin, 1988).

12. The phrase is used in "The Metaphysical Poets," printed in *Selected Prose of T. S. Eliot,* ed. Frank Kermode (New York: Harcourt, Brace, Jovanovich, 1975), pp. 59-67.

13. Matthew Arnold, "The Study of Poetry." Quoted from *Criticism: The Major Statements,* pp. 358-359.

14. See *Ibid.,* pp. 366-371.

15. See Tom Wolfe's account of twentieth-century architecture in *From Bauhaus to Our House* (New York: Farrar Straus & Giroux, 1981).
16. See Myers, *All God's Children and Blue Suede Shoes,* pp. 103-132.
17. Mark Edmundson, "Prophet of a New Post-modernism: The Greater Challenge of Salman Rushdie," *Harper's Magazine,* December 1989, p. 63.
18. *Ibid.*
19. *Ibid.,* p. 64.
20. See Ellul, *The Humiliation of the Word,* pp. 99-100, 165-166, *et passim,* for a critique of structuralist and post-structuralist views of language.
21. Milan Kundera, "Dialogue on the Art of the Novel," quoted by Edmundson, p. 66.
22. In the novel, he debates the merits of weight as opposed to lightness and is unable to resolve which one is better. See Milan Kundera, *The Unbearable Lightness of Being,* trans. Michael Henry Heim (New York: Harper & Row, 1984), pp. 5-6. Kundera's novel should not be confused with the rather salacious movie that was made from it. Again, pop culture and visual icons have a way of trivializing even Postmodernist novels.
23. The term is Edmundson's to describe this new optimistic post-modernism that he sees (p. 62). One wonders what the next literary movement can be called.
24. See Werner Hamacher, ed., *Responses: On Paul De Man's Wartime Journalism* (Lincoln: University of Nebraska Press, 1989).
25. Nolte, *Three Faces of Fascism,* p. 429. See his section "Fascism as a Metapolitical Phenomenon," pp. 429-462.
26. Frederick Buechner, *Brendan* (New York: Atheneum, 1987), p. 76.

CHAPTER TWELVE: *The Makers of Literature: Writers, Publishers, and Readers*

1. See Myers, *All God's Children and Blue Suede Shoes,* pp. 75-87.
2. "Paradise Lost," Book VII, l. 31-33.
3. Major publishers of fiction in effect use agents to screen manuscripts for them. Novelists aiming for the large secular market might do well to try to find an agent. This is less important for nonfiction writers.
4. See Myers's entire list comparing the popular culture to the high culture on p. 120.
5. *Ibid.,* p. 18.
6. Milton, "Areopagitica," in *The Student's Milton,* p. 738.
7. *Ibid.*
8. *Ibid.*
9. For parallels between the Dark Ages and contemporary culture, see Charles Colson, *Against the Night: Living in the New Dark Age* (Ann Arbor, MI: Servant, 1989). See also C. S. Lewis, *"De Descriptione Temporum,"* in *Selected Literary Essays,* ed. Walter Hooper (Cambridge: Cambridge University Press, 1969).

SCRIPTURE INDEX

Genesis

4:1	236
6:5	33
8:21	131

Exodus

20:4	20, 135
20:7	39

1 & 2 Samuel

	87

1 & 2 Kings

	87

1 & 2 Chronicles

	87

Psalms

8:3-4	83
18:28	238
19:5-6	189
24	86-87, 236
33:18	84
119:18	140
119:105	238
119:148	85
126:2-3, 5	104
139:7	41
143:5	85

Proverbs

10:23	46
16:21, 24	211
18:17	169

Song of Solomon

	34
4:1-5	88-89

Isaiah

35:10	104
52:10	84-85

Jeremiah

23:16-32	131
23:25-29	138
50:38	24

Ezekiel

37	97

Zechariah

7:9-12	37

Matthew

5:21-22	32
5:27-28	32
5:29-30	32
5:34	39
5:44	107

5:45	48
7:6	44
15:19-20	32
22:39	37, 107
23:24	43

Luke

| 17:1-2 | 34 |
| 22:19 | 95 |

John

1:1	18
4:24	85
8:12	238
10:9	84
17:14-18	221
19:23-24	242

Acts

| 8:30-1 | xvi |
| 17:24-28 | 188 |

Romans

1 :18	235
1 :19	235
2 :14-15	74
8 :19-22	188, 195
10 :10	39
10 :17	18, 54
12 :15	31
13 :1-7	42

1 Corinthians

| 12 | 221 |
| 12:12-26 | 164 |

2 Corinthians

| 4:6 | 238 |

| 5:21 | 90 |
| 10:5 | 55 |

Ephesians

5:3-6, 11, 12	42
5:19	97
5:31	89

Philippians

| 4:8 | 48 |

1 Timothy

| 4:7 | 139 |

2 Timothy

| 3:5 | 242 |

Hebrews

1:1	137
1:3	231
4 :12	18, 54, 211
5 :14	35
11 :3	18, 231
12 :2	xvi
13 :8	192

James

1 :17	28
1 :23, 24	238
1 :25	238
3 :9-10	39
4: 9	104
5 :12	39

Revelation

3 :15	95
7 :17	103
19 :7	115, 162

GENERAL INDEX

Abortion, 23, 51, 96, 153, 179, 183, 199, 211
Abrams, M. H., 117-118, 243
Addison, Joseph, 173-174
Adler, Mortimer, 46
Aesop, 71
Allegory, 75, 135, 136-137, 225, 226
Anti-hero, 109
Antigone, see *Sophocles*
Apologetics, 54-55, 139-140
apRoberts, Ruth, 86, 236
Architecture, 205
Aristotle, 68, 102, 106-110, 134, 183, 224, 234, 237
Arminius, Jacobus, 201
Arnold, Matthew, 29, 197-199, 204, 205
Arthurian tales, 34, 65-67, 72, 95, 113, 115-116, 136, 153, 174, 222
Auden, W. H., 204
Augustine, 74, 201, 231, 234, 235
Austen, Jane, 122, 176-177

Bach, 165
Bacon, Francis, 239
Barzun, Jacques, 52
Battenhouse, Roy, 238
Battle of Maldon, 61
Beattie, Ann, 123, 238
Beckett, Samuel, 109, 208
Belloc, Hillaire, 229
Beowulf, 61, 64, 79, 133, 136
Bettelheim, Bruno, 142-145
Bible, 17-19, 47, 61, 161, 165, 238
    inerrancy of, 242-243
    influence on drama, 154-160
    influence on fantasy, 134-136
    influence on romanticism, 184-185
    interpretation of, 87

liberal scholarship, 85, 87-88, 177, 178-179, 229, 242, 244
    metaphors in, 84-85
    modern translations of, 235-236, 239
    nonvisual imagery of, 88
    parallelism in, 86-88, 236
    poetry in, 86-89, 184
    unity in, 88
    see also *Word of God*
Billingsley, Lloyd, 128, 212
Blake, William, 95, 181-182, 241
Blasphemy, 40
Boman, Thorlief, 236
Bookstores, 214, 218; Christian, 217, 219-222
Borges, Jorge Luis, 147
Brontë, Charlotte, 28, 184
Brontë, Emily, 28
Browne, Sir Thomas, 162
Buechner, Frederick, 128, 217, 211-212, 222, 228, 238
Bunyan, John, 64, 65, 74-75, 129, 137, 226
Burke, Edmund, 171
Burroughs, William, 208
Byron, George Gordon, Lord, 183

Calvin, John, 186, 201, 211, 243
Calvino, Italo, 147
Campbell, Joseph, 139
Campion, Thomas, 79
Camus, Albert, 201
Capitalism, 193
Censorship, 42-45, 72-73
Cervantes, Miguel de, 174
Chambers, E. K., 233, 241
Change, 149-150, 169, 211
Character, 67-69

Chaucer, Geoffrey, 38, 44, 112-113, 153, 225, 229
Chesterton, G. K., 121, 140, 141, 227
Children's literature, 30, 43-45, 73, 80-81, 82-83, 141-146, 206, 228,229, 240
Cicero, 234
Citizen Kane, 108, 110
Classical, see *Greek*
Coghill, Neville, 238
Coleridge, S. T., 141, 182, 185-186, 243
Colson, Charles, 245
Comedy, 99, 102-105, 111-116, 238
    Christianity and, 103-105, 112
    Dante's definitions of, 102-105
    fairy tales, 145-146
    Greek definition of, 111, 237
    in mystery plays, 159
    in novels, 176
    satire, 111-112
    and sense of life, 103-105, 153
    Shakespearean, 114-115, 238
    violations of, 112
Communism, 124-126, 199
    see also *Marxism*
Computers, 232
Cook, Hugh, 128, 212
Crane, Stephen, 31, 64, 123, 195
Crashaw, Richard, 162
Criticism, xiii, xv-xvi, 45, 204-205

Dante, 40, 95, 102-105, 108, 109, 110, 111, 112, 115, 136, 153, 161, 203, 225-226, 238
Darwin, Charles, 193, 195
Darwinism, 123-124, 128, 153, 193-194
Davies, Robinson, 115-116, 146
Deconstruction, 209, 210
Defamiliarizing, 121, 140
Defoe, Daniel, 174, 242
Deism, 177-179, 185, 191
De Man, Paul, 210
Democracy, 19, 20, 22, 51, 153, 159, 171
Derrida, Jacques, 209
Devotional prose, 162-164
Dickens, Charles, 75, 121, 122, 123, 147, 216, 225
Dillard, Annie, 56-57, 211, 228
Donne, John, 81, 84, 85, 161, 163-164, 203, 226
Dostoevsky, Fyodor, 125, 127, 226
Doyle, Sir Arthur Conan, 69
Dr. Who, 137
Drake, Robert, 76, 235
Drama, 59, 80, 101
    actors, 158
    Biblical influence on, 153-160
    medieval, 113, 154-160

    see also *comedy*, *Greek drama*, and *tragedy*.
Dryden, John, 96-97, 173
Dunlap, John, 240
Dyson, Hugo, 138

Eastern mysticism, 84, 85, 183, 210
Eco, Umberto, 207
Edmundson, Mark, 207-210
Education, 18-19, 21, 24, 61-62, 72, 145, 161, 172, 175, 182, 200, 208, 232
Eliot, T. S., 80, 94-97, 202, 203, 221, 227
Ellul, Jacques, 232, 245
Emerson, Ralph Waldo, 84, 94-97
Empson, William, 241
Ende, Michael, 206
Enlightenment, 130, 169-180, 187, 189-190, 195, 203
    and Christianity, 242-243
    Deism, 177-179
    neoclassicism in, 171-173
    problems of, 177-182
    romanticism and, 181-183
    science in, 171, 177
    skepticism in, 170-171
    utilitarian ethics of, 179
Eugenics, 194, 244
Euphemism, 50-52
Euthanasia, 194, 211
Existentialism, 73, 115, 122, 169, 194, 196-202
    and art, 202
    Christian, 200-201
    ethics of, 199, 200
    and fascism, 201-202
    nature of, 199
    and relativism, 199-200
    and romanticism, 202
Exposition, 62

Fairy tales, 44, 113, 129, 140, 141-146, 153, 240
Fantasy, 32, 69, 70-71, 74-75, 99, 117-120, 129-148, 174, 184, 206, 211
    Biblical influence on, 134-137
    Christian, 135-137
    and occult, 131-134
    problems of, 130-134
    realism of, 119-120, 146-148
    and spirituality, 137-141
    verisimilitude of, 141
Fascism, 194, 201-202, 203, 210, 244
Faulkner, William, 126, 127, 147, 235
Fickett, Harold, 212
Fiction, 59-77
    character, 67-69, 109, 176
    defense of, 59-62

formula, 27-28, 215
see also *popular culture*
and moral education, 61-62
narrative, 62-64
novel, 173-177
plot, 64-67, 109
setting, 69-71
stream-of-consciousness, 203
theme, 71-74
Fielding, Henry, 122, 176
Figures of speech, 83-86
see also *metaphors*
Fitzgerald, F. Scott, 69
Folk culture, 141, 156, 160
Freud, Sigmund, 194-195, 203, 207, 240

Gallagher, Susan V., 34, 231
Graham, Billy 24
Greek drama, 68, 154
decorum of, 35-36, 154, 158
unities, 156-160, 173, 183
see also *comedy, tragedy*
Greeks, comedy of, 111-112
concept of imitation, 120, 134, 185
influence in neoclassicism, 171-173
influence in Renaissance, 159-160
literature of, 99
myths of, 135-136
philosophy of, 117, 134, 135
poetry of, 81, 88
rhetoric of, 49
tragedy, 105-111
see also *Aristotle, Greek drama*
Greene, Graham, 110, 127-128, 228, 237
Gregory the Great, Pope, 104
Griffin, William, 212

Hardy, Thomas, 195-196
Havel, Vaclav, 126
Hebrews, influence of, see *Bible*
and fascism, 244
literature, 86-89, 236
prohibition of images, 134
Heidegger, Martin, 201-202, 210, 244
Hemingway, Ernest, 126, 147, 202, 216
Herbert, Edward, 178
Herbert, George, xvi, 80, 89-94, 161,
178, 222, 226
Herder, von, Johann, 243
High culture, xiv, 29, 36, 160, 207, 217
High Noon, 156-157
Hitler, Adolf, 194, 210, 244
see also *Fascism*
Holocaust, 194, 244
Homer, 31, 61, 64, 66, 85, 203
Hopkins, Gerard Manley, 84, 187-189,
221-222, 227

Horace, 237
Hubbard, L. Ron, 132
Hulme, T. E., 204
Hume, David, 171
Hymns, 79, 80, 172-173

"I Love Lucy," 67-68, 102, 104
Idols, 20-24, 88, 161, 209, 232
Images, 19-24, 88, 161
Imagination, 30-34
Irony, 41-42, 102-103, 116
Irving, Washington, 174

James, Henry, 122, 126
James, P. D., 28
Jefferson, Thomas, 153, 178
Johnson, Samuel, 171, 180
Jonson, Ben, 111, 114, 159, 160, 174, 237
Journalism, 49, 50, 52, 55-56, 62, 173-
174, 242
see also *new journalism*
Joyce, James, 36, 126, 203
Julian of Norwich, 103, 237

Keats, John, 85, 184
Kierkegaard, Soren, 201
Kilpatrick, William Kirk, 37, 61-62
King, Stephen, 131
Kundera, Milan, 209-210, 245

L'Engle, Madeleine, 137, 212, 222, 228
Language, xv, 17-18, 21-22, 25, 39, 50-
52, 71, 81, 82-83, 84, 86, 161, 180,
189, 196, 209, 211, 213, 232
Lawhead, Stephen, 137, 212, 222
Lawrence, D. H., 36
Leax, John, 212, 229
LeCarré, John, 69
Lefebure, Molly, 243
Leibnitz, 171, 242
Lewis, C. S., 28, 43, 53-54, 59, 72, 73,
129, 136, 137, 138-140, 142, 146,
147, 152-153, 185, 203, 226, 227,
229, 239, 241, 242, 245
Lewis, Sinclair, 124
Liberal theology, 85, 87-88, 177, 178,
185, 187, 200, 242
Libertarians, 193
Linguistic analysis, 195
Liturgy, 154-155, 186-187, 241
Locke, John, 171
London, Jack, 123
Longfellow, Henry Wadsworth, 84
Lowth, Robert, 243
Lundin, Roger 34, 231
Luther, Martin, 23, 38, 186, 201, 231,
242-243

MacDonald, George, 129, 137, 139, 185
Madison, James, 153
Malone, Michael, 212
Malory, Sir Thomas, 234
Marlowe, Christopher, 41, 105, 134, 233, 235
Márquez, Gabriel García, 147, 206
Marx, Karl, 124, 194, 207
Marxism, 73, 124-126, 194, 199, 203, 208
Materialism, 71, 123-124, 127, 140, 181-182, 193, 194-196, 198, 203
Maurras, Charles, 244
McMurtry, Larry, 207
Media, and culture, 20-22
    see also *television* and *reading*
Meditation, 85, 163-164
Melodramas, 110, 151, 180, 207
Melville, Herman, 31, 66, 69, 74, 108, 151
Metaphors, 83-86, 117, 172, 187, 189, 235-236, 238
Metaphysical poetry, 161-162, 172
Middle Ages, 151-159, 186
    problems of, 160-161
    and romanticism, 184
    wholeness of, 160
    see also *comedy, mystery plays*
Miller, Calvin, 212
Miller, Arthur, 107, 109, 110
Milton, John, 25, 44, 106-107, 110, 164-167, 170, 173, 179-180, 216, 222-223, 226, 237
Miracle plays, 159
Missionaries, 19
Modernism, 94, 97, 202-204, 211
Movies, 35-36, 46, 68, 72, 101, 153, 154, 156-157
Music, 79, 97
Mussolini, 244
Myers, Kenneth, 207, 220-221, 233
Mysteries, 28, 67, 207, 221, 223
Mystery plays, 113, 154-160
Myth, 134-136, 138-139, 203, 239

Narrative, 62-64, 80
Naturalism, 123-124, 195
Nazism., see *Fascism.*
Nelson, Shirley, 212
Neoclassicism, 130, 171-173, 184-185
    and prose, 173-174
    Romantic reaction, 183-184
New Age movement, 22, 131-134, 183, 192, 200, 210
New Journalism, 55-56, 147
    see also *Wolfe, Tom*
Newman, John Henry, 187

Newman, Edwin A., 234
Newton, John, 171, 181
Nietzsche, Friedrich, 201, 244
Nolte, Ernst, 210, 244
Nonfiction, 49-58
    as literature, 49, 55, 211
    prose, 173, 177
    standards for, 52-53
Novel, 146
    epistolary, 175-176
    Gothic, 184
    origins of, 173, 177
    stream-of-consciousness, 126, 203
    see also *fiction*

O'Connor, Flannery, 41, 65, 75-77, 127, 128, 204, 216, 221, 222, 227, 235
Obscenity, 35-38, 233
Occult, 131-134
Oedipus Rex, see *Sophocles*
Olasky, Marvin, xi, 50, 234
Old Yeller, 103, 237
Orwell, George, 234
Owens, Virginia Stem, 212

Pahlka, William H., 235
Paley, William, 178
Pantheism, 169, 183
Parallelism, 86-89, 236
Payne, Peggy, 212
Percy, Walker, 112, 128, 211, 217, 228
Peretti, Frank, 137, 212
Picaresque tales, 174
Pietism, 186
Plato, 134
Plautus, 224
Plot, 64-67, 109
    conflict in, 64-66
    episodic, 174
    structure of, 66-67
Pluralism, 191-192
Poe, Edgar Allan, 183, 184
Poetry, 47, 79-97
    in Bible, 86-89
    form of, 80-83, 92-93
    free verse, 79, 82, 95, 202-203
    imagery of, 82-83
    as meditation, 85
    and music, 79
    publishing, 216
    and reality, 85
    of Reformation, 160-164
    rhyme in, 79, 81-82, 188
    rhythm in, 188
    stanzas of, 80, 81-82
    syllabic, 80-81
Pope, Alexander, 171, 172, 179-180, 181

Popular culture, xiv, 21-24, 27-28, 29, 36, 45, 64, 70, 73, 79-80, 95, 110, 131-133, 151-152, 191-192, 201, 204, 207, 214-215, 220-221, 223
Pornography, 32-38, 73, 233
Positivism, 195
Postmodernism, xiii, xv, 147, 175, 204-210
  in architecture, 205
  and Christianity, 210-212
  in criticism, 208-209
  in literature, 206-207
  and popular culture, 207
  problems of, 207-210
  in television, 206
Postman, Neil, 20-23, 25, 232
Pound, Ezra, 203, 210, 244
Powers, J. F., 128
Prickett, Stephen, 236, 243
Profanity, 39-42
Propaganda, 49-52
Publishers, 125, 214, 216, 217-222
  Christian, 217, 219, 221
  publishing process, 217-219

Rand, Ayn, 193
Ratushinskaya, Irina, 125, 238
Readers, 214, 216
Reading, aliteracy, 25
  Christians and, xiii, 17-19, 25, 224
  habit of, xiii, xiv, 25, 223
  non-Christian writers, 72-74, 127, 222-223, 235
  works of the past, 149, 151-153
  pleasures of, 28, 29, 36-37
  social implications of, 19, 25
  and television, 21, 30
  threats to, 17, 19-24
Realism, 99, 117-128, 131
  Christian, 127-128
  fantasy elements of, 119-120, 146
  magical, 147
  minimalists, 122-123
  naturalism, 123-124
  Postmodern critique of, 206-207
  prohibited, 135
  psychological, 126
  social dimension of, 120-121
  social, 124, 147
  socialist, 124-126
  varieties of, 123-127
Reformation, 18-19, 160-162
Reiner, Rob, 112
Remarque, Erich, 31
Renaissance, 113, 136, 159
Renault, Mary, 122
Rhetoric, 49-52
Richardson, Samuel, 175-176

Ricoeur, Paul, 207
Robbins, Harold, 241
Romances, 27, 28
  medieval, 113, 129, 136, 153, 174, 184
  see also Arthurian tales
  prose, 174
  and romanticism, 184
  tragi-comedy, 113
Romanticism, 117, 181-190, 195, 203
  Bible's influence, 184-185
  and Christianity, 185-190
  contemporary manifestations of, 182-183, 191
  and Enlightenment, 181-183
  ethics of, 182-183
  and existentialism, 202
  and fantasy, 184
  and fascism, 194
  nature of, 182-183
  organic form, 183-184, 187-188
Rougemont, Denis de, 241
Rousseau, 181
Ruenzel, David, 122-123
Rushdie, Salman, 40, 209-210
Ryken, Leland, xi, 231, 234

Sanger, Margaret, 194, 244
Sartre, Jean Paul, 74, 201
Satire, 111-112, 238
Sayers, Dorothy L., 28, 221, 225, 226
Schaap, James, 128, 212
Schaeffer, Francis A., 192, 196, 232, 242, 244
Schleiermacher, Friedrich, 185
Science, 19, 25, 56, 58, 90, 117, 118, 134, 153, 171, 173, 177, 180, 181, 182, 187, 193, 195, 196, 200, 228
Science fiction, 28, 32, 67-68, 69, 120, 129, 132, 137, 141, 146-147, 157, 207, 223
Scott, Sir Walter, 184
Semantics, 50-52
Setting, 69-71
Sex, 32-38, 96, 194, 211, 214, 215, 217, 228-229
Shakespeare, William, 40, 69, 75, 84, 103, 110, 114-115, 146, 158, 159, 165, 172, 173, 184, 216, 225, 238, 241, 159-160
Shandling, Gary, 206
Shaw, Luci, 212, 229
Shelley, Percy, 182-183, 241
Shideler, Mary McDermott, 227
Shklovsky, Victor, 121, 140, 238
Sidney, Sir Philip, 60-61, 72, 73, 111
Siegel, Robert, 137, 212
Sinclair, Upton, 124

Sire, James, xi, 242
Smith, Adam, 171
Solzhenitsyn, Alexander, 125
Sonnets, 82, 161-162, 188-189
Sophocles, 36, 74, 103, 106, 107, 109, 197, 237
Spark, Muriel, 128
Spenser, Edmund, 129, 136-137, 173, 226
Spillane, Mickey, 36
Spinoza, 171
Star Trek, 67-68, 241
Steele, Richard, 173-174
Steinbeck, John, 43, 126, 147, 235
Sterne, Lawrence, 176
Stevens, Wallace, 202
Stowe, Harriet Beecher, 121
Suzanne, Jacqueline, 241
Swift, Jonathan, 111, 129, 130-131, 137, 171, 174, 180, 195, 225

Tarzan, 30, 69
Taste, 45-46
Tate, Allen, 204
Taylor, Jeremy, 163, 164
Television, xiv, 19-24, 65, 108, 153, 157, 206
    legitimate use of, 24-25
    mind-set of, 21-24
    ministries, 23-25
    politics and, 22
    and reading, 21, 30
    religion and, 22-24
    successful programs, 67-68
Tennyson, Alfred, Lord, 109, 193, 243
Thackeray, William, 122
The Romance of the Rose, 136
Theme, 71-74
Thompson, Francis, 185, 226
Thompson, Hunter, 242
Tolkien, J. R. R., 64-65, 70, 119, 129, 132, 133, 136, 137, 138, 225
Tolstoy, Leo, 125, 127, 147, 229
Tragedy, 68, 99, 101-111
    Aristotle's definition of, 106-111
    Christian, 105, 109, 110
    Dante's definition of, 102-105
    effects of, 106-107, 110
    Greek, 105-111, 237
    hero of, 106
    and sense of life, 103-105
    tragic flaw, 106
Traherne, Thomas, 162
Twain, Mark, 43-44, 72, 216

"Twinkle, Twinkle Little Star," 80-81, 82-83

Updike, John, 128
Utilitarianism, 169, 179

Values clarification, 61-62, 200
Vaughan, Henry, 162
Vicarious experience, 31-35
Violence, 32-38, 143-145, 154, 158, 214
Virgil, 74, 135, 224, 225
Voltaire, 171, 181, 242
Vulgarity, 38

Wangerin, Walter, Jr., xvi, 32, 56-58, 137, 211, 217, 229,
Warhol, Andy, 207
Warren, Eugene, 212, 229
Warren, Robert Penn, 204
Watts, Isaac, 172-173
Waugh, Evelyn, 128, 204
Weil, Simone, 94
Wesley, John, 180, 201
Westerns, 69-70, 156, 207
White, T. H., 234
Whitman, Walt, 121, 183, 239
Wilberforce, William, 180
Wilder, Thornton, 121
Williams, Charles, 146, 226, 227
Williams, Tennessee, 109, 110
Wilson, A. N., 128, 140, 212, 229
Wizard of Oz, 43
Wodehouse, P. G., 223
Woiwode, Larry, 128, 212, 222
Wolfe, Tom, 55-56, 121, 147, 245
Word of God, 18, 92, 97, 139, 209, 238
    as Bible, 18
    as Christ, 18
    as Gospel, 18
    oral proclamation of, 24
    see also *Bible*
    versus graven images, 19-24
Wordsworth, William, 182-186
Writers, xiv-xv, 213-217
    classic Christian, 225-227
    contemporary Christian, 210-212, 221, 228-229
    getting published, 217-219
    modern Christian, 227-28

Yancy, Philip, 212
Yeats, William Butler, 203

Zinsser, William, 55
Zola, Emile, 123-147